D1457343

April 1993

For Prof. James Buchanan,

With warmest regards,

Peter J. Boettke

WHY PERESTROIKA FAILED

The Politics and Economics of Socialist Transformation

Peter J. Boettke

London and New York

First published 1993
by Routledge
11 New Fetter Lane, London EC4P 4EE

Simultaneously published in the USA and Canada
by Routledge
29 West 35th Street, New York, NY 10001

Typeset in Garamond by Witwell Ltd. Southport.
Printed and bound in Great Britain by
Clays Ltd, St. Ives PLC

British Library Cataloguing-in-Publication Data
A catalogue record for this book is available from the British Library.
ISBN 0–415–08514–4

Library of Congress Cataloging in Publication Data
Boettke, Peter J.
Why perestroika failed: the politics and economics of socialist transforma-
tion/Peter J. Boettke.
p. cm.
Includes bibliographical references and index.
ISBN 0–415–08514–4
1. Soviet Union—Economic policy—1986–1991. 2. Soviet Union-
-Economic conditions—1985–1991. 3. Socialism—Soviet Union.
4. Perestroika. I. Title.
HC336.26.B64   1993
338.947—dc20   92–18067
CIP

To Matthew and Stephen

We can get on a bus labelled Economic Reform, but we don't know where it will take us.

George Stigler, *The Citizen and the State*

CONTENTS

ILLUSTRATIONS

PREFACE

Much of my thinking on perestroika has been sharpened by the comments of seminar and conference participants and anonymous referees on several papers over the past few years. The material in the book, in one form or another, has been presented at seminars at New York University, Oakland University, George Mason University, St. Lawrence University, State University of New York at Purchase, Hunter College of the City University of New York, Trinity College, Franklin and Marshall College, Hillsdale College, the Austrian Economics Colloquium of Washington, DC, and the Cato Institute, Washington, DC, and the annual meetings of the American Association for the Advancement of Slavic Studies, American Economic Association, the Association for Comparative Economic Studies, the Eastern Economic Association and the Public Choice Society. In addition, I would like to thank the students in my graduate seminar on Soviet and East European economies at New York University (Fall 1990 and Fall 1991) for their comments and criticisms on the arguments presented in the book. I have published some of these earlier papers in professional journals and as chapters in books. The material for this book, however, was entirely re-written and re-thought, taking into account both criticisms raised on those earlier formulations of the argument and new information concerning the Soviet situation as it evolved.

In addition to their careful and critical comments, my colleagues in the Austrian Economics Program at New York University, Israel Kirzner and Mario Rizzo have provided encouragement throughout the project. I would also like to thank the graduate fellows in the Austrian program for their input at several stages of this project: Juan Cosentino, Sean Keenan, George Pavlov, Gilberto Salgado, Charles Steele and Steve Sullivan. Financial assistance from the Sarah Scaife

Foundation to support the Austrian Economics Program at New York University is gratefully acknowledged.

The economics department at New York University has proven to be a very comfortable intellectual home. In trying to articulate my views I have benefited from several discussions with Andrew Schotter, Jess Benhabib, Jonas Praeger and Roman Frydman. I would also like to thank Gary Anderson (California State University, Northridge), Tyler Cowen (George Mason University), Jeff Friedman (Yale University), Steve Horwitz (St. Lawrence University), Sandy Ikeda (State University of New York, Purchase), Dan Klein (University of California, Irvine), Roger Koppl (Farleigh Dickinson University, Madison), Don Lavoie (George Mason University) and Ed Weick (Weick and Associates) for reading my various papers and helping me clarify my thought on the subject. I would like especially to acknowledge David Prychitko (State University of New York, Oswego) and Mike Alexeev (Indiana University) for their guidance, encouragement, criticisms and for generally trying to keep me on the right track in my endeavor to understand the Soviet situation. I was also very fortunate to work with Alan Jarvis of Routledge. He provided encouragement and guidance from the original inception of the project to its completion. I would like to thank Maureen Cummins for her work on copy editing the manuscript, and Eleanor Rivers and Diane Stafford for their work in overseeing the publication process. Responsibility for remaining errors is my own.

Finally, I would like to express my gratitude to Rosemary, who was patient as ever with my erratic behavior as I had to meet one or another self-imposed deadline. I would like to dedicate this project to our children, Matthew and Stephen, who I hope will grow up to see a more peaceful and prosperous world.

Peter J. Boettke
New York, New York
April 1992

1

INTRODUCTION

Ideas, unless outward circumstances conspire with them, have in general no very rapid or immediate efficacy in human affairs; and the most favourable outward circumstances may pass by, or remain inoperative, for want of ideas suitable to the conjuncture. But when the right circumstances and the right ideas meet, the effect is seldom slow in manifesting itself.

John Stuart Mill[1]

INTRODUCTION

The most dramatic event in political economy to happen since the Great Depression of the 1930s was the collapse of the Soviet system and its satellites in the late 1980s. The Soviet admissions of the failure of their economic system to provide a decent standard of living to its people, let alone keep pace with the technological advances of the West, caught most Western Sovietologists by surprise. Watching the developments (zigs and zags) of *perestroika* and *glasnost* became a full-time occupation for many economists.

The events in the Soviet Union since 1985 have been nothing short of spellbinding. Academics, pundits and the man on the street have been transfixed by the 'Gorbachev phenomenon.' The turning point of the Soviet reform effort, however, came in 1989. One former satellite after another during that fateful year withdrew from the Soviet empire with Gorbachev's blessing. Poland, Czechoslovakia and East Germany dramatically went their own way. The Berlin Wall fell, both figuratively and literally. The Brezhnev doctrine was repudiated by Gorbachev.

On the economic front, the pace of the Gorbachev reforms seemed to quicken (at least in rhetoric) as 1990 approached. No longer did the

1

reform rhetoric limit itself to tactics for improved efficiency of economic administration. Now fundamental systemic issues were debated. Private property, free market pricing, currency convertibility, etc., were legitimate topics of discussion among the Soviet Union's leading economists. These economic discussions culminated in the debate in the late summer and early fall of 1990 over the Shatalin 500-Day Plan.[2] The plan was at one and the same time a draft of a constitution for a new confederation of free sovereign republics, an outline for a market-based economic system for the new confederation and a plan of transition from the old union to the new confederation.[3]

But as is usually the case in political discussions, rhetoric diverged significantly from reality. Gorbachev quickly abandoned the Shatalin Plan and its political and economic program. A compromise Presidential Plan emerged in October 1990, which while maintaining some of the rhetoric of the Shatalin Plan, eliminated all of the details.[4] Both the political and economic reforms in the Soviet Union possessed troublesome paradoxes that simply exacerbated the crisis situation. In the lead up to the failed August 1991 coup, the situation in the Baltic states highlighted the political troubles with the Soviet reforms just as the long lines and empty shelves highlighted the economic woes that continued to plague the Soviet people. Perestroika as an economic reform program failed to bring lasting and systematic change to the moribund Soviet economy.

This book represents a critical assessment of the reform effort (1985–91). The common theme that runs throughout the book is that only on the basis of a sound understanding of the operation of market and political processes can one begin to analyze the Soviet-type system, and the efforts to reform it, with any degree of accuracy. From this theoretical basis, best developed by scholars working within the Austrian (market processes) and Public Choice (political processes) schools of economic analysis, the various proposals and paradoxes of the Soviet effort are examined.

Perestroika failed in large part because it was not tried. Gorbachev between 1985 and 1991 announced at least ten radical plans for economic restructuring, *not a single one was ever implemented*. But even if perestroika – as represented in the major proposals and decrees – had been implemented it would not have produced the *structural* changes necessary to revive the Soviet economy.

Though the events examined are limited in large part to the reform history from 1985 to 1991 – a working knowledge of which would be necessary to examine any direction the former Soviet Union may take in the foreseeable future – emphasis will be on the theoretical problems that economic reform confronts in general. Knowledge of the reasons why perestroika failed may provide us with important general lessons for how to proceed in charting a new course in the former Soviet republics and East and Central Europe.

OVERVIEW OF THE BASIC PROPOSITIONS

There are two general questions which the various chapters in this book attempt to answer. First, if socialism as an economic system was so inefficient, how could it have lasted for seventy-four years? Second, if market reforms are so desirable, why have all the transforming economies experienced an acute economic decline during the reform period? Both of these questions will be answered through a series of propositions which taken as a whole provide the critical answers. Each of the chapters will try to address a specific proposition and tease out its implications.

Proposition 1: Soviet economic strength was an illusion

It has become commonplace among neo-conservative commentators in the West, and even some Soviet intellectuals, to argue that the breakdown of the Soviet empire in the late 1980s was due to Ronald Reagan's military build-up in the early part of that decade.[5] By raising the stakes in the international military game, Reagan put the final strain on the Soviet system. However accurate this perspective is concerning the weight of the military burden on the Soviet economy, it does not address the systemic issues and problems surrounding the Soviet economy. The real question that must be raised is whether the Soviet system could have continued even if no military pressure was exerted by the West.

The neo-conservative perspective on the Soviet problem is untenable because it underestimates the extent to which military power is derived from a prosperous economic base and it overestimates Soviet economic strength. Questioning the neo-conservative hypothesis, however, should not be construed as support for the alternative suggestion that Mikhail Gorbachev was responsible for the break-up.[6] Gorbachev did not become General Secretary to reign over the demise of the Soviet empire. Any view that draws our attention away from the *structural problems* the Soviet system faced throughout its history will fail to grasp the meaning of the Soviet experience with socialism.

Even if the US and the West had reduced the military stakes in the 1980s, the Soviet economy was doomed to fail. The Soviet system was structurally weak since its founding and collapse was inevitable. The economic fact that, as Aleksandr Zaychenko stated, 'Russians today [in 1989] eat worse than did Russians in 1913 under the Czars' had little to do with the military strains of the Cold War and everything to do with the structural problems of socialist economic institutions.[7]

The illusion of Soviet economic growth and progress was due to the failings of aggregate economics, in general, and an odd combination of ideas and interests in academic discussions which did not allow dissenting voices to be heard, in particular. In fact, the whole peculiar art of Soviet economic management amounted to the production, and distribution of this illusion.

To illustrate the conflict between Western perceptions of socialist industrial achievement and the realities of the formerly socialist economies, one need only consider the fact that prior to German unification, East Germany was considered the flagship of the socialist industrialized world. Now it is evident to all that the East German economy was a shambles – incapable of producing anything close to world standards for an industrialized nation.[8] We now know just how inefficient these economies actually were.

It is not at all an exaggeration to say that in economic terms the socialist economies of Europe were Third World economies.[9] As George Orwell pointed out in *Animal Farm*, to the outside world the farm may have appeared as if it was productive and prosperous after the revolution, but inside the farm the animals worked harder and ate less than they ever did before.[10]

Proposition 2: Socialism as originally conceived was (is) an economic impossibility

Soviet-style socialism did not fail because of half-hearted attempts or because of backward political and economic conditions, rather socialism as originally conceived of by Marx, Engels, Lenin and Trotsky was simply a utopian dream incapable of realization in any world populated by human beings. This does not mean that an attempt to realize utopia cannot take place, just that utopia can never be achieved.

In assessing utopias, it is important to clarify two issues. First, the internal coherence of the idea must be examined. Second, the vulnerability of the idea to opportunistic behavior and external invasion must be considered.

If a utopia is internally consistent, then it is said to be theoretically possible. However, if it is internally inconsistent, then it represents a theoretical impossibility. If a utopia is theoretically possible, but vulnerable to opportunistic invasion, then it may simply be impracticable. A utopian system which is both internally consistent and not vulnerable to opportunism, may actually cease to be a utopia, and, instead, offer a vision of a workable alternative social arrangement than that currently present in the world.

Socialism was an example of a theoretically impossible utopian dream. Given socialism's own goals of increased productivity and the moral improvement of mankind (and man's emancipation from the oppressive bonds of man and nature), the institutional demands of its project were inconsistent with the attainment of those goals. The unintended consequence of the attempt to implement this utopian dream in the real world was the Soviet reality of political oppression and economic deprivation.

Proposition 3: Mature Soviet-style socialism, since it could not have conformed to the textbook model of socialism, is best understood as a rent-seeking society with the main goal of yielding perquisites to those in positions of power

Throughout its history the defining characteristic of the mature model of Soviet-style socialism was political and economic monopoly. The vast system of interlocked monopolies, and the *nomenklatura* system, worked to provide perquisites to those in positions of power and controlled access to these positions. The Soviet system created a loyal caste of bureaucrats who benefited directly from maintaining the system. The existence of contrived scarcity rents available to managers and store clerks goes a long way to explaining the persistence of shortages, and the rationale behind many common Soviet practices, such as *blat*.[11]

The narrow interests of the bureaucrats also explains why they did not pay attention to public interest goals such as economic policies which would increase consumer well-being. The main objective of bureaucratic action was not to increase economic productivity *per se*, but rather to increase the rents and perquisites available. Bureaucratic competition substituted for economic competition, and resources were allocated according to political rationales rather than economic ones with the corresponding waste that would be expected. But waste was not penalized in the Soviet system of bureaucratic management. As long as output targets were met, and everyone in the process received the perquisites due to them, then the Soviet manager was judged a success. Certainly such considerations as consumer demand were not to enter the state enterprise manager's calculations.

Economic reform demanded a change in this way of doing things, but change was sure to be resisted. The bureaucratic caste could not be expected to give up voluntarily its privileged position in society.

Proposition 4: The basic organizational logic of politics conflicts with the logic of economic reform

Perhaps one of the oldest debates in the history of political economy is over whether ideas or interests govern policy change. Karl Marx, for example, argued that the economic base determined the super-structure. In other words, ideas flow from economic interests. John Maynard Keynes, on the other hand, argued that the impact of interests was largely overestimated, rather it was ideas that govern the world. Ironically, they both may be right.

The complex interaction of ideas and interests produces an intellectual climate within which the polity exists. Ideas, for example, which demand more government involvement, also create an interest group which will benefit from the intervention. Thus, ideas and interests work together to eliminate the constraints to government involvement in the economy that may exist. The logic behind this is rather straightforward.

It must be recognized that government, whatever form it takes, is an institution that can be, and will be, used by some to exploit others unless effectively constrained. Under democracy, politicians (by definition) seek election or re-election, and in order to accomplish that goal they require votes and campaign contributions. On the other hand, most voters confront a situation where the incentive to gather political information is absent. The expected value of any one vote is usually much less than the cost associated with even the simple act of voting let alone casting an informed vote. The expected value of political information on any candidate or issue is far less than the cost associated with seeking that information unless the voter has a *selective incentive* to acquire particular information. *Rational absten-tion* from voting and *rational ignorance* among voters is a natural outcome of the logic of individual choice within the democratic political process. Well-informed and well-organized political groups are so because the members have a selective incentive to be informed and organized, i.e., they have a *special interest* in the issue under discussion. These special interest groups will supply both the votes and campaign contributions that politicians need to be successful in their bid for office. The main objective of political action, therefore, is to concentrate benefits on the well-informed and well-organized interests which represent a politician's constituents and disperse costs among the unorganized and ill-informed mass of citizens. The bias in government policy-making is, therefore, one that yields short-term and easily identifiable benefits at the expense of the long-term and largely hidden costs. Despite the soundness of an economic policy, unless it can pass that bias test it is most likely destined for the political scrap heap.

Political programs for reducing government involvement in the economy *for any particular action*, for example, entail great costs and offer very little relative benefit in return. A reduction in government involvement in the economy results in short-term and easily identifiable costs to the existing bureaucracy with the promise of long-term and largely hidden benefits to consumers. Stated bluntly, if the logic of politics is to concentrate benefits and disperse costs, then the logic of political and economic liberalization is to concentrate costs on the existing interests who benefit from current government action and disperse benefits in terms of enhanced consumer welfare, and as such, the two logics conflict with one another.

Perhaps a simple example from a democratic regime may illustrate the point. Say a proposition is put forth that teachers will perform better if they receive a $1,000 increase in pay. The cost of the government's education program, however, will be dispersed among tax payers of the state as an increase in their state income tax of $1. In order to be well-informed on the issue and work to defeat the passage of the government's proposed program it would cost the individual opponent of the bill in excess of $100 in terms of time and expense. Such an activity is not economical for most individuals and, therefore, they will remain rationally ignorant of the issue. On the other hand, teachers who expect to receive $1,000 will take the time and additional expense to make sure that the program passes. The interaction of politics under democracy pits vote-seeking politicians and special interest voters on one side against rationally ignorant voters on the other. This interaction produces certain biases in the system which tend to support the ever increasing expansion of government involvement in the economy.

If we reverse the situation so that teachers face a possible cut of $1,000 in their pay and tax payers pay $1 less in state income taxes, then the logic of politics produces strong resistance to reform. The teacher again who expects to lose $1,000 in pay will work very hard to resist the passage of a program that calls for such austerity. On the other hand, tax payers could only expect to receive $1 and as such will again remain rationally ignorant.

To return to the theme of ideas and interests, it does seem that ideas matter in the direction of greater government involvement because they may erode the constraints that existed concerning government action. In other words, ideas can be enlisted in the service of well-informed and well-organized interests when those ideas suggest more government intervention. However, ideas and action in the direction of less government involvement in the economy cannot enlist the service of powerful interests – in fact, the opposite is true since reduction in the size of government requires the defeat of interests.

The basic logic of politics derived from the analysis of democracies is intensified under non-democratic regimes such as the Communist regime of the former Soviet Union.[12] Here, even the façade of public interest quickly disappears. *The sole point of the system was to concentrate benefits on those in power and disperse the costs on the citizens.* The beneficiaries of such a structure were simply not going to give up their privileged positions easily – it would be irrational for them to do so. In fact, endogenous reform would violate the maxims of rational choice because it would require that members of the dominant interest group move in a Pareto inferior manner.

Only an *exogenous* shock, such as war, natural disaster, economic depression or an ideological revolution, could displace the intransigent interest group.[13] At such moments, ideas can play a dominant role by restructuring the basic relationship between the citizen and state. But, without such moments the logic of politics will defeat efforts in economic liberalization.

Proposition 5: Without a credible commitment to economic liberalization, reform efforts are doomed to fail

Even if an *exogenous* shock displaces the dominant interest group and the opportunity for real economic liberalization presents itself,

8

reforms will stall unless the new regime can establish a binding and credible commitment to reform. Only if the reforming regime can convince the populace that it will honor its promise to respect their rights and create a stable environment for economic activity, will the reforms ever get off the ground. Conveying such a commitment, however, is the major problem in establishing a workable constitution of economic policy.

One of the major difficulties facing the reforming regime is somehow signalling to its citizens that it will honor its promise of reform, and not renege. There are two problems confronting the reforming regime. First, a *strategic incentive* game is generated by reform proposals. A policy or promise announced at one time may bring forth a response that in the next time period provides one player with a greater opportunity for personal gain by reneging rather than honoring the promise. When I am having trouble falling asleep, for example, I may attempt to solicit my wife to rub my back with the promise 'I'll rub your back, if you rub mine.' However, if her soothing back rub produces the intended result, then I will be much better off by reneging than honoring my promise – since I will now be asleep. My wife, of course, knows that I will renege on the promise, and therefore, except for the kindness of her heart, will refuse to believe the promise and *not* rub my back.

A similar situation faces the government and its citizens when formulating public policy. Without a binding commitment to honor its promise, citizens will realize that the government may gain in future periods by reneging on the policy, and thus, will not trust the policy announcements of the government unless the government can establish a binding and credible commitment to the policy.

This problem is compounded when we realize that the situation is not limited to the strategic incentives, but also includes an *informational* problem that may be even more difficult to overcome. Faced with a reforming government, the citizen does not really *know* who they are playing with. The citizen's only prior knowledge of the regime was the 'old way' of doing things. Reform signals a break from the past, but why should the citizens believe the regime? Without citizen participation, though, the reforms will stall. The most effective way out of this impasse and to signal commitment by the regime to liberalization is to reject all notions of gradualism and embrace a radical liberalization program that is implemented overnight.

Proposition 6: Only a radical reform that changes the basic relationship between the citizen and the state can get a moribund economy back on track to progress and development

The steps necessary to rejuvenate the Soviet economy are rather straightforward and radical. The government cannot simply copy the Western welfare states because they do not have the economic base which is necessary to establish such a system. The mal-investment that resulted from years of state economic management must be corrected. Unfortunately, most individuals in these economies wake up every day and go to work at the wrong job, in a factory that is in the wrong place, to produce the wrong goods. Many of the firms actually contribute 'negative value added', that is, the value of the inputs in the production process is greater than the market value of the output that is produced. This is the legacy of decades of attempted central administration of the economy.

There is no medicine for this except a strong dose of market discipline. But strong markets will only emerge if a rule of law establishes private property and freedom of entry. All other ideal policies follow from these two principles. The private property order, unlike the communist property order, offers an internally consistent vision of a workable economy.

CONCLUSION

Each of these propositions will be dealt with at much greater length in the chapters that follow. I can, however, offer a brief answer to the original questions posed that derives from weaving these propositions together.

Real existing socialism did not represent Marxian socialism because Marxian socialism was (is) an internally inconsistent utopia. Rather, mature Soviet-style socialism was the unintended by-product of attempting to implement the Marxian dream and the institutional legacy of that attempt. Soviet-style socialism was able to muddle through slowly eroding the accumulated surplus fund it inherited from natural resources, internal imperialism (e.g., collectivization in the 1930s), and external colonialization (Eastern Europe after the Second World War), in large part because of the illicit markets that existed throughout the system and through the use of world prices in allocating scarce natural resources. Thus, Soviet-style socialism was able to last over sixty years because it took that long to exhaust the accumulated surpluses and reach a point of acute economic crisis (I am dating the secular stagnation to the 1970s).

In terms of why market reforms have actually recorded a worse crisis than we had previously believed possible, a few issues need to be addressed. First, because of the previous overestimation of economic capability the costs of the transition are often overstated. In an excess demand economy, like the former Soviet bloc countries, allowing prices to adjust to market clearing levels may appear, according to wage deflated by price index measurements, to decrease the standard of living. In actuality, however, what has happened is the elimination of the queue. Similarly, if previous production measurements concentrated on output targets independent of consumer demand, then the introduction of markets would suggest a reduction in production, when the production of unwanted and poor quality products had simply ceased. The introduction of market forces, when compared to the bogus measurements of the previous socialist regime, would bring with them the appearance of severe reductions in standards of living as a consequence of measurement problems. Eliminating queues and curtailing the production of sub-par and useless products should not be viewed as threats to consumer welfare. Real reforms represent a radical break with the previous system.

In the actual experience of reforming the formerly socialist economies, however, the problem is more severe than just mismeasurement. In the case of the former Soviet Union, reform simply did not take place. As a consequence, while the old regime and old way of doing things had been de-legitimized, no new system had been able to emerge to promote social cooperation under a division of labor. Illicit markets and small-scale markets continued to operate, but large unregulated markets are still a thing of the future. However, without the introduction of large-scale markets and the establishment of a rule of law that protects unfettered markets, the peoples of the former Soviet Union are doomed to continued economic deprivation.

2

THE ROAD TO NOWHERE

The cause of the Party's defectiveness must be found. All our principles were right, but our results were wrong. This is a diseased century. We diagnosed the disease and its causes with microscopic exactness, but wherever we applied the healing knife a new sore appeared. Our will was hard and pure, we should have been loved by the people. But they hate us. Why are we so odious and detested? We brought you truth, and in our mouth it sounded a lie. We brought the living life, and where our voice is heard the trees wither and there is the rustling of dry leaves. We brought you the promise of the future, but our tongue stammered and barked . . .

Arthur Koestler[1]

INTRODUCTION

During the 1990 May Day celebrations Mikhail Gorbachev was jeered by the crowd. Some of the signs of protest read: 'Workers of the World We're Sorry,' 'Freedom instead of Socialism,' and chants of 'Resign' and 'Shame' were heard from the crowd directed at Gorbachev. Perhaps the most telling banner simply read: 'Seventy-Two Years on the Road to Nowhere.'[2]

On 7 November 1990 the celebration of the seventy-third anniversary of the Russian Revolution proved to be a similar experience for the Soviet leader. Gavriil Popov, the mayor of Moscow, had suggested that the celebration be suspended. But Gorbachev insisted that the historic choice of the October Revolution was the correct one and that the spirit of October still remained a great inspiration for his people and the world. So a celebration proceeded.

The seventy-third anniversary parade, however, met with jeering crowds and even a lone gunman who fired two shots but did not harm anyone. The more peaceful demonstrators conveyed their frustrations with the Soviet regime with banners and slogans calling for the resignation of the Communist government. But Anna Pecheikina stole the show by displaying a sickly plucked chicken high above the crowd on a stick. One woman pointed to the bony chicken and said: 'That is what Gorbachev got the Nobel Prize for.' Another man simply hoped he could find the chicken's little brother to eat. The burden of mundane economic survival – characterized by long lines and poor products in the official sector – grew more severe and unbearable under Gorbachev's regime.[3]

At the same time, the historical awakening that represented one of the cornerstones of Gorbachev's policy of *glasnost* increasingly questioned whether the Revolution should be a cause for political celebration at all. Rather, a public mourning would be more appropriate. The movement to erect a monument to political victims of the Stalin era in Moscow by the Memorial Society represented the beginning of a necessary historical cleansing.[4]

Much of the history written by Soviet scholars in the age of glasnost does not support the research of the 'respected' voices in Western scholarship on the history of socialism. In fact, Western scholars such as Robert Conquest and G. Warren Nutter, who were dismissed by some as reactionaries because they recorded the political horrors of Stalinism or challenged the economic claims of socialist planning, were continually vindicated,[5] whereas the historical research of many respected Western scholars of the Soviet system became continually suspect. The work of political historians such as Roy Medvedev and Alexander Tsipko during the age of glasnost confirmed the scholarly findings of Conquest, and economic writers such as Vasily Selyunin and Nikolai Shmelev agreed with Nutter that the growth rates of the Soviet economy were systematically over-stated.[6] The regime had lost its battle to retain the historical lie of achievement born of great sacrifice. The sacrifice was real, but what achievement could this system possibly claim for its people?

7 November 1991 came and went without any official celebration.[7] The Revolution Day holiday was suspended by the ruling government. The attempted coup of August 1991 had destroyed any legitimacy the communist government had retained during the Gorbachev era. Gorbachev's message on his return from house arrest that the Communist Party could still be democratically restructured,

and that the socialist choice of 1917 was still the historically correct one, fell on deaf ears and sealed his political fate. He, like the Communist Party he represented, was simply a dying dinosaur. On Christmas day 1991, Mikhail Gorbachev formally resigned and the Soviet Union ceased to exist as a political entity.[8] Thus ended one of the most closely watched and studied peacetime political eras of the twentieth century.

The Gorbachev period captured the attention of the world. 'Gorbymania' characterized most of the Western press coverage of the unfolding events. All our previous preconceptions of the world were challenged. As the socialist system collapsed, the Cold War was brought to a glorious end. As the iron curtain fell, the horrible economic and social realities could no longer be ignored or apologized for. Reports of economic, environmental and social deprivation were no longer limited to émigré interviews beyond the control of state censors, and Western anti-communist scholars and intellectuals. Soviet bloc officials themselves admitted the failures of the existing system. The socialist reality could be viewed on Western television and Western newspapers carried reports almost daily about some fallen icon of the socialist age or some new historical revelation about the imperfections of the Soviet past.

Unfortunately, the intellectual prejudices of the twentieth century had poorly prepared Western scholars and intellectuals for the task of understanding and interpreting the events of the late 1980s. These prejudices distorted their basic understanding of history, politics and economics, and as result, fundamental questions of social organization lay outside of their grasp. Theorists in both the East and West were at a loss in offering sound analysis of the system that collapsed before their eyes. While the world was swamped with journalistic coverage of the events, there was a lack of deep reflection on the nature of the problem confronting these societies. One reason for this was simply that the speed of the changes from 1989 on were so fast as to not afford such reflection. Another reason, though, was the persistence of certain false prejudices which prevented commentators from understanding.

All historical interpretation is guided by intellectual prejudices for good or bad. The advantage of the bridge to the past provided by the passage of time, in fact, is that it affords scholars and intellectuals a great opportunity in the assessment of which prejudices mislead and which enable interpretation. Obviously, in attempting to understand the unfolding of the Gorbachev and the post-Gorbachev era we do not have the benefit of temporal distance that we do with say the

American, French or even the Russian revolution. But, understanding the reason for the Gorbachev reforms in the first place provides the key to establishing a criteria from which to assess the problems with the Gorbachev reforms and offer advice on how to move forward in a more positive direction in the post-Gorbachev era. But in order to understand the reforms it is necessary to understand the Soviet system and its historical operation. In order to accomplish this task, we must view the grand story of Soviet history through the right pair of theoretical lenses. 'Our understanding of the past,' Douglas North tells us, 'is no better than the theory we use and that theory has been woefully deficient.'[9]

THE POOR PREPARATION FOR UNDERSTANDING

Our ability to understand the Soviet experience has been distorted greatly by the intellectual trends of the twentieth century. The dominant theories in both politics and economics conspired to warp historical interpretations of capitalistic processes and socialist practice. In addition, as the century progressed interest groups developed which served as the guardian of these misunderstandings. Ideas came both to create, and then to serve, the purposes of vested interests which would not allow dissenting opinion to challenge the establishment.

This is not meant to imply that no debate was allowed. Certainly there was debate, but the parameters of the debate were firmly established and unquestioned. For much of the twentieth century the basic consensus on either side of the dispute concerning the grand questions of social organization was that capitalism had failed in providing equity and humane social conditions which progressive legislation must correct.[10] Moreover, the Great Depression of the 1930s supposedly demonstrated that capitalism was not only unjust, but also unstable as an economic system. Capitalism, if it was to survive at all, must be subject to democratic forces of control to tame its operations and protect the populace from unscrupulous business and irresponsible speculation. Socialism, in fact, was viewed as a great threat to those who favored capitalism precisely because it was perceived as offering a viable alternative.[11]

This general intellectual climate was reinforced by the theoretical developments in economics. As academic economic theory became more technically sophisticated and rarified in its presentation of its basic theorems, an appreciative or intuitive understanding of the

15

nature of market institutions and their operation became scientifically suspect.[12] The flip-side of the development of the idea of perfect competition, and the strict conditions established for its attainment, was the development of the theory of market failure. Market failures were said to exist whenever capitalist reality did not meet the conditions of the frictionless textbook model of perfect competition.[13] The concepts of externalities, public goods, monopoly and imperfect competition and macroeconomic instability were developed and used by professional economists to explain why markets may fail to allocate resources in a socially desirable manner. Real existing competitive capitalism generated negative externalities in the form of pollution and other undesirable third-party effects, possessed an inherent tendency toward monopolization and waste, could not provide many basic services such as roads and education and suffered from recurring business cycles. That was the theoretical picture of competitive capitalism that dominated the intellectual landscape for most of the twentieth century.

Obviously, this theoretical perspective colored historical interpretation. The rise of industrial capitalism in the late nineteenth-century United States was viewed as simply a process by which the 'Robber Barons' acquired monopoly power. The banking panics of 1893 and 1907 were viewed as the result of the inherent instability of capitalist industrial processes. The solution to these problems, if one was conservative, was to bring capitalism under the control of democratic forces (preferably dominated by leaders of industry themselves). To eliminate monopoly, the Sherman (1890), Clayton (1914) and Federal Trade Commission (1914) Acts were passed. To eliminate bank panics and regulate business cycles, the Federal Reserve System (1913) was established. Radicals, on the other hand, argued that such reformist measures would not rid society of the ills of capitalism – which possessed inherent contradictions – and that only a transition to a socialist society would accomplish that goal.

The Great Depression shook an entire generation's faith in the efficacy of capitalist markets. Rational planning of the economy came to be viewed not only as the most viable alternative, but the only alternative. The parameters of the debate had shifted drastically by the 1930s. *Laissez-faire* was no longer considered as any kind of option in the economic policy debate. Classical liberal economic policy simply reflected the beliefs of the naive and simple minded. The modern world had become too complex for an eighteenth-century idea to offer anything of value.

John Maynard Keynes went so far as to argue that the great social experiments of the time in Germany (fascism) and Russia (communism) would point the way to the future of economic policy. Country after country had abandoned the old presuppositions of classical political economy. Russia, Italy and Germany had moved towards establishing a new political economy, Keynes argued, and their experience must be watched closely. No one could tell which of the new systems would prove itself best, but they nevertheless successfully persuaded thinking men and women in Great Britain and the United States to strive after a new economic plan of their own. Some may still cling to the old ideas of *laissez-faire* capitalism, 'but in no country of the world to-day can they be reckoned as a serious force.'[14]

Keynes considered himself, and was viewed by others, as a realist in the classical liberal tradition. The Keynesian idea was for government officials to intervene rationally in order to improve the workings and outcomes of the market economy. Keynes's proposal was to combine the socialization of the capital market with the nineteenth-century political traditions of Great Britain. While he saw that the socialization of investment was the only way of securing an approximation of full employment, this change did not require a break with the general traditions of bourgeois society. Moreover, Keynes merely conceived of his theory as an extension of classical political economy and classical liberalism, not a rejection of those systems of thought. Keynes's advocacy of a greater role of government in planning the economy was, in his mind, a practical attempt to save individualism and avoid the destruction of the existing economic system.[15] Keynes's attitude toward *laissez-faire* reflected the general consensus of the times among intellectuals, scholars and politicians.

The spirit of the age led even someone usually recognized as an intellectual leader of classical liberalism, Frank Knight, publicly to declare the virtues of communism.[16] It seemed as if everyone advocated some form of government control and planning of the economy to ensure stability and equity. Paul Homan provided a contemporary overview of the literature on economic planning in 1932 in the *Quarterly Journal of Economics*, and while he criticized various proposals for lacking details, he did not voice any criticism of planning in principle. Contemporary proposals for planning may be faulty, he argued, especially since many disregard the important insights of price theory, but they nevertheless represented the first 'pamphlet' stage of addressing the problems of stability and full employment. Homan pointed out that modern industrial complexity could curiously be employed both as a reason of why we *must* plan the economy, and why we *cannot*. But the idea that industrial relations are too complex to be brought under direct control, though shared by some economists, was the view of an intelligent businessman. Businessmen, however, did not understand the essential characteristics of the problem of economic instability. Their education, according to Homan, was defective with respect to the economics of financial markets, and the fields of money, credit and investment. This businessman's perspective was colored by the American tradition of private enterprise and non-governmental interference. The responsible question of the day was simply which was the best way forward for economic planning, not whether or not the government should engage in planning the economy. The profitable cultivation of the ideas of economic planning will lead to more coherent and comprehensive proposals to solve the problems of stability and equity.[17]

The July 1932 issue of the prestigious *Annals of the American Academy of Political and Social Science* was entirely devoted to national and world economic planning. Not a single criticism of economic planning was voiced in that volume. Instead, planning was lauded as the method by which 'individual and corporate economic activity' could be molded 'into group-defined spheres of action which are rationally mapped out and fitted, as parts of a mosaic, into a coordinated whole, for the purpose of achieving certain rationally conceived and socially comprehensive goals.'[18]

Laissez-faire as a policy was held in disrepute by scholars, intellectuals and politicians. Franklin D. Roosevelt even chose to attack classical economists in his third fireside chat on 24 July 1933. 'I have no sympathy,' he stated, 'for the professional economists who insist that things must run their course and that human agencies can have no influence on economic ills.' On 19 December 1936, Roosevelt expressed his complete agnosticism with regard to the truth of any tenet of political economy in a letter to Joseph Schumpeter. He had studied economics for thirty-six years, Schumpeter was informed, but Roosevelt was 'compelled to admit – or boast – whichever way you care to put, that I know nothing of economics and that nobody else does either!'[19]

In a 1934 book by Rexford Tugwell (a professor of economics at Columbia University and the assistant secretary of the Treasury under Franklin D. Roosevelt) and Howard Hill, the argument against *laissez-faire* was carried further, and included a direct discussion of the Soviet experience. They argued that

> the challenge of Russia to America does not lie in the merits of the Soviet system, although they may prove to be considerable. The challenge lies rather in the idea of planning, of purposeful, intelligent control over economic affairs. This, it seems, we must accept as a guide to our economic life to replace the decadent notions of a laissez-faire philosophy.[20]

Julian Huxley, the noted scientist, argued that the Soviet five-year planning system was simply the 'spirit of science introduced into politics and industry.'[21]

The intellectual *gestalt* of the time could neither appreciate nor tolerate the challenge to economic planning offered by its critics, namely Ludwig von Mises and F. A. Hayek. But without an understanding of even the potential difficulties that economic planning may confront in practice, it would be impossible to make sense out of any real world experiment with economic planning. It should not be a surprise that within such a climate of opinion that Soviet practice could not be properly understood. It was not just a matter of communist apologetics – though, of course, there was some of that – the real problem of interpreting Soviet practice was a sincere blind spot on the part of scholars and intellectuals.[22] It just could not be that economic planning would not work as envisaged. It seemed so rational, so scientific, and it had the great potential of providing economic stability and guaranteeing a more equitable distribution of the social pie.

Not only did this intellectual bias fail to appreciate the *economic* problems of planning, it failed miserably to grasp the *political* problems inherent with planning. In the West, this was due to an utterly naive view of the operation of democracy that dominated political science by the early twentieth century.[23] The textbook model of democracy portrayed the political system as one in which individual citizens could effectively determine the rules by which they would live. The vote process unambiguously conveyed the necessary information concerning the array of public goods and services demanded and the level of taxes that must be paid. Democracy was an ideal model of self-rule. Faced with market failure, democratic governments could easily set the matter straight. If government action failed, it was not due to any structural weakness in the democratic system – political actors would just have to gather more information and try harder next time.

Such a view of democratic processes, however, was woefully deficient. And, it possessed a deleterious affect on interpretations of the institutions of socialist policy. The political problems of Stalinism, which were recognized by many early on, were not attributed to the nature of planning per se, but rather to the lack of a democratic tradition in Russian history. Planning, as such, was not seen to possess any threat to political freedom whatsoever. Economic planning, under democracy, would not face any of the problems associated with Stalinism. Keynes, for example, in reacting to Hayek's *The Road to Serfdom*, wrote that

> I should say that what we want is not no planning, or even less planning, indeed I should say that we almost certainly want more. But planning should take place in a community in which as many people as possible, both leaders and followers, wholly share your own moral position. Moderate planning will be safe if those carrying it out are rightly oriented in their own minds and hearts to the moral issues.[24]

So as long as 'good' people were in charge, nothing was objectionable with economic planning. In fact, economic planning was desirable.

Herman Finer was not as kind to Hayek as Keynes. Finer accused Hayek's *The Road to Serfdom* of being 'the most sinister offensive against democracy to emerge from a democratic country for many decades.'[25] The true alternative to dictatorship, Finer assured his audience, was not economic individualism and competition, but a democratic government fully responsible to the people. Hayek's world, according to Finer, would leave individuals under the control of aristocrats or the moneyed bourgeoisie. But, free people can govern themselves without such masters. Economic planning was simply democracy in action, and it proved itself every time there was a successful government action.

The level of Finer's misunderstanding of Hayek's basic argument was astonishing viewed from our vantage point today, but at the time it was not. The Mises–Hayek analytical criticism of socialist planning was hardly understood by any professional economist and in many respects has not been fully appreciated even to this day.[26] Moreover, the naive view of democracy that Finer defended in his book only came to be seriously challenged as the theory of public choice developed in the post-Second World War era. The mainstream of

THE ROAD TO NOWHERE

thought simply did not appreciate, let alone incorporate, the important insights concerning information and incentives in economic and
political processes that only became evident with the further development of modern political economy.

Why should it be surprising, therefore, that Sovietologists were ill-
prepared to understand their subject matter? They possessed neither
a sound economic or political theory from which to interpret the
unique Soviet facts. The intellectual spirit of the age applauded what
the Soviet Union was attempting even if there existed normative
disagreements about how it was going about it. Economic failures of
the Soviet system were attributed to its backwardness, just as the
political problems of the system were attributed to the lack of
democratic traditions. What was essentially missing from Sovietology
was a thorough examination of the *structural* weakness of socialist
institutions.

THE MALPRACTICE OF ECONOMIC MEASUREMENT

The degree of poor preparation was not just limited to a failure to
recognize that the problems that plagued the Soviet system were not
in the system, but rather were *the* system. Several other developments also conspired that prevented many from even recognizing
that there were problems at all. The emerging hegemony of
macroeconomics in the economic profession and in the public mind
was perhaps the most fateful turn of intellectual events in blinding
observers of the Soviet economy to the reality of the systemic failure
of socialism.

The development of techniques in aggregate economics in the wake
of the Keynesian victory in economic thought drew economists'
attention away from the structural make-up of a system and instead
focused their attention on aggregate figures such as gross national
product (GNP). Beside the conceptual problem of how one aggregates
the data in a world where prices are meaningless, the approach was a
fundamentally flawed one for understanding the industrial structure
of any society. Aggregate concepts, such as price level, national
product, savings rate and levels of public investment, do not allow the
economist to examine how complex production plans in an industrial
economy are continually adjusted to match with consumer demands
through time. But the mutual adjustment of intertemporal decisions
by economic actors to coordinate the plans of producers with

consumption preferences of buyers makes up the unique capital structure of any industrial economy. It is the mutual accommodation of suppliers and demanders through a process of competitive bids and offers that economics must explain, and the techniques of aggregate economics simply drew economists' attention away from this task. As aggregate economics came to dominate the profession in the 1940s, 1950s and 1960s, the problem became even more acute. Not only did economists not pay much professional attention to the dynamics of capitalist processes of production, they ignored them completely.[27]

An example may illustrate the fundamental problem of aggregate economics in assessing economic systems. Consider the case of a fat man and a muscular man. They may both weigh 225lbs, but the composition of each of their bodies is radically different. One is flabby, the other is fit. To understand the health of either individual it does not much matter what the aggregate weight is, the important point is to examine the *structural composition*.

The Soviet economy was similar to the fat man in my story above. Aggregate growth statistics concealed the flabby and faulty capital structure that was born in Stalin's industrialization. But economists preoccupied with such figures did not appreciate the distinction between sustainable development and non-sustainable development of an economy. Western Sovietologists knew of the dangers associated with working with the falsified official statistics on the Soviet economy. But the techniques the United States Central Intelligence Agency (CIA) developed still focused on gaining some aggregate or macroeconomic measure of performance, rather than encouraging detailed microeconomic analysis of the industrial structure of the Soviet Union.

Not only did the CIA develop techniques which were misleading even in the abstract, but they tended systematically to overstate the capability of the Soviet economy on their own grounds. A comparison of alternative measures of Soviet economic growth is found in Table 2.1, and shows that in the late 1970s and 1980s the CIA overstated the growth of the Soviet economy as compared to the estimates of Vasily Selyunin and Grigory Khanin.

But the CIA's performance was actually much worse than these figures would suggest. Whereas the official TsSU figure for the average annual rate of growth of national income in the Soviet economy from 1928 to 1985 was 8.8 per cent, the CIA's estimate was 4.3 per cent, and Khanin's estimate was 3.33 per cent. But this conceals the Soviet decline of the 1970s and beyond. In the 1970s,

Table 2.1 Alternative measure of Soviet economic growth (average annual growth in %)

	Official Soviet statistics (%)	Selyunin–Khanin estimates (%)	CIA estimates (%)
1951–60	10.3	7.2	5.1
1961–65	6.5	4.4	4.8
1966–70	7.8	4.1	5.0
1971–75	5.7	3.2	3.1
1976–80	4.3	1.0	2.2
1981–85	3.6	0.6	1.8

Source: Revisiting Soviet Economic Performance under Glasnost: Implications for CIA Estimates (Washington, DC: SOV 88–10068, 1988): 11.

Selyunin and Khanin estimate that Soviet GNP grew at about 2 per cent annual rate of growth, whereas the CIA estimate was 3.7 per cent. For the eleventh five-year plan (1981–5), Selyunin and Khanin estimate a growth rate of 0.59 per cent, whereas the CIA estimates 2 per cent average annual growth of Soviet GNP.[28]

Moreover, Selyunin and Khanin date the negative decline of the Soviet economy not to the mid-1970s, but rather fifteen years earlier to the beginning of the 1960s. Even if alternative calculations of the Soviet economy may show significant growth, they do not examine the meaning of that growth in terms of the industrial structure created and the employment of scarce resources. As Selyunin and Khanin pointed out, Soviet growth was achieved through

> inordinate resource expenditures. In almost all periods of our history, the use of material resources and fixed assets grew more rapidly than did national income. From 1928 through 1985, material-intensiveness increased by 60% and return on assets fell 30%.

Labor productivity grew only modestly throughout this period. The Soviet method of economic management, they argued, was made possible only because of the abundance of resources at the regime's disposal. 'But the price was high: living standards fell for decades.' [29]

This point, however, does not square well with CIA estimates that Soviet per capita GNP converted at US purchasing power equivalents amounted to $8,370 in 1986 or about 49 per cent of the US.[30] More recent alternative estimates of Soviet per capita GNP challenge the CIA figures significantly by placing the Soviet economy at somewhere around 25 per cent of the US.[31] If the CIA figures were accurate the Soviet economy would have been a maturing industrialized economy, but the reality was that the former Soviet economy provided a standard of living equivalent to a well-developed Third World economy at best. Moreover, if the CIA statistics were correct, then there would not have been any need for a radical economic reform and Gorbachev's rhetoric would have been incomprehensible and unfounded.

Even with revised data international comparisons of per capita GNP systematically overstate the well-being of Soviet citizens. One reason for this bias was that the low quality of Soviet products was not considered. Another reason was that the persistent shortages of goods and the corresponding queuing for even those goods that were available was not reflected in the statistics. And, finally, the per capita GNP statistics do not reveal the low percentage of GNP that went to household consumption in the former Soviet Union. Only about 50 per cent of GNP in the former Soviet Union went to household production.[32] Soviet consumers were far worse off than even revised estimates indicated.

One significant consequence of these mismeasurement problems was that the military capabilities of the Soviet Union were grossly distorted. If the national income of the former Soviet Union was actually less than a third of the US, the military burden of the empire was much greater than ever estimated by Western Sovietologists. Correcting for these alternative calculations of Soviet GNP, and incorporating information from the glasnost era, it is estimated that the military burden represented about 25 per cent of GNP in the former Soviet Union.[33] As a result, most Western estimates of Soviet military strength were seriously mistaken because the military burden (in terms of the explicit and implicit tax on the population) was understated at the same time that the long-term viability of the Soviet economy was overstated. Correcting the figures challenges previous perceptions concerning the capability of the former Soviet system to engage in a sustained military conflict with the West.[34]

These distortions, though, were not simply the product of poor information and inadequate measurement techniques. The distortions served a very important ideological and interest group function. On the one hand, conservative anti-communists supported the bias toward overestimating Soviet economic and military strength because it reinforced their fears of the impending encroachment of communism throughout the world. The statistics justified large military expenditures to fight the advent of global communism. If the Soviet economy was structurally weak, then the threat of communism would have been rather shallow and would not have justified the military conflict of the Cold War. Only a developing industrial power could supply the economic base and technological innovations that would pose a sustainable threat to Western powers. On the other hand, radical intellectuals, even if they despised the Soviet regime, believed in the basic ability of the system of centralized economic planning to promote development. If Soviet economic planning was a failure, then socialism may have been a questionable policy goal to advocate even in more democratic situations. Scholars, intellectuals and politicians of both 'left' and 'right' persuasion, therefore, possessed an ideological stake in the ability of the Soviet economy to develop and prosper.

These ideas about the efficacy of Soviet economic planning also created an extremely powerful interest group, namely the military-industrial establishment in the West. The military-industrial establishment benefited directly from the overestimation of Soviet capabilities.[35] Right-wing and left-wing beliefs about the developing Soviet economy provided the needed justification for large appropriations toward armament productions and military research and development.[36] Thus, an iron-triangle was forged of ideas and interests that simply could not, and would not, allow analysis that seriously challenged the Soviet myth of economic success. But, as we have seen, the Soviet system was far from an economic success. More to the point, the Soviet economy may well be the ultimate political economy tragedy of this century.

A SHORT HISTORY OF SOVIET ECONOMIC FAILURE

Lenin came to power in Russia promising the emancipation of man from the domination of other men and nature. His utopian vision was inspiring and his will to power was resolute. Lenin and the Bolsheviks possessed a concrete vision of the path to a better future. Their plan of social construction after the revolution was not a by-product of improvisation, they knew what they wanted to accomplish and how they were supposed to accomplish that goal. Of course, the civil war influenced the way that policies were implemented, but war had little or nothing to do with the motivation behind the policies. If anything, the Russian Revolution of 1917 was an ideological revolution.[37]

Between 1917 and 1921 the Bolsheviks tried to substitute a unified economic plan for the 'anarchy' of the market. Production for exchange, which characterized the commodity mode of production, would be replaced by production for direct use. The irrationality of the capitalist mode of production would be overcome in strict accordance to Marxian principles.

In economic life the Marxian project entailed eliminating the constant struggle between competing autonomous private interests on the economic scene by bringing economic life under conscious public control. It was this process of bringing all of economic life under conscious control that pre-occupied the Bolsheviks upon coming to power in 1917.

At Lenin's first appearance before the Party after the October revolution in 1917, he gripped 'the edge of the reading stand, letting his little winking eyes travel over the crowd as he stood there waiting, apparently oblivious to the long-rolling ovation, which lasted several minutes. When it finished, he said simply, "We shall now proceed to construct the Socialist order!" '[38]

And proceed they did. Between 1917 and 1921 the Bolsheviks attempted to bring all economic activity under the conscious direction of the Supreme Economic Council. The attempt to abolish money relations and monetary calculation was pursued with a passion. This was quite natural given their ideological program.

The Bolshevik project of rationalization and emancipation was spelled out in the program adopted at the Eighth Congress in March 1919. In the realm of economic affairs, the Party program called for expropriating the expropriators, increasing the productive forces of society by eliminating the contradictions of capitalism, mobilizing labor, organizing the trade unions, educating the workers and, basically, securing 'the maximum solidarisation of the whole economic apparatus.'[39] In order to accomplish this goal the Bolsheviks established the Supreme Economic Council to bring economic existence under rational control, i.e., substitute production for direct use for the chaotic system of production for exchange that characterized the commodity mode of production, and seized the banks and merged them into a single state bank. The bank would become an apparatus of unified book-keeping for society. The bank was to become, to use Lenin's terminology, 'the nodal point of public accounting.'[40] Following Lenin, the Party program of the Eighth

Congress stated that 'Upon the basis of the nationalisation of banking, the Russian Communist Party endeavours to promote a series of measures favouring a moneyless system of account keeping, and paving the way for the abolition of money.'[41]

The rationalization of economic life under communism would eliminate the waste of capitalist production and lead to increased productivity. This burst of productivity would free individuals from the 'chains imposed upon them by nature.' The utopian promise of the project was that 'concurrently with the disappearance of man's tyranny over man, the tyranny of nature over man will likewise vanish. Men and women will for the first time be able to lead a life worthy of thinking beings instead of a life worthy of brute beasts.'[42]

The utopian aspiration, however, resulted in a nightmare by early spring of 1921. In all areas economic output fell far below pre-war levels. In 1921 the Soviet Union, as Stephen Cohen has pointed out, lay

> in ruins, its national income one-third of the 1913 level, industrial production a fifth (output in some branches being virtually zero), its transportation system shattered, and agricultural production so meager that a majority of the population barely subsisted and millions of others failed even that.[43]

The Bolsheviks were forced to retreat from their attempt to implement Marx's utopia and instead re-introduced market relations of exchange and production with the New Economic Policy (NEP) in the Spring of 1921. 'In attempting to go over straight to communism,' Lenin wrote on 17 October 1921,

> we, in the spring of 1921, sustained a more serious defeat on the economic front than any defeat inflicted upon us by Kolchak, Deniken or Pilsudski. This defeat was much more serious, significant and dangerous. It was expressed in the isolation of the higher administrators of our economic policy from the lower and their failure to produce that development of the productive forces which the Programme of our Party regards as vital and urgent.[44]

While the NEP saw a modicum of the rule of law restored within the Soviet Union this period was not without ambiguities.[45] At the same time that Lenin re-introduced market mechanisms he outlawed all political factions within Soviet politics, including factions within the

Party. While denationalizing the majority of industries the Bolsheviks maintained control over the 'commanding heights', e.g., major manufacturing and banking. At the height of the NEP, for example, while only about 8 per cent of industrial enterprises remained state owned, that 8 per cent employed about 85 per cent of the industrial labor force.

The NEP saw a great recovery from the cataclysm of the communist experiment with economic planning, but the system itself was a massive interventionist system possessing its own dynamic. The NEP had its own unintended and undesirable consequences. As Lenin would write of the NEP system in the spring of 1922:

> The machine refused to obey the hand that guided it. It was like a car that was going not in the direction the driver desired, but in the direction someone else desired; as if it were being driven by some mysterious, lawless hand, God knows whose, perhaps of a profiteer, or of a private capitalist, or of both. Be that as it may, the car is not going quite in the direction that the man at the wheel imagines, and often it goes in an altogether different direction.[46]

Not only did the NEP fail to produce the results the Bolsheviks had intended, but the system evolved into a bureaucratic embarrassment. No structural changes were introduced to the economic institutions that were the legacy of war communism. The tasks of economic institutions were re-arranged but they were not dismantled. The problem of bureaucracy in the Soviet Union led Lenin to declare that the 'state apparatus [had become] so deplorable, not to say wretched.'[47] But with Lenin's health failing throughout 1922 and his final stroke on 10 March 1923, which ended his political activity for good, the Soviet regime was left without a leader.

On 21 January 1924 V. I. Lenin died and with him so did the public ideology of Bolshevism. The resulting ambiguity and despair toward socialist construction was the legacy of Lenin. Lenin had criticized political bureaucracy, yet he established a political monopoly for the Party. He argued for concessions to capitalism, but his legitimating ideology demanded an assault on any hint of emerging capitalist relations. Lenin ended his life staring at a stark contradiction. Socialism rather than emancipating man by rationalizing social existence delivered man into a new serfdom characterized by political and economic irrationality.

The revolutionary cadre was caught in despair. 'Lenin had led his followers into the wilderness only to die before he could lead them out.[48] Despair and confusion plagued the Old Bolsheviks from the time of the NEP until their demise at the hands of Stalin in the purges of the 1930s. The Old Bolsheviks thought they had diagnosed the disease that plagued capitalist society, but wherever they applied the healing knife of socialist policy a new sore appeared. They believed that they had brought the truth to the Russian people and the world, but in their mouth it sounded a lie. They promised to bring the living life to the masses, and where their voice was heard the trees withered and died. By the late 1930s, the entire ruling cadre of the Old Bolsheviks – Lenin, Bukharin, Trotsky, Zinoviev, Kamenev, Rykov, etc. – had been eliminated from the political scene by either fate or Stalin's political maneuvering.[49] It was already by this time questionable whether the revolution was worth the suffering it wrought.

In addition to the ideological confusion that permeated the NEP period, the economy was plagued by recurring crises as a result of the government's economic policies. Arbitrary government intervention destroyed the economic incentive to invest and produce in the official market sector. Because of the government's agricultural policy at the end of the NEP, peasants no longer had any incentive to market their grain surplus leading to the 'Grain Crisis' in the winter 1927/28. Net marketings of grain in 1926 and 1927 were only 50 and 57 per cent of the pre-war level although grain output at that time was almost equivalent to the pre-war level. The grain procurement crisis provided the final justification for Stalin to begin his military assault on the Soviet economy. It was the 'Grain Crisis' that gave rise to the rhetorical justification for the 'de-kulakization' drive that brought an end to the NEP.

The poor economic results and the uncomfortable ideology of the NEP, along with fear of foreign intervention, led to Stalin's revolution from above. Stalin with political power firmly in hand by 1927/28 began his military siege of economic life.

Soviet style socialism came to maturity under Stalin. It is important, however, to keep in mind that even at the height of collectivization Stalin never again tried to abolish post-haste and completely commodity relations of production and monetary calculation as the Bolsheviks had sought to do from 1917 to 1921.[50] Marxism became under Stalin merely a mobilizing ideology for power and not a utopian aspiration for man's emancipation. What emerged out of the late 1920s was a *nomenklatura* system whose beneficiaries received ideological justification from Marxism.[51] This has been the case ever since.

The Western textbook image of a rational, hierarchical, planned economy, that was able to achieve tremendous growth (despite its terrible costs) and transform the Soviet Union from a backward peasant economy into a military and industrial power is an illusion. The five-year planning system instituted during Stalin's reign, as Eugene Zaleski points out, could only be referred to as 'planning' with the greatest reserve, and it certainly was not rational.[52]

The Soviet system merely gave the appearance of a centrally planned system, when in reality the system depended crucially upon decentralized decision-making processes to achieve any degree of coordination.[53] There is no doubt that the historical operation of the Soviet system was characterized by strong central power, but that did not affect its fundamental organizational form – at base the Soviet system remained a commodity production economy. The capital structure of the Soviet economy was fundamentally affected by central decisions, particularly those of Stalin, on the direction of industrial development. But, influencing the path of development is not the same as organizing society in strict accordance to a central plan. The US government could decide tomorrow to ban the production of steel and this would radically change the structure of the American economy, but it would not abolish the decentralized processes of market coordination.

The capital market under conditions of public ownership was simply replaced by another decentralized system, one that was more clumsy and less efficient. The 'plan' was built up from the competing requests of the various enterprises and ministries. The political competition among rival pressure groups characterized the 'supreme' economic decisions. The primary function of the planning bureaucracy was to serve as a supply agent and avoid the practice of free price formation and monetary rationing. Capital resources, however, are scarce and, therefore, must be rationed.

If a decree eliminates price competition as the rationing device to coordinate economic decisions, then alternative methods will be relied on to allocate scarce resources. A rent control, for example, which fixes the legal price below the market clearing price will not only lead to shortages of apartments, but also increase the use of non-price competition to allocate scarce apartments. The price control produces costs to the buyer, such as waiting in queues, and so forth, that are not simultaneously benefits to the seller. If the seller possesses any power to transform the deadweight loss into a benefit for themselves they will do so. Problems of discrimination, poor upkeep of apartments, bribing of the landlord, etc., are all common phenomena in areas with rent control. In the Soviet context, both in the consumer and producer sectors, bribing officials, illicit market transactions and special privilege to political elites, emerged as predominant rationing devices.

In addition, despite legal decrees to the contrary, private property in the economic sense was never abolished. Those who exercised control and decision-making power over existing resources were *de facto* private owners, e.g., managers of the factory, etc., even if the claim was made that they acted in the interest of society. These *de facto* private ownership rights of public property, in fact, were the primary source of private benefit from the Stalinist regime to those who 'own' them.[54]

The above only concerns how the official 'planned' sector operates. If we include the unofficial use of the market by planners, then the image of a central, unified and rational plan becomes even more questionable. First, Soviet planners carefully study world markets to aid them in their planning decisions. Thus, as Soviet economic journalist Vasily Selyunin writes, the Soviet planners belie the idea that they can regulate economic life in strict accordance to the plan 'when they carefully study world trends, which are determined by market forces, in order to plan what we should produce.' In doing so 'they tacitly admit that there is a better means than ours for the regulation, or rather self-regulation, of the economy.'[55] Second, the black market is pervasive in the Soviet economy and the coordination of production and exchange activity even within the planned sector, let alone the consumer sector, depends crucially upon its existence.[56]

The Soviet economy never conformed to the ideal picture of a rationally planned communist economy that would abolish completely commodity production because that system is a hopeless and unachievable utopia, as Mises demonstrated in theory in 1920 and Soviet performance demonstrated in practice in 1921. The only attempt to achieve that utopia (1917–21) ended in what William Chamberlin described as 'one of the greatest and most overwhelming failures in history.'[57]

The mature Soviet system evolved into a vast military bureaucratic apparatus that yielded profits to those in positions of power.[58] The root of the Stalinist bureaucracy that plagued the Soviet economy, however, lay in the original Marxian aspiration to plan the economic system rationally even if the original goal was unattainable. Stalinism was, whether intended or not, the logical consequence of Marxist-Leninism. The economic consequences of the Stalinist system were to produce an entirely distorted industrial structure that notoriously disregarded the consumption demands of the populace. In a very important sense, the mature Soviet economy was, and continues to be, a giant mal-invested capital structure where the preponderance of the population goes to work in the wrong place to do the wrong job to produce the wrong goods. Such is the legacy of Stalinist industrial policy.

It is important to understand the history and nature of the system in order to grasp the meaning and task of the reforms under Gorbachev. As Leonid Abalkin, one of Gorbachev's leading advisors, wrote: 'No small number of difficulties arise in the theory and practice of restructuring the economic and management system due to the lack of thoroughly substantiated evaluations of many stages in our economic construction.' Abalkin continued by arguing that at a time when the Soviet government was breaking with existing 'forms, methods, and structures,' they must clearly understand the legacy they were renouncing. It would be 'impossible to assimilate the lessons of the past and to determine the rational avenues of socioeconomic development without substantial reform in economic theory, without the formation of a new type of economic thinking that is radically different from the past.'[59]

Perestroika, it must be understood, did not represent a move away from Marxian central planning – that move was made by Lenin in 1921. Rather, perestroika at best represented a supposed improvement of the bureaucratic system of economic management. But understood at even that level, Gorbachev's reforms did not address the challenge that lay before him from 1985 to 1991.

GORBACHEV'S CHALLENGE

Production and distribution are inexorably connected. Though classical political economists treated production and distribution as analytically distinct that was a serious flaw in their analysis.[60] Market processes of production determine the income and functional distribution of productive factors, such as labor. Within a free-market process there is no distributional process separate from the processes of exchange and production. Factors are paid according to the service they render, or are perceived to render, to others in the market. But in a system, like the former Soviet Union, where the state takes on the role of distribution, wealth is transferred from one class to another based on political rationales. The ability of the state to transfer wealth depends upon its ability to extract economic rents from the productive system without destroying completely the incentive to produce.

The history of the Soviet Union is filled with various 'inventions' by the ruling elite to extract rents from the populace; from the forced grain requisitioning during war communism and the tax-in-kind during the NEP to the collectivization and labor armies under Stalin. The various attempts over the years to reform the Soviet system – Khrushchev's 1957 *sovnarkhoz* reforms; the Brezhnev–Kosygin reforms of 1965; the 1973 industrial reorganization; and the 1979 reforms – were all attempts to improve economic efficiency, expand the productive capability of the economy and enhance the well-being of the *apparatchiks*. Perestroika should be viewed as a further attempt in this Soviet tradition of political economy.

The political distribution of wealth, which necessarily lives off productive output of economic activity in a parasite–host relationship, can be relied upon only to a point.[61] The tax state has its origins in the private property order of the market system. Taxation is derived from the revenues appropriated from the wealth created in the market. Beyond a certain point economic productivity will begin to decline in response to overburdensome taxation, and at that point the economic system enters a crisis. It is probably no exaggeration to say that the most important factor determining economic productivity throughout the world is the system of rules governing the economy. An economy lacking natural resources can flourish if the set of rules governing social intercourse cultivates economic productivity, while an economy rich in natural resources will decline under an unfavorable set of rules.

The peculiar art of Soviet economic policy was to balance an ideological hatred of market relations, which justified the Party's privileged position in society, with the reality of allowing enough market production and exchange so that the Party's ability to extract rents was not threatened. Soviet leaders were chosen for their ability to uphold the fiction that the fictional reality of communism was not fictitious. 'The principle that capitalism (meaning reality) has to be destroyed,' the French Sovietologist Alain Besancon states,

> is therefore capped by another principle – enough capitalism (meaning reality) must be preserved so that the power is not threatened in its material and political base. The whole econ-

33

omic art of the Soviet government consists in combining these two principles so that the socialist design of destroying capitalism is achieved while the strength and vitality of the Party-State on which depends the achievement of this task are preserved.[62]

Besancon concludes that Lenin was the master of this unique Bolshevik art of economic policy. Gorbachev's reforms were consistently in-line with this Bolshevik practice. It was this peculiar Soviet economic tight-rope act that Gorbachev was attempting to master with his zigs and zags between 1985 and 1991.

Gorbachev inherited an economic mess when he rose to power in 1985. 'The problems in the country's development,' Gorbachev stated in his *Political Report of the CPSU Central Committee to the Twenty-Seventh Congress of the Communist Party of the Soviet Union* on 25 February 1986, 'grew more rapidly than they were being solved. The inertness and rigidity of the forms and methods of management, the decline of dynamism in our work, and increased bureaucracy – all this was doing no small damage. Signs of stagnation had begun to surface in the life of society . . .' Gorbachev insisted that the top priority must be to 'overcome the negative factors in society's socio-economic development as rapidly as possible, to accelerate it and impart to it an essential dynamism, to learn from the lessons of the past to a maximum extent,' so that the decisions the party adopted for the future would be absolutely clear and provide a resolute course of action to remedy Soviet society's ills.[63]

In his book, *Perestroika*, Gorbachev stated that the radical restructuring of the economy was 'an urgent necessity.' Any delay in introducing perestroika, he argued, could lead 'to an exacerbated internal situation in the near future, which, to put it bluntly, would have been fraught with serious social, economic and political crises.'[64] In other words, Gorbachev needed to move to introduce enough economic reality (meaning capitalism) to eliminate the threat to the power base that had developed during the pre-Gorbachev era.

Gorbachev found himself in charge of an economy in decline. The Novosibirsk Report by Tatyana Zaslavskaya, which was originally presented in April 1983 at a closed seminar organized by the economics department of Communist Party Central Committee, the USSR Academy of Sciences and Gosplan, argued that the 'social mechanism of economic development as it functions at present in the USSR does not ensure satisfactory results.' Poor labor habits and backward technology, she argued, were a 'result of the degeneration of the social mechanism of economic development' which was structured 'not to stimulate, but to thwart the population's useful economic activity.'[65] The solution to the problem, however, was not to be found in decentralization of economic activity. Rather the solution was to be sought in perfecting the social mechanism of development, i.e., improving the institution of planning to accelerate economic growth.

Abel Aganbegyan, Gorbachev's chief economic advisor in the early years of perestroika, argued that the whole purpose of the new economic strategy was to reverse the declining trend in the rate of growth of basic social and economic conditions in the past fifteen years.[66] By the end of the 1960s, Aganbegyan argued in another essay, measures of economic growth and social conditions in the health and housing sectors had deteriorated far below acceptable levels.[67]

After over 70 years in power the Soviet system had produced for its people a standard of living significantly less than all the major countries of Western Europe, the United States and Japan. As mentioned above, the Soviet economy delivered a consumer bundle to its citizens more appropriate to a Third World country than to a world superpower. Consider, for example, data on motor vehicles per capita. In the United States the number of passenger cars per 1,000 people in 1983 was 540, while in the Soviet Union that figure was 36. Perhaps more importantly, the figure in other Soviet bloc nations during the same year was better than that in the Soviet Union. For example, passenger cars per 1,000 people in Hungary was 118 and Poland 87 in 1983, and 1985 data show that in East Germany that number was 180 and in Czechoslovakia 163. The data on telephones per capita also provides evidence of the failing Soviet economy. In 1984, telephone units per 100 population was 76 in the United States, but only 9.8 in the Soviet Union. At the same time, in East Germany there were 21.1 telephone units per 100 population and 22.6 units in Czechoslovakia. Also consider the evidence on infant mortality. Deaths in the first year per 1,000 births for 1985 were 25.1 in the Soviet Union, 17.5 in Poland, 15.3 in Czechoslovakia, 10.4 in the United States and 9.2 in East Germany.[68]

Even consumption of certain basic food items in the Soviet Union was lower than its Eastern Bloc neighbors. For example, in 1984, as Gertrude Schroeder pointed out, 'per capita consumption of meat in the USSR was 60kg. compared with 75 in Bulgaria, 78 in Hungary, 94 in the GDR, 84 in Czechoslovakia, and 64 in Poland.'[69] Clearly the

Soviet economy that Mikhail Gorbachev inherited was, at best, struggling and, at worst, teetering on the edge of an abyss.

The former Soviet system simply failed to provide for its citizens. There was no systemic connection between production and consumption in the economy. The Soviet consumer simply did not matter. Decent medical care or housing, or even the basic nutritional necessities of life, simply could not be had by the average Soviet citizen through official channels.[70] Data on health and human services in the former Soviet Union document this point in gruesome detail. Since 1964, life expectancy had fallen from 67 to 62 for men and from 76 to 73 for women.[71] Lack of available birth control led to a situation where it was estimated that each woman would have between 8 and 14 abortions in her lifetime.[72]

The housing situation also grew acute. In 1981, 20 per cent of Moscow's population still lived in communal apartments.[73] The housing shortage was a direct legacy of Lenin, who had declared that housing space should be allotted at 9 square meters per head. In 1979 *Pravda* reported that there was 12.1 square meters per person including kitchen and bathroom, one-third the corresponding figure in the West.[74] The system failed at both a microeconomic and macroeconomic level.

It was within this economic context that Gorbachev announced his plans for the radical restructuring of the Soviet economy. The social and political context, in addition, was one of a growing cynicism as the corruption of the Brezhnev era was too blatant to be ignored. The economic stagnation and the social cynicism combined to produce a corrupt situation which, as Konstantin Simis described, infected 'the ruling apparatus of the Soviet Union from top to bottom' and had spread through out the whole society 'to all spheres of life.'[75]

This is why Gorbachev argued that he had 'no time to lose.' Speed was of the essence, he stated, 'to overcome the lag, to get out of the quagmire of conservatism, and to break the inertia of stagnation.'[76] The bureaucracy would resist change, but this obstacle must be overcome if there was to be any chance of real restructuring of the Soviet economy. Perestroika, Gorbachev argued, 'means a resolute and radical elimination of obstacles hindering social and economic development, of outdated methods of managing the economy and of dogmatic stereotype mentality.' He understood that perestroika would affect the interests of many people, in fact, the whole society. And, as he put it, 'demolition provokes conflicts and sometimes fierce clashes between the old and the new.'[77]

Selyunin summed up the problem confronting perestroika nicely. 'The existing bureaucratic machine,' he argued, 'cannot be incorporated in restructuring. It can be broken up and eliminated, but not restructured.' Succumbing to the conservative pressure from the bureaucrats and the ordinary people who 'fear independence' and 'harsh economic realities' and, therefore, argue for gradualism, will undermine and discredit the whole reform package. 'Losing time,' Selyunin argued, 'means losing everything.' It would be 'useless to gradually introduce new rules into the existing system' since the old system possesses tremendous inertia and will reject all challenges to the established order. The only thing that could be accomplished with gradualism was a discrediting of reforms. ' "You see, years have been wasted on talk, and one can't see any changes." History will not forgive us if we miss our chance. An abyss must be crossed in a single leap – you can't make it in two.'[78]

This was Gorbachev's challenge. How does one reform a political economy with such entrenched special interest groups? The planning bureaucrats did not wish to resign their posts voluntarily. But, as Nikolai Shmelev stated, either the Soviet Union would move forward with real reforms and break with the past method of economic administration or the system would 'turn into a backward, stagnant state that [would] be an example to the entire world of how not to organize economic life.'[79] The choice that faced Gorbachev and the Soviet people was clear, Selyunin stated, 'either the feeble but absolute power of administrators and the inevitable collapse of the economy, or restructuring with good chances for salvation.'[80]

Besides fighting a bureaucracy that produced for itself – the economic legacy of the Soviet regime – Gorbachev had to fight against the cultural legacy of the regime.[81] The cultural legacy of Soviet rule was perceived as one of the biggest impediments to real restructuring.[82] Complaints ranged from concern about higher prices and lack of economic security to envy over profit making and income inequality.[83] This should not have been surprising. The Gorbachev reforms, if they had represented a sincere effort at 'marketization,' would have brought with them, at least temporarily, the so-called three worse sins of capitalism: *higher prices* as the market adjusted to years of artificially suppressed prices, *unemployment* as some of the previously subsidized firms were forced out of business and *income inequality* as entrepreneurs earned profits by satisfying consumer demand.

Perestroika, therefore, confronted both an economic legacy of a distorted industrial structure with entrenched special interests, and a cultural legacy which resisted change. This is the essence of the challenge Gorbachev confronted. He tried to enlist the Soviet intellectuals through glasnost to aid him in the endeavor. But the ambiguity and paradoxes within perestroika eventually undermined the alliance with liberal intellectuals through glasnost. The paradox in perestroika, as Gorbachev perceived the reforms, was that he needed strong central control to accomplish a great decentralization of economic decision-making. If he was successful he would lose centralized control to forces that could threaten his political authority. Gorbachev was certainly aware of the risks of his strategy and, therefore, must have believed that either he could withstand the pressure or he did not really intend systematic reform.[84] If no systematic reform was forthcoming, though, then he ran the risk of alienating his strongest supporters – Soviet intellectuals who enjoyed the fruits of glasnost.

Gorbachev's challenge was real. We know from the study of public choice that policy formation within democratic regimes tends to produce policies that possess a bias toward short-term and easily identifiable benefits at the expense of long-term and largely hidden costs. What Gorbachev's professed perestroika promised – if it was to be a sincere effort at marketization – was short-term and easily identifiable costs and long-term and largely hidden benefits. Within a democratic regime, despite the economic logic of such a program, that would mean political suicide. Perhaps an examination of the reform package Gorbachev introduced will give us an indication of how he intended to confront that logic and why his approach ended in failure.

THE GORBACHEV REFORM PACKAGE

The system Gorbachev inherited was economically and politically bankrupt. Both internal and external debt were enormous, persistent shortages and poor quality products characterized economic life, a tremendous technological gap existed between the Soviet Union and the West and the promise of an integrated European Economic Community in 1992 would highlight the Soviet economic failure. Gorbachev's strategy, decidedly different from the reform path chosen in China, was to institute political, cultural and economic reform. *Perestroika* (restructuring), *glasnost* (public frankness), *Noyoe Myshleniye* (new thinking) and *uskorenie* (acceleration) became the 'buzz-words' of the Gorbachev era. Beginning with the

'Principles of Restructuring: Revolutionary Nature of Thinking and Acting,' *Pravda* (5 April 1988) the Gorbachev era was defined, at least in rhetoric if not always in practice, by radical reform in the political economy of Soviet socialism.

There was, though, a fundamental ambiguity within the reforms from the beginning. The ambiguity was apparent within Gorbachev's words and deeds. Gorbachev's first policies for renewal were an anti-alcohol campaign, and industrial and agricultural centralization with super-ministries. Not exactly an auspicious start for a liberal reformer. Decentralization efforts in economic reform really only emerged in 1987.

Moreover, Gorbachev wanting to reduce the Soviet burden had *de facto* repudiated the Brezhnev doctrine. In fact, he applauded the reforms in Eastern Europe of 1989. At the same time, however, he acted with hesitation and trepidation toward the independence movement in the Baltic nations.[85]

In addition, while the rhetoric of perestroika from 1987 to 1991 moved beyond calls for worker discipline and industrial intensification, and instead demanded the freeing of economic life to stimulate private initiative, Gorbachev continually postponed fundamental economic reform claiming that the people would not tolerate economic change.[86] This constant shifting of policy cost Gorbachev his credibility. For all the talk about renewal and restructuring, Gorbachev had nothing to show on the economic front.

The program of perestroika was filled with ambiguities and inconsistencies and on several levels never did get at the real problems confronting the Soviet economy. Alice Gorlin upon examining the original Gorbachev strategy concluded that his efforts would have only a marginal impact because they did not address the real problems within the system.[87] The basic economic institutions would remain intact. The system would remain much too bureaucratic to expect any significant change. Second, even though new individuals have replaced the previous ministers and bureaucrats, they have as much a vested interest in preserving the current system from which they benefit as did their predecessors.

The Gorbachev reforms, as represented in some of the crucial documents and reforms – specifically, the Law on State Enterprises and the Price Reforms – reveal no coherent strategy for economic renewal. For example, the Law on State Enterprises, which as Gorbachev stated, was of 'primary importance' to the economic reform, was instituted on 1 January 1988.[88] The law was supposed to grant financial autonomy to enterprises. Firms that could not cover their expenses were no longer to receive subsidization from the state. The intent of the law was to transform firms into fully self-accounting, self-financing and self-managed entities. But enterprises were still subject to state control both in their pricing and output policy. Despite the rhetoric and promise of enterprise autonomy the Law on State Enterprises did not go nearly far enough to meet the objectives of real economic reform.

An even bigger ambiguity within the Gorbachev reform process was probably in the area of price reform. Initially, price reform was to come in 1989, then 1990, and finally it was postponed with the disclaimer that the Soviet people would rather wait on line than pay higher prices.[89] Every time Gorbachev debated freeing up prices there was a run on the state run stores. This just exacerbated the shortage problem already plaguing the Soviet system. Shortages of everything at the state stores became the common condition.[90] So Gorbachev promised to bring relief through subsidized basic products and the whole process of reform was stalled.

Moreover, what was meant by price reform under Gorbachev was never very clear. Aganbegyan, for example, stated that under perestroika a 'radical and total reform of price formation is envisaged' but this did not include the wholesale adoption of free pricing. Prices instead of established

> in a voluntaristic fashion . . . will be based on social costs and will take into consideration the cost effectiveness of production and the level of world prices shaped by the relations between supply and demand. The prices will be reviewed at least once every five years and will be closely tied to the indicators of five-year plans . . . The state will set up a certain method for calculating prices, and the Prices Committee is being invested with the task of assessing the rationale for contractual and free prices. In particular, speculative price increases aimed at excessive profit will not be permitted.[91]

In other words, perestroika did not include a proposal to allow freely fluctuating prices to guide exchange and production in a complex economy, but rather it included a call for a better administration of prices. Such a system of price administration should not have been expected to produce any significant desirable results in terms of restructuring the Soviet economy.

These ambiguities were reflected in the economic policy debates and the speed with which different positions seemed on the rise only to be defeated the following week.[92] In October and November 1989, for example, it appeared as if Leonid Abalkin would push through a radical reform package, including the full adoption of private property and free market prices.[93] Abalkin's program, however, was defeated in December 1989 by the more cautious program of Nikolai Ryzhkov.[94] Then again in March 1990 it seemed that Ryzhkov would be removed from power and that radical economic reforms would be instituted at the urging of Abalkin and Gorbachev's personal economic advisor Nikolai Petrakov.[95] Even in early April 1990 Soviet officials were arguing that there was a good chance they would institute radical economic reforms similar to the program instituted in Poland as of 1 January 1990.[96] But by the end of April 1990 market reforms were postponed indefinitely.[97] And, then, in August and September 1990, it was reported that Gorbachev had finally decided decisively for radical market reforms with the adoption of the Shatalin '500-Day' plan. However, as with all the other reform packages the 500-day plan was rejected in favor of a Gorbachev compromise program with the old Soviet institutions of economic management which basically amounted to no reform at all.

This inconsistency, coupled with the incoherent reform package, resulted in lackluster economic results. The economic performance of the official sector under perestroika was less than desirable. As Aganbegyan admitted in his book, *Inside Perestroika*, from 1985 to 1988 policy-makers had not been able to reduce the problem of shortages and pent up consumer demand.[98] Moreover, the 1990 plan admitted that 'of the 178 highly important types of output that are under state statistical monitoring, the production of 62 was lower in the first eight months of this year than during the same period of last year.'[99] Such basic items as petroleum, coal, gasoline and diesel fuel, fertilizers, chemical fibers, sawtimber, pulp, cardboard, hosiery, sugar and flour were all in short supply. The Soviet economy by 1989 was in even worse shape than it was in 1985. The living standards of the people had not improved. There were shortages of almost everything in the official market, even in Moscow. The collapse of the official market continued throughout the history of perestroika. By the summer of 1990, most products were acquired outside the official state retail distribution system. It was estimated that 42 per cent of meat products, 55 per cent of vegetables, 20 per cent of milk, 75 per cent of potatoes and 44 per cent of eggs were sold outside the state distribution system.[100]

Gorbachev's own hesitation and inconsistency contributed to the problems of reform – which would be difficult enough under even the best of conditions.[101] Gorbachev and his advisors were prisoners of a mode of thinking which could not grasp the basic functions of capitalist markets, nor could they appreciate the institutional preconditions necessary for the successful functioning of markets. This inability resulted in conceptual weaknesses in the reform package which undermined perestroika.[102]

The reforms introduced during the Gorbachev era did not represent a radical restructuring of the Soviet economic system. More accurately they represented a radical realignment of special interest groups from those who benefited under Brezhnev to those who would benefit under Gorbachev.[103] One must infer from his efforts that Gorbachev's intent was simply 'a revitalization of the old regime.'[104] Nothing in the reform package would have been able to overcome the basic structural problems facing the Soviet system. As Marjorie Brady, deputy director of the Russian Research Foundation in London, pointed out, Gorbachev neither rejected the socialist system of planning nor embraced the idea of a free market. Gorbachev envisaged, instead, a 'law-governed economy'; a 'corporativist ideal' if you will. Gorbachev, she stated, was 'bent on creating economic structures of a kind that would scarcely find favor with the Austrian or Chicago schools of economic thought.'[105] In this assessment she was quite correct. And, unfortunately for the peoples of the former Soviet Union, not only did the reforms fail to restructure the system, they actually accelerated the decline of their standard of living as officially measured.[106]

DOES ECONOMICS HAVE A USEFUL PAST?

One of the most common complaints heard concerning the transition of the economies in East and Central Europe and the former Soviet Union, is that there does not exist a transitional model. But this overlooks the several experiences in history in which strong central governments have been turned back and market economies have flourished.

Yuri Maltsev argues that the models of Spain, Taiwan and Korea are suggestive.[107] Post-Second World War reconstruction also offers several historical models of transformation. The West German 'economic miracle' of Ludwig Erhard speaks well of the positive effect of immediate abolition of price controls.[108] The Hong Kong 'miracle' is also suggestive. Alvin Rabushka contrasts the economic development of the three Chinas – mainland China, Taiwan and Hong Kong – in the post-Second World War era. By analyzing three jurisdictions with a common cultural heritage, Rabushka demonstrates that prosperity depends far more upon economic institutions than cultural traits or natural resources.[109] The institutional rules that govern economic activity either promote or discourage economic prosperity. The economic benefits of a free market require the underlying institutions that sustain the system: free entry and private property protected by a rule of law. These are indispensable insights for drawing up a workable economic and political constitution for the post-communist world.

Another suggestive approach to the problem of the transition from strong central government to greater economic freedom that has direct relevance to the economies in Eastern Europe and the Soviet Union is Hernando DeSoto's *The Other Path*.[110] DeSoto documents the vast underground economy in operation in Peru. Peru's economic problem is not the people's lack of initiative nor any cultural resistance to capitalism but an over-regulated economic environment. Productive activity flees to the underground to escape the regulatory and taxing power of a bloated bureaucracy. The underground economy was also a staple part of the Soviet-type economy as well, representing in some estimates up to 30 per cent of GNP and employing over 20 million in the Soviet Union.[111] Would-be reformers must provide the incentives to economic actors to bring the vast energies devoted to the underground economy to the legitimate economy. In order to do that, firm rights to private property have to be established, consumer and producer subsidies must be eliminated, prices must be completely deregulated and taxation must be limited.

The characterization of the situation in the East as one of trying to make an aquarium out of fish soup is not as apt as it is literary. Economic life was not destroyed in the former Eastern Bloc, just channelled in a different direction. The reform task is one of redirecting the economic energy of the population toward productive activity that has something to do with the satisfaction of consumer demand.

CONCLUSION

If the disease that plagued the former Soviet economy was misdiagnosed, then that was because the basic anatomy of the Soviet system was little understood by the doctors of Sovietology. Gorbachev's policy of glasnost eliminated the ability to attribute the failure of the Soviet system to the historical backwardness of the country. Life under the Czars certainly was not very good, but in many respects, life under the communist system was even worse. Throughout its history much of the Soviet population lived in a state of constant fear brought on by the reality of arbitrary political terror.

On the economic front, Soviet citizens did not fare much better. It is a mistaken argument to suggest that Soviet citizens traded-off Western style consumerism for Soviet style security. Sure enough, the society enacted a cradle to the grave security blanket. But that blanket did not provide much comfort. Soviet consumers were forced to wait in long queues in order to acquire products of poor quality. Pride in one's work and the psychological benefits of self-fulfillment were suppressed by an institutional structure which discouraged an ethic of workmanship. The social compact in the former Soviet Union was 'we pretend to work and you pretend to pay us.'

The labor situation in the distorted industrial structure of the Soviet economy represented an implicit welfare system. Workers received salaries to work in jobs at state run enterprises that could not survive a market test. Pavel Bunich, a reform economist in the former Soviet Union, has remarked that the Soviet Union had the highest unemployment in the world. Unfortunately, he added, the unemployed all get salaries.[112] The structural incentives for enterprise managers rewarded conformity with the gross output targets as opposed to cost minimization. As a result, the Soviet labor market was characterized by an excess demand for labor. Overmanning resulted, but simultaneously so did underemployment of workers as they produced goods which were not valuable to consumers. With a near guarantee of employment, and the low official pay differentials that existed between employment grades, Soviet workers simply had no incentive to exert much effort in their official state jobs.

The official low prices on Soviet products did not offset the low salaries the state employees received. Low prices for goods that cannot be bought at that price are economically meaningless. The failings of the official system to provide goods and services to Soviet consumers forced everyone to rely on the illicit market to purchase basic necessities and augment their paltry official work income. 'Criminal' economic behavior in the black market was both a normal way of life and an albatross around the average citizen's neck. This economic situation simply reinforced the Kafkaesque environment within which the Soviet people found themselves.

Gorbachev promised to change both the political and economic landscape of Soviet life. To a large extent he did through glasnost. But his success was also his failure. The Soviet system was simply not reformable. The political and economic irrationality that Soviet citizens had to cope with was inherent in the institutional structure of the system.

The establishment of civil society and the unleashing of the productive capacity of the population required a complete break with the old regime. Such a complete break, however, was not a task which the Gorbachev government was up to, and as a result, the situation merely grew more acute from 1985 through 1991. Any claim to legitimacy eroded from the official sector in both politics and economics. The situation of 'dual power' between the official state and the underground society that had always existed implicitly throughout Soviet history emerged explicitly in the late 1980s as dissident intellectuals and politicians vied for intellectual and political power and a new breed of entrepreneurs sought their millions in the embryonic private market economy. This explicit challenge to the ruling order was a necessary condition for the resurrection of a society that had followed the 'road to nowhere' for over seventy years.

During the Gorbachev era, it seemed that the old order withstood the challenge. But it turned out that the ruling *nomenklatura* had won several small battles only to lose the war as the Communist Party was replaced in December 1991 by Yeltsin's democratic Russia. It is not yet clear whether the Yeltsin government will succeed in its endeavors. Moreover, we still do not have a clear picture of the drama of the Gorbachev years. The two 'plays,' however, are connected. We must understand the moral of the story of the one, before we can begin even to construct the tale of the other.

3

THE THEORETICAL
PROBLEMS OF SOCIALISM

It has become general practice to criticize the deformed, barracklike, leveled-off socialism built in the thirties. But this criticism painstakingly passes over the structural reasons why socialism was barracklike. And it shies away from the key question of whether we can feasibly build nonbarrack, democratic socialism on a noncommodity, nonmarket foundation. This is really the million-dollar question, both for those who think about the future and for those who try to understand the past. Why has the antimarket and fiscal-commodity relationship campaign in all cases, without any exception, in all countries . . . always entailed autocracy, infringement on human rights and personal dignity, and omnipotence of administration and the bureaucracy? . . . Why have all known historical attempts to eliminate free circulation and the producer's economic autonomy, ours included, ended in failure that ultimately urged a retreat?

Alexander Tsipko[1]

INTRODUCTION

Without doubt the twentieth century has been the age of socialism. The socialist idea promised a social order that was both more productive and moral than the capitalist system. 'Whatever our view of its utility or its practicability,' Ludwig von Mises wrote, 'it must be admitted that the idea of Socialism is at once grandiose and simple. Even its most determined opponents will not be able to deny it a detailed examination. We may say, in fact, that it is one of the most ambitious creations of the human spirit. The attempt to erect society

46

on a new basis while breaking with all traditional forms of social organization, to conceive a new world plan and foresee the form which all human affairs must assume in the future – this is so magnificent, so daring, that it has rightly aroused the greatest of admiration.'[2]

Socialist governments were established throughout Europe, Asia, Latin America, Africa and elsewhere. In fact, the entire world experienced socialism to some degree or another. Yet the empirical reality of the system, wherever and whenever it has been implemented, was political and economic ruin. Despite the fact that the idea of a socialist order captivated many of the brightest minds and some of the most idealistic hearts it has been responsible for some of the most horrible crimes of this or any century.

Socialism's failure was not due to half-hearted attempts or lack of political will on the part of its adherents. Nor did the system fail to produce humane results because of a poor choice of leaders or historical accident.[3] The problem lies within the idea of the social system itself. But this conclusion is one that does not go down easily with the idealist who dreams of the more rational and moral universe that socialism promised.

The paradox of socialism – that a system inspired by a desire to provide a more humane existence could result in mass oppression and economic deprivation – is a theoretical puzzlement. Why, as Soviet philosopher Alexander Tsipko asks, have all known historical attempts at socialism failed so miserably?[4]

THE IDEA OF SOCIALISM

Socialism simply means a social system of production based on public ownership as opposed to private ownership. The idea has a history that goes back much further than the nineteenth century and Karl Marx. Marx, however, is a useful spokesman because he systematized socialist thought.[5]

It is commonplace to argue, though, that Marx's analysis was confined to a critique of capitalism and did not really address the nature of socialism. This assertion misses a fundamental point about Marx. No doubt Marx did not wish to write 'recipes for the cookshops of the future,' but his reluctance to provide blueprints had more merit to it than is usually understood. He was not avoiding the problem of examining socialist society, but advocating a particular method to social theory.

Marx in this fashion moved beyond the utopian socialists. He did not criticize the utopians for examining the future socialist society, but rather for the way in which they conducted their examination, and for their incoherent and contradictory descriptions. Scientific socialism was not simply Marx's excuse for avoiding any detailed or blueprint description of the future socialist society. Rather, it reflected Marx's advocation of a particular method, i.e., dialectical criticism, to such an examination. Socialism was to be described through the systematic critique of capitalism. The critical examination of capitalism and the development of a positive theory of socialism were seen as two aspects of the same social theory project. Marx sought to conduct a critique of capitalist society that would as a by-product reveal the main features of the future socialist society.[6]

Contrary to received wisdom, therefore, implicit in Marx's work is a coherent and consistent view of socialism. Socialism is what capitalism is not. Whereas capitalism is a chaotic and anarchistic method of production, socialism would be orderly and rational. Production for direct use, rather than production for exchange (and profit) on the market, would become the overriding organizational principle of economic life under socialism. And the corresponding contradictions of capitalism would be overcome.

As Marx argued in *Capital*, 'The life-process of society, which is based on the process of material production, does not strip off its mystical veil until it is treated as production by freely associated men, and is consciously regulated by them in accordance with a settled plan.'[7] The abolition of private property in the means of production and the substitution of a settled plan for the market would result, according to Marx, in rationalizing economic life and transcending man's alienated social existence. Marx's economic project promised emancipation from alienation and exploitation through rationalization of the social forces of production.

Modern socialism, despite moral posturing, still clings to the rationalization project. Alan Ryan, for example, has argued that

> No matter what the actual follies of Soviet attempts at central planning, and no matter what the theoretical difficulties of gathering the sort of information that a planned economy needs, the ideal of replacing social accident by social reason is anything but absurd.

What is sought, according to Ryan, is a social system of production in which there is 'room for growth and imagination but in which we might get more of the answers right *before* trying them in the market place.[8]

The organizational form the rationalization project takes can be of various types. Workers' self-management as well as the extreme administrative command planning system attempts to pursue the rationalization of economic life.[9] Production for use, not exchange, is the only organizational rule for socialist rationalization. The logic of complete rationalization demands the liquidation of market forces in total.

Market socialism is simply incoherent from the point of view of rationalization because at least some degree of the plan coordination necessary for social production will rely on the anarchistic operation of the market.[10] Market coordination cannot operate effectively in environments of public ownership, instead bureaucratic coordination takes over. This is the conclusion of both theoretical and empirical investigations of alternative economic systems of production that many leading economists have now reached. 'The basic idea of market socialism,' Janos Kornai states, has 'fizzled out.' The history of Yugoslavia, Hungary, China, the Soviet Union and Poland 'bear witness to its fiasco.' An examination of the facts, Kornai concludes, suggests that it is time to 'abandon the principle of market socialism.'[11]

A consistent definition of socialism, therefore, is a social system of production based on public ownership of resources and coordinated through a planning system of some sort or another. There are fundamental theoretical problems that this system confronts. There are problems of the mobilization and utilization of diffuse knowledge within the economic system to coordinate plans and there are the problems of political organization and incentives. These problems thwart attempts to realize the socialist goal of a more productive and humane society.

THE THEORETICAL PROBLEMS OF SOCIALISM

While several thinkers had previously dealt with the problem of incentives with collective ownership and the political problems of strong central control, Ludwig von Mises was the first theorist to address the problem that the socialist system confronts in mobilizing the 'intellectual division of labor' that exists within an advanced industrial society.[12] Mises's argued that a full understanding of the problem of utilizing the division of knowledge within society was made possible only with the further developments of economic theory which arose out of the subjectivist revolution of the late nineteenth century. 'To understand the problem of economic calculation,' Mises wrote, 'it was necessary to recognize the true character of the exchange relations expressed in the prices of the market. The existence of this important problem could be revealed only by the methods of the modern subjective theory of value.'[13] The exchange ratios established on the market, according to Mises, were the result of a process that was 'anchored deep in the human mind.'[14]

The freely established exchange ratios on the market, while certainly not perfect conveyors of information, nevertheless serve as 'a guide amid the bewildering throng of economic possibilities.' The money prices formed in the market, by translating the subjective assessment of trade-offs by some into effective knowledge for others, provide the social context within which individuals make economic decisions. Absent this context and individuals are left groping in a deep fog. Monetary calculation, despite its imperfect character, and profit and loss accounting separate out from among all those technologically possible projects those which are economically feasible from those which are not. Monetary calculation provides all that practical life demands. 'Without it, all production by lengthy and roundabout processes of production would be so many steps in the dark.'[15] With the growing division of labor and the lengthening of the process of production that accompanied advanced industrial development, Mises argued, monetary calculation had become 'an aid that the human mind is no longer able to dispense with.'[16]

Without any means of economic calculation, socialism was doomed to economic irrationality. Mises argued that the universal call by socialists for the abolition of private property in the means of production sealed the fate of their proposal for social betterment. Without private property in the means of production, Mises argued, there could not be any market for the means of production. Without a market for the means of production, money prices for capital goods could not be established. And, without money prices reflecting the relative scarcity of capital goods, there would be no guide or signal available to individuals to aid them in assessing whether investment projects were allocating resources in a profitable manner or not. Economic calculation would be absent from such a situation, and without this component in the process of social appraisement the rational allocation of scarce resources would be an impossibility.

In addition to the problem of economic calculation, however, Mises also restated the problem of organization and incentives. Previous attempts to tackle the problem had been 'deplorably inadequate.' The attempted solution was always couched in terms of a 'better selection of persons.' 'It has not been realized,' Mises argued, 'that even exceptionally gifted men of high character cannot solve the problems created by the socialist control of industry.'[17] The problem is not that humanity has not been able to live up to the moral imperatives of socialist organization. Rather, it is socialist organization that does not live up to the demands of humanity and delivers man into an irrational political and economic existence. 'The problems with which we are concerned do not arise from the moral shortcomings of humanity,' Mises states. 'They are problems of the logic of will and action which must arise at all times and in all places.'[18]

To sum up, Mises's argument concerning the fundamental problems of socialist organization was that without private ownership in the means of production, there can be no market for the means of production. Without a market for the means of production, there can be no money prices for the means of production. Without money prices reflecting the relative scarcities of capital goods, there would be no signal to guide economic actors about alternative uses of resources. And, without a signalling device, rational economic calculation would be impossible. In other words, without the freely established exchange ratios of the market to guide economic actors, there would be no effective way to appraise the relative economic merit of the numerous array of technologically feasible production projects that lay before the economic planners. Technological information is one thing, the economic problem of the effective use of resources is quite another. Whereas the price system translates the subjective assessment of trade-offs by some into effective knowledge for others, socialism possesses no similar procedure. Without the ability to appraise the alternative use of scarce resources, economic decision-makers will not only squander scarce resources, but they will receive neither the information nor possess an incentive to correct the faulty pattern of resource use. As a result, persistent error will be structurally imbedded in the social system.

These Misesian insights into the fundamental problems facing the political economy of socialism received increased theoretical attention in the work of several scholars in the Austrian and Public Choice schools of economics. F. A. Hayek, perhaps more than any other figure, has contributed to our understanding of the epistemological (or knowledge) and political problems that socialism confronts.

Socialism is logically impossible, Hayek argues, because of the social system's inability to access the requisite economic knowledge for economic coordination.[19]

Nevertheless, economic planners once in power must find some rationale upon which to base their decisions, and since economic rationales are out of the question, decisions will be based instead upon political rationales. As a result, those who have a comparative advantage in the political game, and in exercising discretionary power, will rise to the top of the planning apparatus. This is, as Hayek showed in *The Road to Serfdom*, the basis for the totalitarian tendency within socialist economies.[20]

The Mises–Hayek knowledge and political problems are interconnected. The bureaucratic planner, necessarily ignorant of the privately held assessment of trade-offs that economic actors possess, cannot obtain the economic knowledge necessary to accomplish the task he sets before himself and must, therefore, base his decisions upon the information readily available, i.e., political rationales. The epistemological problem suggests that no proponent of planning can access the knowledge necessary to plan comprehensively, or interfere optimally with, advanced industrial economic activity. The political problem 'constitutes a warning that since the case for any particular use of the planning power lies beyond the capacity of human reason to establish, that power will instead be wielded in response to political clout rather than careful debate.'[21]

It is these theoretical difficulties that the socialist organization of society must confront which render it completely impracticable. The problems with socialist planning consist of four (conceptually separate, but logically connected) arguments: (1) property rights and incentive problems, (2) problems of informational and computational complexity, (3) epistemological problems and (4) political organization problems. Each leads logically to the next one. Perhaps by examining each in isolation, and in a little more depth, the Mises–Hayek critique can be more fully appreciated.

Socialist managers do not face the same incentives as capitalist managers do to insure efficient allocation of resources. Public ownership produces a situation where since everyone owns everything nobody owns anything. As a result property is not cared for and resources are wasted. The incentive problems associated with collective ownership is one of the oldest arguments in intellectual history. Aristotle, for example, employed this argument against the communism of Plato's *Republic*.[22]

Even if we assume that this incentive problem is overcome, say by postulating the evolution of socialist man, the task of collecting and processing the necessary information for the coordination of plans presents us with a new difficulty. If the socialist planner could gather the information required to insure the efficient allocation and use of resources, the amount of information necessary to complete the task in a reasonably efficient manner would be too vast and the computations too complex.

Vilfredo Pareto recognized this complexity point with regard to the mathematical system of general equilibrium. The solution of the system of simultaneous equations cannot, and should not, be taken as a numerical calculation of the prices that would coordinate the economic system. Let us assume, Pareto stated, that 'we have overcome all the difficulties in the way of acquiring knowledge of the data of the problem, and that we know the ophelimities of all the goods for each individual, all the particulars pertaining to the production of goods, etc.' Even with this 'absurd hypothesis,' he argued, we are still not provided 'with the practical possibility of solving the problem.' Take an example of an economy of 100 individuals and 700 goods. The coordination of such a small economy would require us to 'solve a system of 70,699 equations.' A task, Pareto pointed out, that 'is beyond the power of algebraic analysis, and it would be still further beyond it if we considered the fabulous number of equations which a population of forty million individuals, and several thousand goods would entail.' The only means for solving such a vast system of equations, Pareto concluded, 'would be to observe the actual solution which the market gives.'[23]

But beyond the problem of informational and computational complexity lies a deeper epistemological problem that socialist planners must overcome. Assume that a modern supercomputer can solve any system of equations presented in a matter of seconds.[24] Even with this assumption granted, socialist planning confronts an insurmountable difficulty. The relevant economic knowledge for decision-making is *contextual* knowledge and not abstract data of the kind that could be fed into a computer. Economic circumstances change daily, and information gathered yesterday may not be relevant for tomorrow. Appraisement of such information is only possible within the context of the competitive market process. Moreover, much of the knowledge that is essential for the social appraisement process cannot be treated as data since it largely consists of tacit, or inarticulate, knowledge. Judgement, expectation, conjecture and perception are just some of the crucial aspects of economic decisions that lie beyond full articulation. Furthermore, this aspect of economic decision-making cannot be divorced from the competitive struggle for profit.[25] Absent the process of competition and the establishment of monetary prices, the subjective assessment of alternative uses of resources by some agents cannot be conveyed as effective knowledge to others. As a result, rational economic calculation will be hindered to the point of non-existence.

Finally, the nature of economic planning confronts us with a political problem of great proportions. To engage in socialist economic planning, certain institutional structures have to be established and discretionary power has to be turned over to someone or some group.

For the moment let us put aside the problems that time dimensionality presents to discretionary planning,[26] and simply examine the logic of discretionary control. We cannot model policy-makers as benevolent despots and make sense of the world. Rather, economists must view political actors in the same manner as they view economic actors – as self-interested individuals.[27] In planning environments this argument is intensified, for now the very institutions of political control require the concentration of power in the hands of a few individuals.[28] We should expect that those individuals with a comparative advantage in exercising discretionary power will rise to the top of the planning apparatus. Unfortunately, skill in exercising discretionary power is not usually a character trait of the fair and open minded. An evolutionary process of survival insures that only those with such political skills will emerge from the process of competitive struggle for power. Totalitarianism is the logical, though unintended, consequence of establishing the political institutions of socialist planning.

CONCLUSION

The theoretical problems that socialist planning confronts prevents that ideological system from realizing its ends. The means of collective ownership and economic planning are ineffective in obtaining the end of a more productive and moral universe. The unintended by-product of pursuing the socialist ends with the means of collective ownership and economic planning has proven time and time again to lead to economic deprivation and political repression. The expected rationalization of the social system is defeated by the realization of political and economic irrationality. Socialism, as understood historically, simply possesses no weapons to combat the organizational difficulties presented by property rights and incentives, computational complexity, the underlying epistemics of economic coordination and political control.

On the other hand, capitalism does possess weapons to combat at least three of the problems. Private property rights have the effect of mobilizing individuals to husband resources effectively. The price system by reducing information concerning the relative scarcities of resources to a monetary price economizes on the amount of information that economic actors must process in making decisions. In addition, the price system through the incentives of profit and loss mobilizes individuals to discover new ways of arranging or rearranging means to obtain ends. In other words, the interaction between *ex ante* expectations and *ex post* realization in the market process motivates individuals to learn how better to pursue their ends. The ability of the entrepreneurial process of competitive markets to reveal error and motivate learning is perhaps its most significant weapon in combating the epistemic problem of economic coordination.

But, real existing capitalism in Western Europe or the United States, however, has not found a way to insulate its operations from the political demands of democratic politics, and the corresponding effects of rent-seeking behavior.[29] Thus, despite the relative economic success of Western democracies they do not represent an ideal model for the formerly communist countries of East and Central Europe and the Soviet Union.

The more immediate problem, however, is how do we understand real existing socialist economies, and specifically the former Soviet Union? I have argued that socialism, understood as a system of collective ownership and economic planning, is organizationally incoherent and operationally impossible. Real existing socialism, while a consequence of attempting to pursue the ideals of socialism, has little in common with the textbook depiction of it. In order to understand the forces that have come to bear on the reform efforts it is important to understand how the system really works and not how it might work if we could assume away all the problems mentioned above.

A sound understanding of the Soviet system, both in its historical operation and at the present time of reform, is only possible when both the economic and political problems confronting socialism, and their intersection, are understood and appreciated. As F. A. Hayek wrote several years ago in the foreword to Boris Brutzkus's *Economic Planning in Soviet Russia*:

> Even the most careful study of the Russian facts cannot lead very far if it is not guided by a clear conception of what the problem is, i.e., if it is not undertaken by a person who, before he embarks on the investigation of the special problems of Russia, has arrived at a clear idea of the fundamental task that economic planning involves.[30]

4

THE NATURE OF THE SOVIET-TYPE SYSTEM

The modern world could no more get along without
accumulated capital than it could get along without police or
paved streets. The greatest change imaginable is simply the
change that has occurred in Russia – a transfer of capital from
private owners to professional politicians.

H. L. Mencken[1]

INTRODUCTION

If the argument presented in the last chapter that socialism is not only an
inefficient form of economic organization, but literally impossible is
correct, then we are presented with an immediate conceptual difficulty in
analyzing the history of socialist practice. If the Soviet-type economy
was not actually an example of socialist central planning – because that
social system is an impossibility – then what was it?

This question has rarely been asked by either proponents or
opponents of socialism. Among proponents of socialism, as well as
traditional comparative systems analysts, the question is not raised
because socialist central planning is assumed to be possible (and
perhaps desirable). Even though Marxist critics of the Soviet Union
have challenged the conceptualization of the Soviet Union as centrally
planned, they do so from the perspective that this is evidence of a
perversion of socialism by Stalin.[2] The workers' revolution was
thwarted by bureaucratic intrigue, and the forces of state capitalism.
On the other hand, traditional comparative systems analysis (whether
conducted by a proponent or opponent of socialism) argues that the
conceptualization of the Soviet Union as centrally planned was
essentially correct.[3]

Central planning was portrayed as an alternative to market exchange. Economic activity was viewed as strategically controlled by the center, which directed the development of the economy. Details of the institutional structure of the Soviet system were analyzed, but little attention was paid to the actual processes of decision-making within the system and how the decision-making process related to the conceptualization of the Soviet system as centrally planned.[4]

Some critics of socialism, such as Ludwig von Mises, have argued that comprehensive central planning is impossible, but that Soviet-style socialism was simply an inefficient form of incomplete socialism. Only the full-blown international socialism, which was advocated by the Marxist revolutionaries, is an impossibility. Incomplete socialism would only be seriously impaired economically, not utterly chaotic. Such a system of economic organization would eventually exhaust the social surplus fund (provided by nature's endowment of resources and/or built over generations of economic growth) through waste, but it could stumble along for quite some time. As long as planners could rely on world prices to aid in the allocation of scarce resources, attempts at central planning would merely lead to economic inefficiency and not the breakdown of social order that would follow from the absence of any means of economic calculation.

But this argument did not go far enough in explaining the actual operation of the Soviet-type system. However sound Mises' argument may be, it lacked both a detailed examination of the institutional structure of Soviet-type economies and the incentives within the system that are necessary for an adequate understanding of that system. Much of the *implicit* economic relationships that were vital to the operation of the Soviet system are glossed over in the Misesian analysis. As a result, Mises's discussions of Soviet practice seem somewhat odd.[5] They leave the impression that he was denouncing the Soviet government for doing what he had argued in 1920 was impossible for them to do: centrally plan an advanced industrial economy.

Traditional comparative systems theorists do not fare any better. The *de facto* establishment of property rights and the pervasive operation of illicit markets, as well as the system of special privileges for the Soviet elite, simply did not receive the attention necessary to understand the system as it actually operated.[6] And in the Marxist analysis, where these factors were emphasized, their existence is seriously misunderstood. The Stalinist command economy was not a perversion of socialism, but the logical, though unintended, consequence of attempting to institute a central planning regime in strict accordance with socialist principles.

Understanding the task of reform and what pressures would bear on the reform movement, requires a clear picture of what it is that is supposed to be reformed. In order to gain such an understanding we must begin by looking at the real, existing system that was in place when Gorbachev initiated perestroika, and not some system that we imagine theoretically to have been in operation. The illusion of central planning must be rejected. Illicit markets existed both inside and outside of the 'plan' and, in fact, were vital to the operation of the system. In reality, the Soviet system remained at heart a commodity production economy that depended on the decentralized decisions of individuals to coordinate economic affairs in an *ex post* fashion.

The Soviet system was best characterized as a market economy dominated by monopoly producers and subject to vast and arbitrary government interference. This chapter seeks to justify this characterization and provide the appropriate backdrop for analyzing the problems associated with reforming the Soviet system and why all historical attempts to do so have failed so miserably.

THE INSTITUTIONS OF SOVIET CENTRAL PLANNING

The Soviet system of economic planning was basically implemented right from the beginning of communist rule.[7] On 15 December 1917, for example, the Bolsheviks established the Supreme Council of the National Economy (VSNKh) that would rationally plan and direct the development of the economy. The establishment of the VSNKh was followed by further economic decrees which nationalized the banks (27 December 1917), foreign trade (22 April 1918), large-scale industry and railway transportation (28 June 1918) and small-scale industry (29 November 1920). Though the New Economic Policy of the 1920s attempted to liberalize the economy and reduce the administrative burden of the bureaucracy (through repeal of some of the decrees, e.g., the 29 November 1920 decree), the major economic centers of the national economy remained under government direction and control. In other words, despite the NEP reforms the basic institutional structure established after the revolution remained intact. The Soviet state as it matured under Stalin, despite some shuffling, renaming and realignment of the institutional

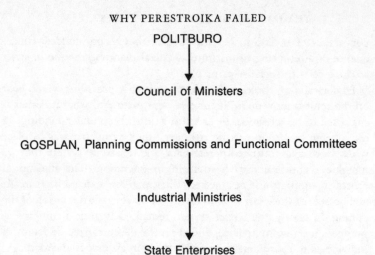

Figure 4.1 The decision-making hierarchy of the Soviet economy

structure, simply reinforced the basic institutions of administrative command that originated with the Bolshevik attempt to construct the new socialist order. The institutional hierarchy of the economic bureaucracy was firmly implanted in the Soviet structure of governance by the 1930s and has remained basically intact ever since.

The planning bureaucracy of the Soviet economy can be represented by the rough organizational chart shown in Figure 4.1. This decision-making hierarchy was supposed to coordinate economic activity in an *ex ante* manner so as to maintain a balance of society's resources.[8] Theoretically, *ex ante* coordination would better serve the interests of society by eliminating the waste and inequities in economic affairs associated with the *ex post* coordination of economic plans by the price system. By bringing economic decisions under conscious regulation, the planning apparatus was supposed to balance the supplies and demands for society's scarce resources in a more effective manner than accomplished by the price system. Supply and demand would be brought into balance by rational and democratic administrative procedures, rather than the chaotic process of price adjustment that occurs in a market economy.

The Politburo and the Central Committee first decide the priorities for the planning period, and set output targets. These output targets are then communicated to Gosplan which in turn establishes control figures and estimates of the required inputs to meet the control figures. Ministries are then informed of the projected material constraints they will have to face, and they will begin negotiating with Gosplan over the control figures and the availability of resources. After this initial phase of negotiation, the ministries will inform the enterprises of the control figures.

Now a new stage of political bargaining begins as the enterprises negotiate with the ministries over output targets and input requirements. During this stage of the planning process information flows up from the individual enterprises to ministries to Gosplan. At each stage, the requested inputs by subordinates are checked against the input needs as estimated by the superior office. If a discrepancy exists, then the subordinate must defend the deviation from the superior's estimate. Gosplan serves as the final arbitrator of this process by assessing the competing requests. As the bargaining process comes to an end, Gosplan must make sure that planned supplies of each commodity match their planned demand (input requirement and final use). In this manner, Gosplan develops a binding economic plan that assures the *ex ante* coordination of economic activity in society. At least this is how it was supposed to work.

THE ECONOMICS OF ILLUSION

This portrait of political economy decision-making at successive stages of the planning hierarchy over output targets and input requirements did not engender the rational allocation of scarce resources in either theory or practice. In fact, the system generated economic irrationalities throughout the entire process. Plan failure among economic agents was a staple part of Soviet economic life for managers of enterprises as well as consumers. Obviously, the Soviet planning system possessed a certain rationality, but it was not economic rationality.

The ideological illusion of a rationally planned economy had to co-exist with the reality of systemic economic failure.[9] Without the ideological illusion, the Party's economic monopoly could not be justified. As a result, the Soviet people had to live a lie. This was not a normal lie, however, in that it was the peculiar Soviet false reality that had to be protected to legitimate the revolution and the Party. Soviet citizens spoke in one language that conformed to the pseudo-reality of Soviet socialism, while they lived within an entirely different reality. There was one lie, but two realities.[10]

The problem with the planning system was not limited to the vast amount of information that was supposed to be processed by the center, and the sheer complexity of that task. Rather, the *quality* of the information available to economic planners in the absence of free market prices would prevent any mind or group of minds from assessing the economic allocation of scarce resources among alternative uses even if the most advanced computational technology was available to them. This fundamental problem with central planning of the economy has often been overlooked because analysts and planners confuse technical and economic efficiency. It is one thing to determine that platinum, steel or cement, could be used to build a bridge, it is quite another to discover which material would be economically employed in that use. The technical problem concerns achieving one end and allocating means to obtain that end given certain physical and engineering constraints. The economic problem, on the other hand, is one where scarce means must be allocated among competing ends, and the knowledge required to accomplish this allocational task economically is dispersed throughout the economy in scattered bits and pieces. In other words, the economic problem of a complex industrial economy is one of mobilizing the private information that is embedded within the various, and often conflicting, plans of economic actors in a way which translates that information into effective knowledge for others so as to promote the coordination of economic plans between actors.

The functional significance of economic calculation in the market economy is that, despite its imperfections, it allows the social system to select out from among the numerous array of technologically feasible projects those which are economic. In economic calculation, the market system possesses a weapon to combat the general knowledge problem that all social systems confront in attempting to mobilize the dispersed and incomplete information that exists throughout the economy and is not available to anyone in its entirety.[11] Through a process of error detection and the corresponding opportunity for economic profit, the market system motivates learning among economic agents so they may discover how better to allocate scarce resources to satisfy consumer demand. The hierarchical planning system does not possess similar weapons.

Not only does the planning hierarchy lack the requisite information rationally to plan the economy, but it also does not possess the disciplinary devices that a market system does to overcome strategic incentive problems.[12] Consider, for example, the principal/agent problem that exists whenever a principal relies on an agent to carry out her goals. In such situations, the agent because of informational asymmetries may find it in his interest to act in a manner inconsistent with the goals that the principal has set. Unless the principal can effectively monitor the activity of the agent, her goals will not be achieved.

A large corporation potentially faces this problem because of the separation of ownership from control. The owners (shareholders) may desire that management only act in a manner as to increase the profitability of the firm. Management, however, may wish to pursue an alternative course of action that maximizes their perquisites independent of the goal of profit maximization. Without effective monitoring, management can act in a manner that diverges significantly from the goals of the owners. But the market system provides a disciplinary force through the capital market that compels management to act in line with the goals of the shareholders.

A decline in the stock price of a corporation signals to economic actors that the expected future profitability of the firm has declined. If individuals believe they can increase the profitability of the enterprise, then they will buy up shares, take over the enterprise and restructure management. Takeovers and mergers discipline managers to act in accordance with the interests of owners through the market for corporate control. Market competition from new groups of would-be managers in addition to competition within the firm by those who want to climb the corporate ladder present challenges to existing management whenever they behave contrary to the interest of the principal.

Well-established and freely functioning labor and capital markets, however, are a prerequisite for this disciplinary device to exert the corrective monitoring of agent behavior necessary to overcome the problem of strategic incentives. Without these markets, or similar devices, agents will strategically act in a manner that diverges from the interest of the principal.

In a democracy, for example, politicians are supposedly the representatives of the electorate. Elected officials, in other words, are the agents while the citizenry are the principals. The vote mechanism supplies the monitoring device to discipline the behavior of politicians. The problem that exists within democratic procedures, however, is that the phenomena of rational abstention and rational ignorance among voters seriously questions the ability of the voting system to convey accurately information about voter preferences. Moreover, there does not exist in the political process the kind of error detection and learning mechanism that do exist within the market process to motivate a quick adjustment of behavior among political actors so as to conform to the expectations of the electorate.

This potential problem of agency is compounded within government decision-making when it is recognized that there are also deeper layers of the principal/agent problem throughout the system. Most functional tasks of governance are not carried out by vote-seeking politicians who must face re-election, but by a non-vote-seeking bureaucracy. Beyond the principal/agent problem that exists between voter and politician, there is another principal/agent problem between the politician and the bureaucracy and another between the head of the bureau and her subordinates.[13] Political actors must devise monitoring mechanisms to make sure that the bureaucracy acts in line with their goals. But there are definite limits to the supervisory capacity of officials (or the electorate). And, these limits vary inversely with the degree of coordination required to accomplish the task assigned. In a large organization, the higher the degree of coordination required the lower the limit of supervisory capacity.

Whereas the price system can achieve a high degree of coordination of economic plans in the complex task of advanced industrial production by summarizing the terms of exchange (and, thus, economizing on the amount of information actors must process), politics does not have recourse to any analogous procedure. A free market provides the incentives and information for the mutual adjustment of behavior among participants even though no single mind or group of minds consciously directs the flow of resources for the system as a whole. Bureaucratic organization of the economy, however, would require the superior consciously to coordinate the activities of all subordinates.

Under Soviet rule, even the potential check of the electorate was absent from political economy decision-making.[14] The Party, and the Party alone, was the principal and the planning bureaucracy was the agent. Most Soviet economic practices, in fact, can be explained as attempts by the Party to monitor effectively the behavior of bureaucratic agents. Soviet practices, from the periodic purges within the Party and the elaborate *nomenklatura* system of patronage to the five-year plans and gross output success indicators, can be explained as the rational outcome of attempts to reduce the agency costs associated with centralized economic administration of the economy.[15]

The sole purpose of the Soviet economic administration was to maintain monopoly control over resources.[16] In this way, the Party could treat all economic problems as technological ones. The Party leadership would decide priorities and dictate that resources flow in a direction that would achieve those priorities. Such a wartime approach to the allocation of scarce resources cannot persist indefinitely since it tends to disregard the economic cost of resource use.[17] Throughout their history, Soviet economic planners possessed neither the information nor the incentive to appraise the alternative use of scarce resources in production. Without any method to assess the opportunity cost of resource use, waste and mis-allocation inevitably result. In other words, the Soviet system was in a state of perpetual economic crisis.[18]

This crisis, however, could not be revealed otherwise the leading role of the Party would be questioned. The underlying ideology of the Soviet system promised a more moral and efficient society. Unfortunately for the peoples of the Soviet Union it produced neither. But, that could not be openly admitted or the system would lose legitimacy.[19] The major function of the economic bureaucracy was transformed into the production and maintenance of the illusion of rational economic planning that achieved tremendous economic growth.

THE DUAL REALITY IN POLITICS AND ECONOMICS

The official version of the economic structure of the Soviet economy was justified on the grounds of its rationalizing effect on the social system of production. Central planning would eliminate the chaos and waste of capitalism, including the business cycle. But, the central planning system was theoretically incoherent. Such an administrative command system of economic organization could not engender the incentives or mobilize the information necessary to coordinate successfully the multitude of economic plans required in an advanced industrial economy.

Alongside the official economy emerged a *de facto* economy that attempted to fill in the gaps created by the failed official system.[20] Markets are like weeds, they spring up all over and are impossible to stamp out completely. Wherever there is a gap, alert economic actors will attempt to grasp the opportunity available for personal gain. In the production process, special middlemen (the *tolkachi*) were relied on to gather resources (inputs) so enterprises could meet plan targets. The *tolkachi* worked on behalf of state enterprises selling surplus commodities on the one hand and purchasing needed products on the other. There emerged an entire secondary supply system around the *tolkachi*.[21] On the consumption side, illicit market transactions attempted to correct for the long queues and poor quality of consumer goods found in the official state stores. Private market activity enhanced consumer well-being by increasing the flow of goods and services available and by offering an additional source of income.

The dual reality that Soviet citizens dwelled within was not limited to economic activity, but also extended to their cultural, intellectual and political life.[22] Jazz music, for example, was for a long time an underground phenomenon. Books and articles suppressed by state censors circulated *samizdat* among scholars and intellectuals. And, the dissident movement arose to challenge the governing authority of the ruling elite on several fronts.[23]

There is, however, a significant difference in the experience of this duality within the economic sphere from that in the cultural and intellectual realm. The underground culture emerged not to 'correct' the failings of the official system, thus propping it up. Rather, the *sub-rosa* culture challenged the official system. Its function was to break the official system down and offer an alternative social order.

The monopolistic grip of the Party over the economy was more difficult to break. The Party's monopoly was its main source of privilege and power. Party officials did not have to wait in queues, they shopped in special stores, lived in nice *dachas* and drove their *zils*.[24] The underground economy existed to correct for the failure of the official system, not to replace it.[25] The ruling elite could co-exist with a system that appeased the population, but they could not co-exist with an economic system that would have threatened the monopoly status of the Party.

Illicit market exchanges propped up the faulty structure of the planned economy. The *tolkachi*, for example, made the appearance of conformity to the planned targets easier; they did not compete with the official industrial supply system. The underground market in consumer goods aided individuals in obtaining desired goods without waiting in queues, but again it did not compete with the official system.

From high officials to bureaucratic functionaries, the failure of the official economy presented opportunities for economic gain. Basically, the official Soviet economy was a non-price rationed economy. If prices are not allowed to tell their story about relative scarcities of goods and ration scarce goods among alternative uses through monetary bids and offers, then some other rationing device will emerge to allocate scarce resources.[26] Queuing, of course, rationed scarce goods and services in the official economy. But, the existence of queues automatically presented an opportunity for store clerks and others to transform the non-monetary costs to consumers of obtaining goods into economic gains for themselves. Barter or outright bribing could obtain goods that could not be obtained through official channels. Living *na levo* (under the table) was the mainstay of Soviet economic existence. From a taxi cab ride across town to admission to university, from obtaining an apartment to receiving anesthesia for an abortion, securing goods and services required side payments (monetary or otherwise).

In addition, without stable and enforceable property rights, the unofficial economy was forever vulnerable to opportunistic behavior. The discipline of repeated dealings provided an incentive for most individuals to act in a cooperative fashion. But the opportunity for strategic cheating was always there. As a result, illicit enforcement mechanisms emerged to police contracts.

An example may clarify this point. During prohibition of alcohol in the US, drinking did not cease.[27] Rather, an illicit market for alcohol quickly arose to meet consumer demand. But several things were undesirable about the characteristics of this particular market. First, the quality of the product sold changed radically, increasing in potency and, thus, risk to consumers. The high cost of transporting the product (which now had to include the cost of evading the police) dictated that per unit potency must increase in order to maintain profit margins. Beer and wine almost disappeared from the market as pure grain alcohol was transported and mixed at points of distribution. Second, the private mechanisms for enforcing contracts increased the criminal element in the production and distribution of alcohol. In other words, prohibition did not eliminate alcohol consumption, but it did create 'bathtub gin' and Al Capone.[28]

Without clear property rights and contract law, product quality cannot be guaranteed and the market environment may deteriorate due to the criminal element. The underground economy of the former Soviet Union cannot be relied on completely to transform the economy into a functioning free market system. The unofficial economy existed solely because of the failures of the official economy brought on by the prohibition of free market exchange and production, and, thus, lived in a symbiotic relationship with the official economy.[29] Transformation required the abolition of prohibitions against market activity and the establishment of well-defined and strictly enforced property rights. In other words, transformation required the preponderance of the *sub-rosa* economy to cease to exist. Not because of a government 'crack-down' on corruption and theft of state property, but because individuals would be allowed freely to produce and exchange goods as they saw fit. Competition from an above-ground and legitimate free market sector would overtake the state sector in the production and distribution of goods.

Socialist theorists traditionally did not predict that this would be the outcome of a competition between the private and state sectors. Fabian socialists, for example, argued that the laws of economics were on the side of socialism. Basically, their argument was that since state enterprises could sell their products at cost and not for a profit, they would undersell and thus out-compete capitalist firms. The Fabian strategy for social change, as opposed to the Marxist strategy, was one of gradual encroachment by the state sector. Public production of goods and services would eventually crowd out capitalist production as public enterprises proved to be the superior producer of the good.

After the collapse of the Russian economy as a result of 'War Communism' in the Spring of 1921, the Bolsheviks introduced partial market reforms with the New Economic Policy. While retaining their Marxists credentials, the Bolsheviks were implicitly engaging in a controlled experiment with the Fabian idea of a socialist encirclement of capitalism as opposed to an immediate revolutionary abolition of capitalism. During the NEP in the 1920s, the old Bolsheviks introduced the concept of 'socialist competition.'[30] The socialist sector of state-owned enterprises would compete with the small-scale private enterprise that was allowed to exist legally. The state sector would eventually defeat the private sector because of the efficiency of large-scale industrial planning, and then socialist economic planning could be fully implemented throughout the entire economy. This competition was cut short by arbitrary intervention into the economy by the Soviet government throughout the 1920s which destroyed the incentive to engage in above-ground, private capital accumulation and investment, and finally, by Stalin's revolution from above beginning in 1928 in which all private market transactions sought refuge in the underground economy from then on. The state socialist sector 'won,' not by outperforming the private market in economic competition – this, contrary to socialist expectations, it could not do – but by destroying the legal private market altogether.

That was the basic economic system Gorbachev supposedly sought to reform. The Soviet social system of production was characterized by the pseudo-reality of a rational, hierarchical planned economy, co-existing with the reality of plan failure and illicit corrective measures on both the producer and consumer side of the market. The Soviet system not only relied on the decentralized decisions of thousands of economic actors to coordinate plans that were supposed to be pre-reconciled by the organs of central administration, but it also remained at heart a commodity production economy.[31] Production was not for direct use, but rather was divided into two categories: production for production's sake (to maintain the illusion) and production for exchange (to sustain the population). Bargaining and haggling were a way of life for those who had to subsist by living *na levo*.

In other words, the Soviet economy was not a centrally planned economy radically different from any other economic system witnessed in history. It was over-regulated, abused and distorted, but it was, nevertheless, a market economy.[32]

THE SOVIET ECONOMIC SYNDICATE

The Party elite watched over this market economy as if it was their own private domain – which it was. They were the *de facto* owners of Soviet society's scarce resources. As Milovan Djilas pointed out a long time ago, they were the 'New Class' of propertied owners under socialism.[33] Each layer of the Party elite, from Politburo bosses to local Party officials to enterprise managers, was a feudal lord. They benefited directly from both the successes and failures of the official economic structure.

The central planning bureaucracy simply represented the central office of an elaborate system of interlocked industrial cartels in the Soviet economy.[34] The ministerial organizational structure established barriers against competition from other producers. The market was segmented and the central office monitored the cartel.[35] The persistence of excess demand for products caused by artificially low official prices produced a sellers' market. The shortage economy in combination with the monopoly status of producers simply reinforced the power of the managers of the state economy. The seller in such an environment can insist on whatever terms of trade he desires.

As a method of monitoring the cartel arrangement the Communist Party exercised tight control over managerial appointments.[36] Approval of the Party district committee was necessary to change jobs. Party organizations were responsible for creating a 'managerial reserve' list of qualified individuals for management positions. Party organs maintained the right to veto any appointment made to posts listed in the *nomenklatura*.[37] Loyalty to the Party and political reliability were the critical factors in the criteria for selection to managerial posts.

The mature Soviet economy was simply a syndicate or 'ultramonopoly' created and enforced by the organs of centralized state power. 'The *nomenklatura* class,' Michael Voslensky writes, 'exercises unlimited sway over the huge syndicate of which the Soviet economy consists. That is the principal feature of the country's economic organization. Nevertheless, the outside world goes on believing that its chief characteristic is economic planning.'[38]

CONCLUSION

The revolution of 1917 did not usher in a new era of social justice and economic rationality. Rather, the economic system born in the Russian revolution was the twentieth-century version of the 'old regime.' Political and economic privilege was granted to those in positions of power, and the organs of state power were employed to defend those positions. The countryside was brutalized into a new form of serfdom and forced to finance the ruling elite's preoccupation with building industrial cities. Moreover, citizens throughout the Soviet Union were compelled to shoulder the burden of a military empire that was ridiculously expensive.

The Party's influence was felt in every area of life. Those beholden to the system existed throughout every layer of society from Party boss to local school teacher. The conceptual difficulty of reforming such a social system was not that this was an entirely new adventure in economic restructuring. All that needed to be done was to eliminate the leading role of the Party and its monopolistic grip over the economy. The conceptual difficulty lay in mobilizing a people that had been culturally conditioned to submit to authority to challenge the main beneficiaries of the system.

The challenge of reforming the Soviet system was not one of pure economic theory as is suggested in the usual conceptualization of the problem as a move from a centrally planned non-market economy to a private market economy. A private market economy, in a fundamental sense, does not need to be created. A market economy evolves spontaneously wherever opportunities for economic gain present themselves as is evident in the continued existence of the *sub-*

rosa economy of the former Soviet Union even at the heights of 'war communism' (1918–21) and Stalin's assault on private economic activity in the 1930s. Well-functioning markets, however, do require the establishment of rules which protect private property and ensure the freedom of entry. Without these institutional constraints, individual economic activity cannot be guaranteed to move in directions that will be viewed as socially desirable. Within the proper institutional constraints, however, the profit-seeking activity of individuals will tend to generate an overall economic order that allocates scarce resources in a manner which will enhance the economic welfare of citizens.[39] Policy choices should be limited to the choice of the institutional constraints, i.e., the general rules, within which economic activity will transpire.

Changing the general rules in the former Soviet Union, however, amounted to recontracting the basic social compact that had existed from at least the 1930s.[40] Some would certainly gain with the new regime, but many would lose. And, those who had the most to lose were those in positions of power. That was the conceptual problem associated with reforming the former Soviet Union.

The problem was one of *political economy* and could not be addressed otherwise. But in order to begin to address the problem, it was necessary first to understand what was supposed to be reformed. Unfortunately, standard Sovietology did not pay enough attention to the unofficial system that sustained the official Soviet system. The reasons for this failure to examine in detail the real operation of the Soviet system can be attributed to: (1) a disregard among economists for evidence other than measurable statistics; (2) the elegance of the formal structure of central planning and the balancing of inputs and outputs; and (3) the preoccupation with aggregate measures of economic growth as opposed to detailed microeconomic analysis of the industrial structure. Any one of these intellectual prejudices, let alone all three in combination, would possess a deleterious effect on the attempt to understand the Soviet system.

The Soviet economy simply was not a centrally planned economy where the leading stratum sought to employ society's resources in an efficient manner, but just failed to do so for lack of ability or effort. Rather, the system that evolved out of the attempt to realize the Marxist dream of a more rational and just society was a caste society of political power and economic special privilege. The Soviet reality, as opposed to the pseudo-reality often portrayed in Soviet propaganda and Western textbooks, was represented in the interconnection between the official and unofficial economies and the economic self-interest of those who benefited from that structure. Understanding the real Soviet reality is a necessary prerequisite for satisfactorily examining the difficult problem of transforming the former Soviet economic system into a thriving and prosperous market economy.

5

THE LOGIC OF POLITICS AND
THE LOGIC OF REFORM

A nation so unused to acting for itself was bound to begin a
wholesale destruction when it launched into a program of
wholesale reform . . . An absolute monarch would have been a
far less dangerous innovator. Personally, indeed, when I reflect
on the way the French Revolution, in destroying so many
institutions, ideas, and customs inimical to freedom, abolished
so many others which were indispensable to freedom, I cannot
help feeling that had this revolution, instead of being carried out
by the masses on behalf of the sovereignty of the people, been
the work of an enlightened autocrat, it might well have left us
better fitted to develop in due course into a free nation.

Alexis de Tocqueville[1]

INTRODUCTION

In accomplishing any difficult task, recognition of the problem to be
solved is one thing, providing a workable solution is quite another. A
clear conception of the problem, however, is a necessary prerequisite.
In fact, one of the major stumbling blocks to the transformation to a
more liberal and civil society in the former socialist countries has been
the failure to appreciate the depth and nature of the problem at hand.
Moreover, the cultural legacy of the previous system of economic
organization – the administrative command economy – has been
misunderstood.

Not only were scholars, intellectuals and political actors confused over
the nature of the Soviet-type system, people in both the East and West
were generally confused over what the economic organization of a liberal
and civil society would look like.[2] This confused state is a result of a

failure to understand the historical lesson offered by twentieth-century economic policy. The experience of the economic systems in both East and West have more in common than is generally recognized.

The historical experience of government-managed economic policy in both East and West has much to offer for developing sound and liberal economic policy in the twenty-first century. Recognition of the structural problems confronting government-managed economies provides the basis upon which we can begin to understand the political realities that liberalization policies will face.

RENT-SEEKING: EAST AND WEST

Difficulties in government economic management are not peculiar to the Soviet-type economies. The failure of economic policy in Western democracies also illustrates the fundamental problems of government management of the economy.[3] Budget deficits, public debt, monetary and credit manipulation, disruptive taxation and failed public services are facts of life in the West and are consequences of economic policies that demanded an active role of the government in managing the affairs of capitalism.[4] Western consumers are ridiculously well-off compared to their East and Central European counterparts, but that should not dissuade us from examining our own deep structural problems and providing information to would-be reformers about the failures of Western political economies.

While most commentators discuss what the East can learn from Western democracy and managed market capitalism, we still have much to learn from the East that relates to our own problems. And, rather than learn from our legislative economic 'successes' the East could learn a lot from our failure to protect our constitutional heritage. As John Kenneth Galbraith has reminded us, the political and economic systems of the West are not examples of *laissez-faire* capitalism, but are forms of incomplete social democracy.[5]

While *laissez-faire* capitalism does provide answers to the economic problems of incentives, information and dispersed knowledge discussed in Chapter 3, the constitutional democracies of the West have failed to address the political organization problem in any lasting way.[6] The noble and inspiring original attempt at constitutional democracy derived from the work of Montesquieu has failed to produce the polity it envisioned because of the internal workings of democracy.[7] The rule of factions that James Madison warned us about has become the norm of governmental practice in the West.[8]

The rule of factions is a logical outcome of representative democracy. Good politics does not always make for good economics. Rational abstention and rational ignorance on the part of voters undermine to a considerable extent the preference revelation function of electoral campaigns. Moreover, democratically elected politicians, who by definition must rely on votes and campaign contributions to get elected, cater to those who have a selective incentive to cast informed votes. As a result, the bias in policy-making under representative democracy is to concentrate benefits on the well-organized and well-informed and disperse costs on the ill-organized and uninformed mass of citizens. The best way to do this is to sponsor policies which yield short-term and easily identifiable benefits at the expense of long-term and largely hidden costs. Continual deficit financing or financing government activity through the hidden tax of inflation are just two of the tools that politicians have at their disposal for pursuing such a course. Public policy in the Western democracies, therefore, contains both a concentrated benefit and a short-sightedness bias.

Western institutions such as the United States Federal Reserve System, Federal Trade Commission, etc., even though they are lauded as fundamental institutions for regulating the excesses of capitalism are quite susceptible to political influence. Much of the evidence of the history of these institutions, in fact, suggests that they were instituted for the purpose of protecting special interests from the rigors of free-market competition.[9]

We are, therefore, faced with a peculiar situation in assessing comparative political economies in East and West. On the one hand, complete and comprehensive socialism is simply an economic impossibility. The economies of the East did not conform to the ideal model of socialism. This was not because of political perversion of the ideal by the leaders, but for the simple reason that the socialist model cannot exist in reality. Instead these economies were commodity production systems that relied on the decentralized decisions of the market (however deformed) as the basic coordinating mechanism. The system granted *de facto* ownership of scarce resources to members of the bureaucracy who derived profits from their positions of power through artificial scarcity rents and patronage rents.[10]

On the other hand, Western economies do not conform to the ideal model of capitalism. *Laissez-faire* capitalism, unlike socialism, however, *is* an economic possibility. But, individuals find that through the use and manipulation of government they can achieve and protect contrived scarcity rents that competition would otherwise disperse

among consumers. From an organizational viewpoint, the real existing economic systems in East and West are the same – the difference
lying in degree not in fundamental kind – and can be studied and
criticized by employing the same principles of economics. The
economies of East and West are quasi-mercantilist, rent-seeking
societies.

Whether we call these economies state capitalist or state socialist
(deformed capitalism or incomplete social democracy) the main
problem facing the reform of the government-managed economy in
both East and West is the powerful vested interests that benefit from
the pre-existing organizational arrangement. The failure of both the
Thatcher and Reagan 'revolutions' to produce any lasting structural
change should warn the would-be reformers in the East of the
difficulty in turning back the state.[11] As Anthony deJasay has
concluded: 'Democracy's last dilemma is that the state must, but
cannot, roll itself back.'[12]

Within a democratic regime such as the US, as Milton and Rose
Friedman have argued, an iron triangle consisting of politicians,
beneficiaries and the bureaucracy forms which produces a bias toward
the status quo.[13] Moreover, as Racquel Fernandez and Dani Rodrik
have argued, even in cases where the welfare implications of a policy
change are unambiguous, such as trade liberalization, reforms will be
resisted by the polity.[14] The bias toward the status quo results not only
because of the interest group pressures that the Friedmans discuss, but
also can be shown to follow logically from the asymmetry that exists
within the political process. Informational uncertainty about
individual gainers and losers from political economy reform prevent
desired reforms from ever being adopted in the first place even if they
would receive popular support after the fact. And, once a reform is
rejected it is unlikely to ever be accepted.

In other words, even assuming away pressure groups, voter
preferences may still be revealed in a manner which possesses a status
quo bias. An electorate, for example, that rejects a policy reform will
not possess any incentive to change its vote in the future for the
simple reason that no new information about the efficacy of the policy
will be provided by the passage of time. Information concerning the
rejected policy will not be readily available and, thus, there will be no
reason why the electorate would change their behavior. A rejected
reform will remain rejected, whereas an accepted reform will either be
supported as it proves effective or it may be reversed in the future if it
proves to be unpopular.

The incentives and information generated by voting procedures, as well as interest group pressure, generate a bias toward the political status quo and the rejection of welfare enhancing economic policies. Only a shock to the system coupled with a major reform package can break this hold that existing political structures have on the economic system. The upshot of this analysis is that public policies that generate economic inefficiencies can have a rather long life once they are instituted. Moreover, the focus of reformers should not be on correcting past inefficiencies because the difficulties of reversing the particular policy will be considerable. Rather, reformers should be concerned with establishing institutions which protect against economically inefficient public policies from being accepted in the future.

The reformers in the East would do well to learn from the failure of Western democracies to check the encroachment of the state into economic life and the apparent inability to reverse the process. And the West would do well to acknowledge intellectually that the same pretense of knowledge that inspired the socialist experiment in the Eastern Bloc also inspired, and continues to inspire, our attempts at managed capitalism and social democracy.

THE PROBLEMS AND PARADOXES OF REFORM

Perhaps the most common complaint one hears concerning the transition of the economies in East and Central Europe and the former Soviet Union, is that there does not exist a transitional model. While the transformation task is daunting, the mainstream perspective tends to overstate the difficulty.

There should be real concern on how to get there from here. But, the economic problems of reform are systematically overstated in the conventional wisdom because of erroneous comparisons between the real levels of output, employment and prices in a market environment with the spurious levels recorded under the previous administrative command system. For example, there is a standard of living measurement problem in the reform process. Traditional measured real incomes are nominal incomes divided by prices, but in an excess demand economy (i.e., where prices are fixed below market clearing levels) incomes divided by prices do not measure actual living standards. A rise in prices that brings forth supply may actually increase well-being whereas the measurement would show a decrease. A similar problem is associated with standards of economic growth. The previous system valued production independent of the net market value produced and as such overstated economic growth. Moreover, the gross output targets provided an incentive to include physical, but valueless, bulk output in measurements of growth. A decline in measured growth during the transition, therefore, might actually correspond to increased coordination of production with consumption and satisfaction of consumer demands, including an increase in product quality. Needless to say these problems are further compounded if we include the problem of falsification of economic statistics. From a purely positive economic perspective reform is much more tractable and the attendant costs much lower than are usually stated. The political economy problems of reform are real enough without including bogus economic costs.

Moreover, while there appears to be an intellectual consensus about the failure of the old regime in East and Central Europe, a similar consensus has not emerged concerning where the transformation should lead. Therefore, the two major difficulties confronting structural reform are: (1) ideas concerning the nature and logic of economic organization; and (2) the vested interests of the old regime.

At the level of ideas there are those experts from the West who continue to voice opposition to unfettered capitalism.[15] The majority of Western economists, especially those advising the governments in transition, such as Jeffrey Sachs and Stanley Fischer, are convinced that the problem with the formerly socialist economies was that the planning principle was pursued too comprehensively and vigorously, thus confronting the bureaucracy with an overly complex task. In those cases where partial marketization had occurred (such as Hungary), the problem was simply that East European economists did not learn how to manage their economies effectively. With the right institutional framework, e.g., a central bank, a Federal Trade Commission, an Environmental Protection Agency and so on, the task of managing the economy could be accomplished efficiently and the anarchy of unfettered markets could be controlled. The context and implementation of planning under the old regime is challenged, not the principle of planning and government management of a market economy. That is the logic of the position of the mainstream reformer even if they do not state that position explicitly.[16] Mix macroeconomic stabilization policies with microeconomic regulation and the conventional wisdom espoused by Western advisors for economic transformation emerges.

Western institutions, such as the World Bank and the International Monetary Fund, continue to provide aid for the planning and management of economic development to some 75 governments around the world, including former socialist economies. Continuous appeals have been made by American politicians and intellectuals throughout the Gorbachev, and now Yeltsin, period to aid the East European economies in this period of transition along the lines of the Marshall Plan.[17] On 1 April 1992, President George Bush and Chancellor Helmut Kohl of Germany unveiled the plan for a $24 billion aid package to the Russian government to assist the process of economic reform.[18]

This practice persists in spite of the overwhelming evidence of the failure of government planning of economic development and foreign aid programs.[19] The very aid package offered would, by subsidizing existing political/economic structures, undermine the revolutionary transformation necessary for the formerly communist economies to become prosperous and thriving.

These ideas and practices concerning government management translate into two trends in policy-making that undermine even the best intentions of reform. It is argued that what is needed is a careful and detailed plan for the transition, which is envisioned as a process of phasing in reforms. Drawing up a detailed plan requires the specification of hundreds, perhaps thousands of laws concerning the regulation of markets. Phasing in requires deciding on economic priorities, e.g., which subsidies stay, which go, what firms are privatized, which ones are not and so on, before market competition is introduced. Both trends in policy-making tend to undermine structural reform.

Rather than concentrate on working out details of economic regulation, reformers should commit themselves to fundamental change in the structure of the polity's relationship to the economy. The problems with the phase in strategy are twofold. First, the time lag gives opposition forces the opportunity to organize and develop their counter-strategy to reform. Second, if the government could outline priorities and select out the economically strong companies from weaker ones and enact 'hard' budget constraints in the absence of free market processes then there would be no need for reform in the first place. But only real market competition can provide the discipline of the hard budget constraint. Politics, on the other hand, in both East and West leads to 'soft' budget constraints and their corresponding inefficiencies as politics dominates economics.

Thus, the reform decrees should neither be overly detailed nor come in a series of small steps. The decrees must come, as it were, overnight. Immediate and unconditional repudiation of government planning and management of the economy must be instituted. Protection of private property, the elimination of consumer and producer subsidies, the elimination of all restrictions on labor mobility and the elimination of all restrictions on currency exchange are just some of the decrees necessary. But in order to accomplish such a reform the political actors need to have tremendous conviction and power.[20] This, of course, is potentially one of the great paradoxes of reform.

Great centralized power may be necessary in order to implement a great decentralization of the power of the government over the economy. Such power would be needed because the very reason why reform is necessary, i.e., the dominance of bureaucratic interests over economic, also provides the strongest resistance to reform. The vested interests of entrenched bureaucracy provide formidable obstacles to fundamental change.[21] Bureaucratic inertia, as the reform economist Vasily Selyunin pointed out in 1988, possesses the potential to undermine any effort at change. 'Today,' Selyunin stated,

> this uniquely large and uniquely impotent apparatus is engaged in translating the Party's decisions on restructuring into the language of various instructions and directives. Since bureaucrats' chief concern is self-preservation and, therefore, the preservation of administrative management methods, it is not hard to guess what the results of this process will be. The existing bureaucratic machine cannot be incorporated in restructuring. It can be broken up and eliminated, but not restructured.[22]

This problem of bureaucratic inertia and the paradox of centralized power to accomplish decentralization are not phenomena new to the post-communist political economy. They actually represent the fundamental problem and paradox of all attempts to change governmental structures in a direction that reduces their scope and power. Ironically, for example, trade liberalization in Taiwan and South Korea in the 1960s and Chile in the 1970s was imposed by authoritarian regimes. Unfortunately, authoritarians often claim power with a statement of good intentions, but rarely live up to them.[23]

SOVIET BUREAUCRACY AND PERESTROIKA

Since its inception, the Soviet state was an autocracy, although not necessarily a dictatorship. Ultimate authority usually was shared by a small group. At times a single individual, such as Stalin from 1928 to 1953, exercised approximate absolute power. But the Soviet political system would best be described as rule by a small clique centered in the Politburo.

The political structure of the mature Soviet system was established by Lenin in the spring of 1921. In order to alleviate the economic catastrophe of 'War Communism' and eliminate the political challenge to power that had emerged, Lenin introduced the partial economic liberalization of the New Economic Policy, but simultaneously he decreed absolute political power to the Communist Party. Not only were opposition political parties effectively eliminated, but even free debate within the Party was decreed illegal. Though many Western observers of the Soviet scene, such as Stephen Cohen and Jerry Hough, refer to the 1920s as a period of cultural liberalism and as a sort of 'Moscow Spring,' this overstates the freedom of that period. Surely, the NEP period could be characterized as one of relative freedom compared to the period of 'War Communism' that preceded it or the Stalin period that came immediately after, but it was not a period of political liberalization as is sometimes suggested. It was, rather, a period of solidifying an authoritarian political monopoly. That was the political system that Stalin inherited and manipulated in his struggle for succession after Lenin's death in 1924 and subsequent consolidation of power in the late 1920s.[24]

Stalin simply became the sole power within a monopoly of power. Lenin's 'testament,' which has been a subject of controversy for years, warned against this outcome.[25] But Lenin did not at any time suggest that the Bolsheviks should forsake their privileged political position. Rather, his letter to the Congress could be interpreted as suggesting that leadership should be a collective leadership and not controlled by any one individual in order to prevent a split of the Central Committee. Stalin had concentrated enormous power, but Lenin was not sure he knew how to use that power wisely, besides which Stalin was 'too rude.' Trotsky possessed exceptional abilities, but was too attracted to the purely administrative side of affairs. Zinoviev and Kamenev could not be fully trusted because of their hesitation in October 1917. Bukharin was the most valuable theoretician in the Party and considered by many the favorite of the whole Party, but he was too scholastic. No one man, in Lenin's assessment, had the characteristics to rule effectively. They must rule collectively and avoid a split. Nevertheless, Stalin was able to outmaneuver his political opponents and consolidate his power by the 1930s.

One of the consequences of Stalin's purge of the 1930s was the creation of a loyal cohort. The average age of members of the Soviet bureaucracy fell drastically as younger individuals assumed their purged seniors' former positions. 'In 1930,' Michael Voslensky points out,

> 69 per cent of the regional and district secretaries and secretar-
> ies of the central committee of the Union's constituent republics
> had joined the party before the revolution. In 1939, 80.5 per
> cent had joined the party only after 1924, i.e., after Lenin's
> death. Of the 1939 secretaries, 91 per cent were under forty; in
> other words, they were adolescents at the time of the revolution.
> The figures for the secretaries of regions and towns are similar.
> In 1939, 93.5 per cent had joined the party only after 1924, and
> 92 per cent were under forty.[26]

A comparison of the Seventeenth Party Congress in 1934 and the Eighteenth Congress in 1939 also demonstrate this purge effect. At the 1934 congress 80 per cent of the delegates had joined the Party prior to 1920, but at the 1939 congress 50 per cent of the delegates were under 35 years old. Stalin's purge of the 'Old Bolsheviks' served, among other things, to create a layer of very young and loyal apparatchiks.

In representative democracies government bureaucracies grow slowly over time and members tend to be of various age cohorts. The process of hiring and retiring is continuous, but gradual. The situation in the former Soviet Union prior to Gorbachev was quite different. The Communist Party closely controlled the appointment of person-nel to positions of power through the *nomenklatura* system and political patronage. Moreover, since the bulk of the state bureaucracy came to power at about the same time, the same cohort controlled the strategic positions within the bureaucracy. This system could be expected to be extremely stable in its ordinary operations until that cohort began to retire or die of natural causes.

In addition, the Soviet state had been an exceptionally stable autocracy because of its method of succession. The usual route to autocratic power is either military coup or dynasty. A third route avoids many of the problems associated with either the coup or dynasty models of political succession, and has proven very stable in the few cases that it has been successfully implemented.[27] The major characteristic of this system is that a voting body is appointed to determine the autocrat's successor after the autocrat's death or retirement. Like his predecessors, Gorbachev rose to Chairmanship of the Communist Party of the Soviet Union (CPSU) as the result of a Politburo vote.

This system of succession effectively screened candidates for their ability to rule in the interest of the cohort who elected them. At the time of Gorbachev's ascension to power, the Soviet economic bureaucracy consisted of over 400 state committees, union ministries, union-republic ministries and regional ministries and authorities. And, each of these organizations had its own bureaucracy. The Soviet economic bureaucracy employed millions of people and permeated the entire industrial and agricultural systems from top to bottom.[28]

Many interpreters have viewed Gorbachev's efforts from 1985 to 1991 as a revolutionary challenge to the Soviet bureaucracy.[29] In this interpretation, Gorbachev is seen as an enlightened autocrat bent on modernizing and liberalizing the Soviet political economy. Perestroika was said to have a net decentralizing effect on the management of the economy.[30] But this 'decentralization' never did represent a movement toward *laissez faire*. The basic structure of the Soviet political economy remained the same.[31]

What Gorbachev was up to can perhaps better be understood as a redistribution of patronage perquisites.[32] Unlike his predecessors, Gorbachev faced significantly lower transaction costs in redistributing patronage opportunities because of the demographic transition of the bureaucracy. Finally, by the mid-1980s the cohort which had collectively controlled the bureaucracy since Stalin's rule began to die or retire. With them went the structure of informal quasi-contracts within and between the bureaus which formed the basis of the stability of the Soviet power structure.

Gorbachev liberalized government restrictions in some ways. But much of perestroika seems to have been primarily an effort to reallocate patronage opportunities to consolidate his power base, a rather routine practice of fresh autocrats throughout history. His redistribution of political rents, however, was couched in liberalization rhetoric. The market-oriented rhetoric of the Gorbachev period bore little resemblance to the reality of continued bureaucratic management of the economic system. No serious effort was made to end the domination of the economy by the central government.

Gorbachev's activities, however, unintentionally conflicted with the long-run stability of the Communist political and economic system. He presided over the demise of Soviet state socialism as an unintended consequence of the exploitation of opportunities to reallocate positions of privilege in the Soviet bureaucracy.[33] In other words, Gorbachev's perestroika never was an attempt to change the basic political and economic system of Soviet rule. He was not an agent of change, but rather a guardian of the structure of the old regime – even if populated with new faces.[34]

THE CLASH OF LOGIC

Conceptually, economic reform is a fairly simple matter. Private property in resources must be established and protected by a rule of law, consumer and producer subsidies must be eliminated and prices must be free to adjust to the forces of supply and demand, responsible fiscal policy should be pursued that keeps taxation to a minimum and reigns in deficit financing, and a sound currency should be established. Introducing such reforms – even within Western economies – is anything but simple. And the major problem is not just another conceptual one of designing the appropriate sequence or plan of reform.

One of the most important insights derived from academic research in modern political economy is the potential conflict that exists between good economics and good politics as discussed above. To reiterate, in democratic regimes, where politicians depend on votes and campaign contributions to remain in office, research has shown that the logic of politics produces a concentrated benefits and short-sightedness bias with regard to economic policy. Popular economic policies are those that will tend to yield short-term and easily identifiable benefits at the expense of long-term and largely hidden costs.

In the formerly communist political economies this argument about the logic of politics can be intensified. The benefits of public policy fell mainly on the only constituency that mattered: the descending layers of the Party bureaucracy that permeated society. From the nice *dacha* to special access to stores, the Party elite were the primary beneficiaries of the system. Economic reform promised to disrupt the old system and yield very real short-term costs. Structural economic reform promised short-term and easily identifiable costs to be born mainly by the Party bureaucracy and long-term and largely hidden benefits in terms of increased economic efficiency and consumer well-being. The logic of reform was in direct conflict with the logic of politics.

Real reform of the basic structure of the constitution of economic policy *within* any given polity seems to face a daunting task. Endogenous reform seems impossible because it would violate the basic maxims of voluntary exchange since it would require that some individuals, namely current beneficiaries, agree to a Pareto inferior position. Gradual and marginal policy change cannot do the job either. Only a large policy change preceded by an exogenous shock could move the system in the desired direction.

Even though the ruling elite in the former Soviet Union fought real economic reform at every step, they could not repudiate economic reality.[35] The Soviet economy had exhausted its accumulated surplus in terms of natural resources and Western technology and was unable to continue to develop.[36] The economic situation simply grew worse under Gorbachev and the demand for structural reform grew louder and more threatening to the old system. Glasnost, in addition to the events of 1989 – from Tiananmen Square to the Berlin Wall – mobilized the intellectual and cultural elite into opposition against the Gorbachev government and the Communist Party.[37]

But an exogenous shock, in the form of either an ideological revolution, a natural disaster or an economic collapse, can precipitate the regime change necessary for reform. The problem with reform within any political and economic system is that, as Mancur Olson argued in his *Rise and Decline of Nations*, as political stability occurs entrenched interests form, which through their rent-seeking activity eventually retard the further economic development of a country.[38] Reform in a situation with such entrenched interests is a near impossibility. The logic of reform runs directly contrary to the logic of politics. If the logic of politics is to concentrate benefits on the well-organized and well-informed and disperse costs on the ill-informed and unorganized masses, then the logic of reform is actually to concentrate costs and disperse benefits. As long as the entrenched interests are not displaced, reform measures within a system will continually stall. Empirical illustrations of this simple point can be found in the failure of both Reagan and Thatcher, and the troublesome reform efforts in the Soviet Union from 1985–91.

Another side of Olson's argument, however, points to the window of opportunity that exists when for reasons of an exogenous shock the dominant interest groups are displaced. At such moments, when the dominant interest groups are dispersed by some exogenous shock, intellectual entrepreneurs can act in a manner which changes the basic structural rules governing a society. The failed August coup provided the shock necessary.

Liberalization demands legal protection of private property and freedom of entry in the economic arena. Free trade, i.e., freedom of exchange and production, as a principle must be held as an absolute rule of social interaction and be codified in the body of law.[39] In order to transit the path from powerful central government to governance structures more amenable to economic freedom the reformers (in both East and West) will need a vision of a workable utopia. Such a transition will require an evolutionary development of ideas and revolutionary political action to overturn vested interests no less dramatic than the previous revolution that got us here in the first place.

CONCLUSION

Gorbachev's dithering with the Soviet economic bureaucracy, while winning him great praise abroad, totally discredited him at home. Elena Bonner, the widow of Andrei Sakharov, argued in November of 1988 that she had lost faith in perestroika. Western intellectuals had not framed their questions concerning the ability of perestroika to succeed correctly. The real question was whether there was anything in content within perestroika that compelled people to believe. 'I always was a believer . . .,' she stated, 'but today my faith in perestroika is waning.'[40] In 1990, Bonner voiced her disillusionment with perestroika in even stronger terms. The credit given to Gorbachev in the West, she argued, was 'false credit.' Perestroika was a vague and ever-changing policy without a goal or even direction. Moreover, Gorbachev had failed to establish any political base for perestroika. After an initial two-year period of success with glasnost – freedom for most prisoners of conscience, changes in emigration and travel policy, disarmament and the withdrawal of Soviet troops from Afghanistan – the ambiguities of perestroika began to undermine efforts at transformation of the Soviet system. All that five years of perestroika brought was empty shelves, decreased production, inflation, budget deficits, unlimited presidential powers and a complete loss of faith in political authority per se.[41]

The original program of perestroika did not represent a coherent agenda for economic transformation. Perestroika never was formulated in a manner which would introduce the discipline of unfettered markets as was necessary. Rather, decentralization simply meant a movement of the state's economic management functions from the center to lower levels of government supervision, such as the republics. And, destatization did not exactly translate into privatization of state enterprises.[42] Moreover, perestroika possessed no strategic vision for wresting power from the vested interests of the old regime.

These failings of perestroika as a program for economic transformation are perfectly understandable because the intention never was to introduce market discipline nor was it meant to defeat the vested interests of the old regime. From the beginning to the end, Gorbachev was quite clear that what he intended to accomplish was to modify, not fundamentally change, the Soviet system of state socialism. The goal was to make the Soviet system more humane and more efficient, but not to transform the system into a market economy with a limited government. His rhetoric and, even more so, his actions never suggested otherwise.

As a result, perestroika did nothing to instill trust in the population. Fundamental economic change, however, required that trust be established. Without establishing trust, as will be discussed at length in the next chapter, the economic transformation could not even begin to get off the ground.

6

CREDIBILITY IN SOVIET REFORMS

It must not be. There is no power in Venice
Can alter a decree established.
'Twill be recorded for a precedent,
And many an error by the same example
Will rush into the state. It cannot be.

William Shakespeare[1]

INTRODUCTION

After six years of Mikhail Gorbachev, and despite all the talk about renewal and restructuring, the Soviet economy was worse off and the Soviet Union no longer existed as a political entity. As a program of economic restructuring and renewal, perestroika must be judged an absolute failure.[2] Glasnost to be sure produced a political and cultural awakening of sorts unknown during the seventy-four years of communist rule, but perestroika simply failed to deliver the economic goods.

As events in the former Soviet Union are continually unfolding it is rather difficult to get a handle on the full significance of current policy statements and initiatives and analyze them from an economic point of view. With the failure of the August 1991 coup, we have entered the post-perestroika era. We now know that reform communism has been rejected.[3] But as for what will emerge, we will have to wait and see. What we do know, however, is that the perestroika period (1985–91), along with previous attempts at reform such as the New Economic Policy (1921–8), the Khrushchev's sovnarkhoz reforms (1957) and the Brezhnev–Kosygin reforms (1965), can now be safely treated as history.

Fortunately, sometimes the historical experience of one period provides insights for understanding more contemporary situations. One such example is the Soviet experience with the New Economic Policy (NEP) in the 1920s and its parallels with perestroika. Many Sovietologists have pointed out the connection between the NEP and perestroika. Gorbachev himself argued that perestroika represented 'the most important and most radical reform our country has had since Lenin introduced his New Economic Policy in 1921.'[4]

Both the NEP and perestroika were broadly heralded as liberalization policies, and both came to an abrupt end less than a decade after they were initiated. The NEP and perestroika were simply not sustainable economic policies. The NEP, for example, was reversed in 1928 when Stalin began his 'revolution from above.' And, despite the collapse of the communist system, the consequences of the failure of perestroika are yet to be fully realized. Food shortages, declining production and social unrest are just some of the economic problems that the new leaders of the former Soviet republics will have to confront in the immediate future.

Understanding the reasons why both these liberalization attempts failed is important, not only for antiquarian interests, but also for what such an understanding can tell us about the general theory of social organization and public policy. An examination of the failing of the NEP and perestroika may offer invaluable insights for constructing a workable post-perestroika constitution of economic policy.

EXPLANATIONS OF THE FAILURE OF NEP

There is, as of yet, no professional consensus on what caused perestroika's unravelling, but for the NEP there does exist competing hypotheses. The *traditional* explanation is that the NEP failed because free markets cannot be relied on to provide the basis for industrial development.[5] A backward country cannot be expected to develop without a massive and concerted industrialization program. The consequence of this line of reasoning is the 'Big Push' theory of economic development. Despite whatever excesses Stalin may have committed, it is argued that he was necessary to lift the Soviet Union from a backward peasant economy into a major industrial and military power. Alec Nove, one of the most respected Sovietologists, endorses this position when he argues that 'the survival of the regime, given the Bolsheviks' aims and their rapid industrialization program, required a harsh autocratic type of regime.'[6]

The traditional explanation has been challenged by the *reformists*.[7]

Reformists have argued that the NEP failed because of the political intrigue of Stalin. The NEP, they argue, would have developed the appropriate base for sustainable development and the advance toward a market socialist economy. In the reformist formulation, the personality of Stalin corrupts the revolution. Stalin was simply a 'bad' leader, who led the revolution astray from its humanitarian goals. The humane socialism of the 1920s, and specifically the alternative of Nikolai Bukharin, was sustainable, but co-opted by Stalin's ruthless quest for power. This line of reasoning, however, leads analysts away from focusing on the operation of the system and its institutional demands. It fails to appreciate the internal contradictions of interventionism that plagued the NEP with recurring economic crises throughout its history.

The *revisionist* interpretation attempts to avoid the failings of both the traditional and reformist explanations and offers a more telling narrative of the Soviet experience with the NEP.[8] The focus in the revisionist interpretation is on the institutional structure and its impact on economic processes. The internal contradictions of the NEP, and the inability of the regime to establish a binding commitment to economic reform, are seen as the major reason for its failing as a liberalization policy.

The NEP failed neither because of the failure of unhampered markets to promote economic development, nor because of the political intrigue of Stalin, but because its institutional design was inconsistent with economic incentives and, therefore, could not mobilize the information that existed within the economic system and was necessary for the coordination of economic plans. In other words, the institutional structure of the NEP did not provide the appropriate environment for individuals to solve the coordination problem of economic development, and as such was doomed structurally to failure. The ensuing instability caused by a discretionary policy regime undermined attempts at liberalization. The same argument can be applied to perestroika.

INFORMATION AND INCENTIVES

Public policy must be constructed in a manner which recognizes the obstacles presented by information and incentives. Policy must first and foremost be incentive compatible with basic economic motivations. Policies that are based on notions of public spiritedness and humanitarian goals, but disregard economic motivations are most likely to be doomed to failure. Moreover, even if public policies offer rewards to those who perform as expected, economic actors must possess the relevant information to act appropriately. If actors have the motivation to 'do the right thing,' they must nevertheless have access to information about what the right thing to do would be in their present context. The problem of obtaining relevant economic information is one that confronts even a benevolent ruler or regulator.[9]

The problem is that relevant economic information is dispersed throughout the economy in scattered bits and pieces and is not available to anyone in its totality.[10] The price system, through the constellation of relative prices and the calculus of profit and loss, allows individuals to use this dispersed information in an economically effective manner. The social learning process of market competition reveals errors and motivates individuals to be alert to opportunities to correct their previous mistakes concerning the use and allocation of scarce resources. The daily changes in market conditions set in motion a process of mutual accommodation that translates the subjective assessment of trade-offs by some into effective knowledge for others. Within the context of the competitive market process individuals are able to discover and learn how to use information that is essential for the coordination of the production plans of some with the consumption demands of others.

Private property is a fundamental precondition in this social learning process because it affords market experimentation. Since private property, in effect, places the sphere of accountability for decision-making on the owner, this encourages risk-taking and innovation. The owner receives the rewards or suffers the losses of decisions in the market place. This context motivates individuals to be alert to, and learn of, opportunities for pure profit. The system of private property establishes a context in which various individuals are free to pursue all kinds of ideas. Accountability amounts to a legal responsibility not to infringe on the property rights of others, and the financial risk implied in the market experiment. With community property, however, the manager neither reaps the increase in the value of assets nor suffers the loss of asset depreciation. Decisions are accountable to committees and bureaus that decide 'social' goals.

The whole justification of substituting community property for private property is to somehow arrive at an *ex ante* criterion for eliminating mistaken decisions concerning resource use. But, such a substitution of community for private property stifles the experimentation and learning processes that constitute the market economy. The trial and error experimentation by individuals within a market economy engenders a process of learning and discovery without which new methods and technologies for the use of scarce resources would lay hidden. Error, while costly to the individual market participant, is a fundamental driving force in the market system as a whole. The ability of the private property order to reveal errors and motivate learning is perhaps its most important function.

Policy should be structured in a manner which does not distort this social learning process. Unfortunately, the problem of constructing an optimal governmental policy that intervenes properly without distorting the flow of information is compounded by the passage of time. For one, relevant economic data is contextual and not abstract. Information gathered yesterday may be irrelevant for decisions today because of changing conditions. The price system overcomes this problem by alerting individuals to these changes through the adjustment of relative prices. Activity outside of the context of the market, however, does not have access to such a register of accommodating changes in intertemporal decisions. Even in cases where discretionary intervention might be desired to correct for perceived market failures, the problem remains as to how to acquire the requisite knowledge to intervene properly. Ignorant or haphazard intervention will simply lead to further destabilization and exacerbate the problem it sought originally to correct.

The dynamics of change associated with the passage of time also presents a timing problem for public policy, as Milton Friedman pointed out a long time ago. A long and variable lag exists between: (1) the need for action and the recognition of this need, (2) the recognition of a problem and the design and implementation of a policy response and (3) the implementation of the policy and the effect of the policy.[11] Because of these lags, Friedman argued that discretionary public policy will often be destabilizing. For this reason, he argued the case for *rules* rather than discretionary public policy.[12]

Finally, the passage of time introduces strategic problems for policy-makers. Policies that seemed appropriate at t_1 may not be deemed appropriate at t_2. In fact, a basic presupposition of the argument for discretion is exactly that policies accepted for one period may prove to be inappropriate for another, and, therefore, policy-makers must possess the ability to shift policy as circumstances change. Such shifts in public policy (coupled with the impact that these shifts have on the expectations of economic actors), however, may prove destabilizing to the overall economic environment.

THE ISSUE OF CREDIBILITY

Recognizing the temporal dimensionality of choice is one of the most fundamental issues in establishing viable economic policy.[13] The analysis of both private and public choice must recognize the paradox that the passage of time presents to actors. Individual behavior, such as leaving credit cards at home when shopping or joining a drug rehabilitation center, are just some examples of attempts to solve the problem of 'multiple selves' as individuals construct themselves through time.[14]

Our concern here, however, is not with the individual choice problem, but with the public choice problem that follows from the strategic interaction between rulers and citizens. A fundamental problem faces public choosers when a policy that seemed optimal when introduced, appears less so as time passes.[15] Without a binding commitment to the policy, the government will change policy to what now appears to be optimal. The problem is that economic actors who realize this will anticipate the policy change and act in a counter-productive manner from the perspective of the policy-maker.

Optimal intervention, by definition, requires that a large degree of discretionary control be entrusted to government decision-makers.[16] The expectational problems of discretion, however, generate difficulties for government planning in general.[17] Optimal intervention is simply not a possibility because of the problems of information and incentives discussed above. One reason discretionary control does not work is because current decisions by economic actors depend on expectations concerning future policy and those expectations are not invariant of the policies chosen. For example, if for whatever reason (either an increase in demand or reduction in supply) market conditions produced a windfall profit for the oil industry, the government could respond by proposing to tax away those profits with the argument that this will not affect the current supply of oil because it is the result of a past decision. But such a policy would lead oil companies to anticipate that similar expropriations will occur again in the future, and this expectation will impact on their investment decisions in a manner which will reduce the future supply of oil. Policy decisions and social rules create expectations and expectations guide actions.

93

These insights are directly applicable to the NEP and perestroika situation. The NEP period, for example, was one plagued by legal ambiguity toward private enterprise just as the position of the cooperatives was precarious at best under perestroika. During NEP

> the population lived in uncertainty, fearful of breaking the law, afraid of what was to come. Paradoxically, those who were considered the victors (the workers) lived in poverty, although without fear, while those who knew they were the vanquished (the middle peasants, Nepmen, intellectuals) enjoyed material comfort, but lived in fear.[18]

The legal ambiguity toward private trade led Boris Pasternak to describe the NEP in *Doctor Zhivago* as 'the most ambiguous and hypocritical of all Soviet periods.'[19]

But while most scholars recognize the conflicting expectations between current market conditions and a possible future crack-down by the ruling regime, it is rarely systematically addressed within the usual analysis of the NEP or perestroika.[20] The establishment of a binding commitment which limits the regime's discretion is a fundamental prerequisite for successful market reforms. Without such a binding commitment reform efforts fail to produce the desired outcomes.

Perhaps the following scenario between the citizen and the ruler will illustrate the basic policy dilemma clearly. The ruling regime, which can either be sincere or insincere, announces a plan to introduce an economic liberalization policy. The citizen now must decide either to enter the market or stay out of the official market. A major problem confronting the citizen, however, is not knowing whether the regime in question is sincere or insincere. The citizen's only prior information concerning the regime is policy history, but the reform announcement was presumably intended to signal a break from the old way of doing things.[21] If the citizen decides to enter the official market in expectation of continued liberalization, then the regime must decide either to continue the liberalization policy that was announced or renege on the announcement and tighten political control in the second round, for a host of ideological and short-term financial considerations, by cracking down on individual economic activity.

If the ruler is following a discretionary policy, then the citizen will foresee that the ruler may be likely to choose to crack down in the second period of this game, and therefore will choose to stay out. But if the ruler can convey a credible commitment, he would announce liberalization, and the citizen would choose to come into the official market. The ruler's payoff, independent of whether the regime is sincere or insincere, will be higher with commitment conveyance than it would be without it, but the insincere ruler would be better off once the announcement of liberalization elicited citizen market participation to pursue crack-down in the form of increased taxation, regulation or confiscation. The sincere reform regime, however, will not crack down and will continue to pursue liberalization policies.

In such situations, though, since the citizens are uninformed about the sincerity of the ruling regime, and given certain probabilities that are derived from their previous experience with the regime's efforts at reform, it may be rational for them to expect that the rulers will go back on their announcement to pursue economic liberalization. If this is the case, citizens will choose to stay out of the economic game, and, thus, defeat both the short-term and long-term goals of the ruler.[22] The only way out of this policy dilemma for the ruler is to establish a binding and credible commitment to liberalization. Establishing just such a commitment, however, is the major problem of constitutional political economy.

The ruling regime's problem is even more difficult than solving the basic paradox in establishing constraints on their activities that do not deter their positive ability to govern. In order to get liberalization off the ground, the rulers have simultaneously to establish binding constraints on their behavior and signal a sincere commitment to reform to the citizenry. During war, for example, if his troops crossed over a large river to do battle with opposing forces, the commanding officer may order the bridge burned – thus pre-committing his troops to the battle ahead by eliminating the only possible escape. At the same time, however, opposing troops witnessing the smoke have received a signal that the other side will fight a hard battle. The reforming regime must do something similar to establish trust and bind themselves to the liberalization policy.

This simple illustration of the basic problem of policy design and the failure to solve the dilemma goes a long way toward providing an explanation of the failures of the NEP and perestroika. Specifically, an examination of the tax and license fees of the Nepmen (private traders) and the grain policy during the NEP and the policy toward individual labor activity and cooperatives during perestroika highlight the explanatory power of this simple game.[23]

ILLUSTRATIONS OF THE PROBLEM

The policy game under the NEP

The introduction of the NEP in the early spring of 1921 represented a drastic reversal from the previous policies pursued by the Bolsheviks. During 'War Communism' the Bolshevik regime had pursued policies of extreme centralization that sought to eliminate completely market exchange and production and establish a centrally planned economy.[24] The 'War Communism' policies had to be reversed as they resulted in a drastic reduction in production and threatened the political alliance between the peasant and the proletariat. The NEP represented, in large part, a policy of economic liberalization that was intended to restore partial economic freedom to the peasants so as to appease the political unrest and spur the farm production that was necessary to feed the emerging industrial strata of society.

On 24 May 1921 a decree from Sovnarkom (Council of People's Commissars) permitted not only the sale of surplus food by peasants in farmer markets, but also trade by others of goods produced by small-scale private manufacturers. Whereas private trade during 'war communism' was basically outlawed – though it did continue in the form of black market bazaars – under the NEP sales could now be conducted from permanent facilities. Decrees concerning hired labor (not more than ten or twenty laborers), the leasing of factories, etc., followed throughout 1921 and 1922.

> The property rights and legalized spheres of business activity that had been granted to Soviet citizens during the first two years of NEP were collected and set down in the Civil Code of the RSFSR, which went into effect on January 1, 1923. Although not a dramatic extension of the rights of private businessmen, the Civil Code . . . represented a clear reversal of the policies of War Communism.[25]

This policy shift to partial liberalization was meant as an inducement to private economic initiative, and it worked to an extent. But the policy signal was not unambiguous. Nepmen were subject to many taxes and fees, including business and income taxes. The most substantial of these was the fee for the use of business facilities. In fact, this fee accounted for twice as much revenue from private traders as the business tax did in 1922. In January 1923, it was announced that the fee would be increased. At this time, applications to rent facilities for private business declined 20 per cent.[26]

The legal ambiguity of the Nepmen was highlighted in the laws against speculation and price controls. 1924, as a result of this, saw a marked decline in the economic activity of private traders. The government tried to reverse this downward trend by providing more favorable treatment to the Nepmen – for example, easy state credit. But this policy was again reversed in 1926/27. State credit to private business, for example, was cut by 25 per cent in 1926. The administrative tool that proved most devastating in the war against the Nepmen was taxation. There was a 50 per cent rate increase in the tax on profits of urban private traders from 1925/26 to 1926/27 (12.9 per cent to 18.8 per cent). In the Sokol'nicheski quarter of Moscow, for example, in 1929/30 private traders and manufacturers represented 1.7 per cent of the region's income tax payers, with 8.2 per cent of the total taxable income, but accounted for 55 per cent of the region's income tax receipts.[27] The tax burden, in combination with their political status as *lishentsy* (the deprived), assured that Nepmen were most vulnerable.[28] By 1928, as Aleksandr Solzhenitsyn points out, 'it was time to call to a reckoning those late stragglers after the bourgeoisie – the NEPmen. The usual practice was to impose on them ever-increasing and finally totally intolerable taxes. At a certain point they could no longer pay; they were immediately arrested for bankruptcy, and their property was confiscated.'[29]

The cumulative effect of these policies was simply to discourage individuals from investing resources in the official market even though liberalization policies had been announced by the regime with the introduction of the NEP. Economic actors chose to withdraw from the economic game, despite the pleas from the Bolsheviks for them to 'enrich yourselves, accumulate, develop your farms.'[30]

Price controls on grain provide another example. After the initial announcement of price liberalization, the government reversed course. In 1924, the People's Commissariat of Internal Trade attempted to fix a maximum price for grain. But over the years peasants had learned that grain was a good hedge against inflation. Tax pressures to enforce sales were enacted, but peasants did everything to pay the tax in anything other than grain. A private market developed where grain was sold above the maximum price – creating parallel markets, one state-regulated prices, another free prices.

In response, regional authorities attempted to issue orders declaring it obligatory to deliver 25 per cent of all flour milled in a region to the state-purchasing authority at the fixed price, but this merely led to a cessation of milling operations. By December 1924 the state had collected less than half of its projected amount of grain (118 million pods out of 380 million). Moreover, the grain stocks of the state declined from 214 million pods on 1 January 1924 to 145 million pods on 1 January 1925. Price fixing policy by the state had been defeated.[31]

Foreign economic relations also provide another example of where despite the announcement of liberalization the inability of the regime to bind itself to a credible commitment undermined the reform effort. At the Genoa Conference (April–May 1922), for example, the Soviet delegation refused to conclude an agreement with Western powers on the question of Russia's debts.[32] In addition, at the end of 1922 a proposal for relaxing the foreign trade monopoly was rejected. Prospects for the expansion of foreign economic relations were, therefore, reduced considerably. Without such ties, long-term economic development was unlikely. Foreign governments simply had no reason to trust the Bolsheviks in economic deals.

Exchange rate policy also hindered economic development and ran counter to the intentions of the NEP. The hard currency reforms in the beginning of the NEP – the chervonets reforms – were a major accomplishment, but they did not last even two years. The low levels of gold reserves, the unrealistic exchange rate and the small volume of Soviet exports, all undermined the monetary reform. Moreover, beginning in 1928, Gosbank refused to exchange Soviet money for foreign currency.[33]

Finally, the general policy of grain procurement under the NEP illustrates the problem most clearly. The cornerstone of the NEP was the substitution of the tax in kind for the grain requisitioning of 'War Communism.' Peasants, though, with the war communism period still fresh in their memories had to be convinced that arbitrary requisitioning was not a policy option, i.e., the government had to make a credible commitment to maintain the NEP. However, as we have briefly seen the Bolsheviks did not commit to any such binding constraint. As a result, by the end of the 1920s (i.e., 1928) peasants no longer had an incentive to market grain surplus. From the peasants' point of view, the market was simply not a secure outlet.[34]

Thus the NEP was abandoned in 1928 and Stalin ruled over the Soviet system until his death in 1953. The reversal from the quasi-liberalization of the NEP to the authoritarian measures of collectivization is one of the most drastic and fateful turn of events in the twentieth century. The abandonment of the NEP, though, did posses both an economic and political logic. Not because market institutions cannot provide the basis for economic development, or because Stalin's personality was one that thrived on political authoritarianism. Rather, the internal contradictions of the NEP led to an ever-increasing reliance on the substitution of political rationales for economic rationales in setting economic policy. The shifting policies produced an expectational regime which worked against the goals of policy-makers. Since the Bolsheviks were not willing to construct a binding commitment to economic liberalization, the only way out of the policy impasse was complete authoritarianism. Stalinism was the unintended consequence of the failure of the discretionary regime of the 1920s to cope with the obstacles that information and incentives present to political economies.

The policy game under perestroika

The Gorbachev period (1985–91) offers a further illustration of the basic insight of the 'reason of rules.' For all our justified euphoria about the collapse of communism and the change in the landscape of global conflict, a fundamental uneasiness remains about the prospects for a peaceful transition to a market economy and constitutional democracy.

Just like the NEP, perestroika suffered from internal contradictions that precipitated its unravelling. Perestroika began as a policy of renewal and acceleration. It represented Gorbachev's public policy program to reverse the decline of the Soviet economy. Perestroika ended up, however, simply precipitating the crisis and collapse of the Soviet regime.

Cornerstones of perestroika included the law on individual economic activity (1986), the law on state enterprise (1987) and the law on cooperatives (1988).[35] Despite the rhetoric and promise of these laws, they did not go far enough to meet the objectives of economic reform. The laws contained contradictions and ambiguities that prevented their achieving desired results. Furthermore, they failed to convey any binding commitment on the part of the Gorbachev regime to real market reform. Rather, the decrees of perestroika left the clear impression that they were written on a word processor. From 1985 to 1991 Gorbachev introduced at least ten major policy packages for economic reform under the banner of perestroika; not a single one was implemented fully.

The law on state enterprise, for example, as discussed in Chapter 2 was supposed to introduce self-accounting, self-financing and self-management. But, unwilling to move too quickly with the reform of state enterprises, the government decided to stagger conformity to the law. Some enterprises would operate under the new guidelines as of 1 January 1988, others would do so the following year, January 1989. Such a staggered reform was similar (in both content and effect) to announcing that in order to improve traffic conditions the British system of driving on the left will be followed. But, in order not to disturb infrequent drivers (who may need time to adjust to the new rules of the road) it is decided that taxis and buses will drive on the left while ordinary drivers should continue to drive on the right until they have had time to prepare for the change to the new system.[36]

In addition, given the commitment to full employment by the regime, there was no way to introduce self-financing in a manner consistent with a 'hard budget constraint.'[37] Enterprise managers and employees knew that despite whatever announcement was made concerning self-financing, that as long as the regime was committed to full employment, enterprises would possess a 'soft budget constraint' with all the corresponding inefficiencies.[38] Bankruptcy would not be tolerated and state subsidies would continue as before.

Not only did the law on state enterprises fail to aid the move to the market economy, it contributed to the economic problems of the already struggling official industrial sector. Managers in an effort to return the favor to workers for whom they owed their jobs, and since they did not face hard budget constraints, readily approved wage increases. Average wages rose by 8 per cent in 1988, and 13 per cent in 1989.[39] Thus, state enterprise costs increased and with that so did the demand for increased state subsidies from the enterprises. This, in turn, put an increased strain on the state budget, and, consequently, the monetary system as the printing press was employed to monetize the debt. The persistence of microeconomic inefficiency bred increased macroeconomic destabilization as economic agents responded rationally to the contradictory rule changes.

The law on private economic activity was passed in November of 1986 and became effective in May 1987. This law allowed individuals to engage in activities which previously had been deemed illegal. Despite several restrictions – such as the limit of time that state employees could devote to individual enterprise – the intent of the law was to encourage individual economic enterprise and market experimentation. Family members of state employees or individuals such as students, housewives and pensioners were allowed to work full-time if they desired. In order to do so, though, individuals had to apply for a license granted by local authorities and pay either an annual income tax or a fee. The fee applied, in particular, to cases where it was difficult to monitor income, such as driving a taxi. The fee for a private taxi, in 1987, was 560 roubles, which meant that a worker who was 'moonlighting' as a taxi driver had to earn the equivalent of three months' wages before driving the taxi would cover its costs.[40] The perverse consequence of this policy in terms of the persistence of a 'black market' in taxis is described by William and Jane Taubman in their book *Moscow Spring*. The private market for taxi services had gone on for years. The law on individual enterprise, in this case, amounted to simply regulating and taxing an activity that had gone on 'unofficially' for years. As a consequence, very few if any of the Moscow *chastniki* (private taxis) they encountered were registered and, therefore, official. 'Registration,' they point out, 'required burdensome medical exams, payment of a fee, and of course heavy taxes . . . But most burdensome was the requirement that all individual labor activity be moonlighting; the workers must have primary jobs in the state sector.'[41]

An even more fundamental problem with the law on private economic activity was the existence of the campaign against unearned income.[42] The campaign required individuals to have appropriate documentation explaining how they had made their money. A natural market response to this was the emergence of an illicit market in documentation. A less desirable consequence was a decline in economic well-being as the informal networks which historically filled the gaps caused by the inefficient official system were disturbed.[43] The attitude of the regime conveyed by the campaign simply reinforced the lack of trust citizens possessed concerning the commitment of the government to reform. Without a credible conveyance of commitment to market reform, farmers, workers and so on, did not have any incentive to invest in the above-ground market.

This is clearly seen in the development of cooperatives in the Soviet Union under Gorbachev.[44] The law on individual enterprise (adopted November 1986) provided the legal foundation for the cooperative movement since it permitted family members who live together to form businesses. Formal recognition of cooperatives came with the Law on Cooperation in the USSR, adopted 26 May 1988. Whereas the number of cooperatives was 8,000, employing 88,000 on 1 October 1987, by 1 July 1989 there were over 133,000, employing 2,900,000. The output of cooperatives amounted to an estimated 350 million roubles for 1987, 6 billion roubles in 1988 and was estimated to be 12.9 billion roubles by June of 1989. Despite this explosion in cooperatives, hostility, from the public and the government, toward the economic success of cooperatives threatened their long-term viability.[45] Since this hostility resulted in accusations that cooperatives' financial gains were made without any real effort – just exploiting the shortage situation – the threat of the campaign on unearned income was very real. Often, state shortages get blamed on the cooperatives. A state shortage of buns, and a state shortage of sausage, translates into a cooperative sandwich with its corresponding high price – at least that is how some described the situation.

The precarious position of cooperatives was compounded because they had to rely almost exclusively on the state sector for supplies even though they were not hooked up officially to the central supply network. Thus, cooperatives had to rely on illicit transactions, such as bribes and agreements with state enterprises, to obtain resources which simply increased their vulnerability to 'blackmail' both by officials and criminals. In fact, cooperatives were often assumed to be fronts for criminal activity.

In addition, the legal status of cooperatives and the tax policy to which they would be subject has changed often. Even before the end of 1988 a resolution was passed which sought to restrict the activities of cooperatives. In February 1989, republican authorities were given the authority over taxation policy toward cooperatives and were encouraged to set differential rates based on the type of cooperative, its pricing policy and so on. The 'speculative tendencies' of cooperatives were subject to criticism and authorities were encouraged to take steps to bring cooperative pricing more in line with state pricing. Cooperatives were subject to taxes ranging from 25 to 60 per cent of their income depending on their pricing policy. The August 1989 law on cooperative taxation, for example, established new regulations on cooperatives and tied taxation of cooperatives to the relationship between state and cooperative prices.

By constraining the freedom of cooperative and private market experimentation, the Gorbachev government prevented the market from serving one of its most vital functions – inducing an increase in the supply of goods in response to excess consumer demand. The demand side of the market bid up the price of goods in short supply, but the supply side was not free to respond. With the failure to increase supplies, it was inevitable that cooperative prices would rise. Consumers, therefore, could either wait in long queues at the state store and attempt to purchase goods that became increasingly non-existent at the fixed state prices, or they could go to the cooperative market and purchase goods at high market prices until the shelves in these private stores were emptied. That is what the average consumer saw as the benefit of perestroika. Either way, expectations of a better future were dashed and the credibility of the reforms was irreversibly damaged.

The undesirable effect of the policies adopted under perestroika was not just limited to their incentive incompatibility with entrepreneurial activity. It went much deeper, and undermined the basic constitution of economic policy. The continual flux in the legal environment for the cooperatives conveyed a lack of commitment on the part of the regime to private sector experimentation. But, without such a commitment to protect the legal rights of the private sector, there was no way to induce the investment and hard work that were needed to develop the Soviet economy.[46] So, in addition to incentive incompatibility, there was the additional debilitating problem of adverse reputation that results from policy reversals and the failure to commit.

The inability to convey any kind of commitment to reform sealed perestroika's fate. The reforms simply could not get the economy going and the consumer crisis grew more acute.[47] The political instability of failed reforms, alongside deflated expectations on the part of the population, produced a highly troublesome situation for the Gorbachev regime.[48]

In the fall of 1990, when Gorbachev backed out of his commitment to the radical 'Shatalin Plan' and moved to the right, he blew his credibility with his liberal allies. But perestroika had already cost him his credibility with communist conservatives. So the winter zig to the right did not gain Gorbachev much. As he tried to zag to the left in the spring of 1991, especially with the April compromise with Yeltsin, the right prepared for one last effort to regain control.

First, they sought to regain control through 'constitutional' means, and when that failed, they resorted to the August coup. Even though the coup failed, the failure certainly cannot be attributed to the success of perestroika. It was the failure of perestroika, in fact, that resulted in the coup attempt. As the regime kept on introducing liberalization policies only to go back on them, the official economy sank deeper into an abyss. The bureaucracy which was threatened by reform knew that more and more radical measures would be necessary to get out of the abyss. However, those measures would be clearly undesirable from their point of view. So they sought to resist one more time. Fortunately, the effort was neither united nor skillful, and it fell apart in three days.

The unravelling of the Soviet Union as a political entity, however, is the unintended by-product of Gorbachev's policy of perestroika. The failure of the regime to convey the kind of commitment to economic liberalization that was necessary to reform the Soviet system proved to be perestroika's undoing.

CONCLUSION

One of the most basic insights of constitutional political economy is the necessity of rules to govern over economic activity. It is a research program which focuses our inquiry on the working properties of rules, and the processes of social interaction that take place within rules. By examining both the rules of social interaction and their impact on social processes, scholars can begin to develop ideas about workable constitutions of economic policy.

In developing a workable constitution of economic policy it must be recognized that the obstacles that incentives and information present to discretionary behavior are formidable. The Soviet experience shows that without effectively signalling and establishing a binding and credible commitment to broad liberalization, the behavior of the government simply destabilizes the situation.[49]

The argument against government intervention in the free market process does not amount to asserting that government intervention must necessarily lead to totalitarianism. That was a misunderstanding of the argument on the critics' part. Rather, the argument suggests that interventionism produces unintended results which will be viewed as undesirable from the government's own point of view. Thus, interventionist policy constantly forces upon government officials the choice of either rejecting their previous policy or intervening even more in the attempt to correct the past failing. The argument is a stability argument. Intervention is just not stable as an economic and political system. The discretionary behavior of the government results in situations that undermine their own initiatives.

Whereas the instability of the 1920s in the Soviet Union led to Stalinism, the instability of the late 1980s has led to the dissolution of the Soviet Union. In either case, one a normative nightmare whereas the other offers normative hope, the experience illustrates the basic point: discretionary behavior on the part of the government fails to produce the stable environment that is necessary for economic prosperity. The insights that the Soviet experience offers should become basic material in developing a workable constitution of economic policy in the post-perestroika era.

7

CHARTING A NEW COURSE

One morning . . ., according to a much-loved anecdote . . ., Lenin woke up in his mausoleum on Red Square. The father of the revolution made his way up to the street and started to look around. He spent all day walking and talking to people, reading newspapers, even watching this new-fangled television. At the end of the day he was seen in the Kiev Railroad Station – the station for trains to Poland and the West. 'Vladimir Ilyich,' someone asked, 'where are you going?'

'Back to Zurich,' he replied, 'to start over again.'

Robert Kaiser[1]

INTRODUCTION

Several years stand out in history: 1688, 1776, 1789, 1917 – and now 1989 can be added to that list. 1989 was a year of tremendous change and the images that flashed before our eyes shall be etched in hearts and minds for a long time. From the lone unarmed protest student facing off the tanks in Tiananmen Square to the joyous dance on top of the Berlin Wall, from the accession of Solidarity in Poland and the Civic Forum in Czechoslovakia to the execution of the tyrant Ceausescu in Romania, the images of 1989 were an overwhelming affirmation of humanity's universal struggle for freedom.

These images of 1989, however, have to a large degree given way to the sober reality of the 1990s. The road from serfdom is tough going. The path from communist domination to economic and political freedom is one fraught with difficulty. The conflict between economics and politics is highlighted along this road. As the adjustments in the economic structure proceed to correct for the previous distorted order citizens will experience overtly unemployment, higher prices and discrepancies in income levels that previously were only experienced in an implicit manner. This occurs at the same time that new-found political freedoms give greater voice to complaint. The danger in this situation is that the emerging democratic forces can potentially derail the emerging economic freedoms and lead back to the dominance of politics over economics.

While 1989 clearly saw the end of communism as a legitimizing ideology, the economic and political transformation of the former communist bloc is still far from completed. The political hypocrisy was best represented in the Soviet Union from 1989 to 1991, where the communist government remained formally in power until Gorbachev's resignation on Christmas day 1991. In addition, on the economic front each Gorbachev announcement of economic reform was followed by a reversal of the reform program so in the end no official reform had taken place and the Soviet economic situation grew worse.

In the Soviet context this led to a competitive duality in both the economic and political sphere. While the official economy grew worse, the unofficial economy maintained the population.[2] State supplies disappeared, but market bazaars emerged. The state budget became more out of line and roubles were printed at an ever-increasing rate, but the black market exchange rates for currency reflected the declining value of the rouble and citizens increasingly relied on alternative currencies and barter arrangements to satisfy their market demands. In the political realm, while power remained in the hands of the Party it was continually slipping through their fingers. The political forces unleashed with *demokratizatsiya* grew in legitimacy. And, with the failed coup of August 1991 the communists lost any remaining power they had. From August to 25 December 1991 all that remained of communist central power was symbolic.

Many observers saw this as tragic, but this was not tragic at all. The crucial lesson of the emergence of Western civilization is the importance of competition among governance structures for the development of peaceful co-existence and economic development.[3] Competition is one of the most important processes through which we learn how to live and organize our affairs. Economic competition and the recognition of the benefits of exchange provide the foundation for social cooperation not some mythical notion of communal belonging.[4]

The Soviet experience with socialism did not eliminate competition or the gains to be had from exchange, but it transformed the competitive struggle and the gains that were to be had. Political competition and political privilege substituted for economic competition and profits in the mature Soviet society as discussed in Chapter 4. Soviet socialism was a failure because politics completely dominated economics as the pre-eminent organizing principle of society. In order to correct the situation – to chart a new course – economic forces must be unleashed from political forces, even if those political forces are democratic. If the main failing of previous policy can be found in rules of the game which perverted the incentives and impeded the flow of vital information, then reform entails establishing rules of the game which provide high-powered incentives to actors to discover and use economic information effectively. Competition among alternative market experiments is the best way to assure that new ways to satisfy market demand are discovered and that power is divested from any single entity in society.

The problem with central planning never was in the idea of planning per se, but rather in the fact that planning was limited to the imagination of state authorities. Planning within a market environment is vast, but decentralized at the level of the firm or individual entrepreneurs that actively participate in the market process. Market competition, guaranteed by a rule of law which protects the freedom of entry, sets in motion a process of learning and discovery that government planning simply cannot replicate.

The discovery procedure of competition is also vital in the political realm. Competition among localities, provided citizens are free to move, sets in motion a discovery process that provides an incentive to individuals to reveal information about the level of public services and role of the state.[5] *Freedom of competition*, both economic and political, should be the operative phrase along the road from serfdom.

FIRST PRINCIPLES

As socialism declines as a social theory, liberalism necessarily ascends as the only viable alternative. The grand debate in social theory boils down to the contrast between socialism and liberalism. This debate, to a large degree, was one over means and not ends. Promoting public welfare and eliminating poverty, ignorance and squalor are not only the ends of socialism, but also the ends of liberalism. The peculiar characteristic of the socialist solution to the social problem lay in the means advocated to reach that end.[6] Socialists argued that by bringing social life under the conscious and planned control of associations of men social problems could be eliminated. The broadening of the public life, to such a degree that eventually eliminated the autonomous struggles of the private life, would rid society of the social problems of poverty, ignorance and squalor, and promote the public welfare. Emancipation from the dominance of both other men and nature was the promise of the socialist project. Historical experience has seriously called into question the efficacy of the socialist means to obtain the stated ends.

Just as there are variants of socialism (from the real existing models of Stalinist, Maoist and Yugoslavian, and the theoretical systems of classical Marxism, humanistic Marxism, market socialism and so on) there are also variants of liberalism (from the real existing liberal democracies of the US, Western Europe and the Scandinavian countries, and the theoretical systems of classical liberalism, modern welfare state liberalism and radical liberalism of the libertarian variety). The negative argument of this book, while directed mainly at the Soviet experience, implies that all variants of socialism confront the same fundamental structural failing of an inability to provide the incentives and information necessary to coordinate advanced industrial activity. On the other hand, some variants of liberalism suffer from the internal contradictions of democracy which allow politics to dominate economics with the consequence of perverting economic incentives and distorting the flow of economic information.[7] The task is to articulate a version of liberalism which corrects for the fundamental flaws of socialism and the flawed variants of liberalism.

Just as Marx's vision of socialism was implied in his negative assessment of capitalism, the positive vision of liberalism can be found in the critique of socialism I have offered. Positive liberalism strives to be what socialism and weaker versions of liberalism are not. The dialectic of social theory teaches through contrast and critical examination.

Justifications for the liberal order can be found normally in one of two directions, the Locke–Nozick natural rights justification or the Hobbes–Buchanan contractarian justification. Both of these justifications, however, are flawed.[8] A more satisfying alternative perspective for examining the properties of the liberal order can be found in the Hume–Hayek tradition.

The Locke–Nozick formulation of the liberal order begins with an assertion and not an argument.[9] The natural rights position of self-ownership is justified by Locke on religious grounds and Nozick simply begins with the Lockean position and attempts to derive the implications. The basic problem with this approach is not limited to the difficulty in its justification, but rather lies with the difficulty associated with delimitating the nature of the rights under consideration. The distinction between negative and positive rights does not seem to do the trick. What we want to achieve by delimiting rights is the 'good' society, i.e., a society in which the consequence of following the rules is beneficial. A moral society that yielded bad consequences would be neither desirable nor 'good.' In other words, what we expect from rights is increased opportunities to better ourselves, i.e., positive liberties. But once the desire for positive rights is recognized the limiting questions of which rights, and whose rights, are to be respected requires an alternative criterion for adjudication. Settlement of competing rights claims cannot be resolved by reference to natural rights alone.

The social contractarian approach of Hobbes–Buchanan tries to resolve the problems associated with natural rights theory by way of the social compact.[10] In Buchanan's scheme, for example, the leap out of Hobbesian anarchy is accomplished by individuals coming to agreement behind a Rawlsian 'veil of ignorance' as to the basic organization of society. But despite the logical rigor of Buchanan's analysis the system lacks any endogenous process by which individuals come to adopt rules of behavior.

In large number settings individuals treat rules as parametric, similar to how agents within the perfectly competitive model of general equilibrium treat price as given. But, in the perfectly competitive model if agents treat price as given, then how do prices ever adjust to clear the market? Price adjustments in the Walrasian model occur by invoking the extra-economic character of the auctioneer. In other words, the model fails in one of its most important tasks – explaining the process by which equilibrium could ever be achieved.[11] Buchanan's discussion of the social contract is vulnerable to a similar argument since he explicitly builds his Hobbesian model on the basis of the perfectly competitive model.[12] Since rules are treated as parameters in the Buchanan description of pre-constitution interaction, then how is it possible that individuals could ever come to observe social rules? Just like the Walrasian counterpart, the Hobbesian sovereign must be invoked in order to establish the appropriate rules. No endogenous process of rule formation is possible within this system.

In addition to this logical untidiness, the Buchanan formulation also confronts a problem of constructivism. If a constitution could emerge in such an ahistorical fashion as is suggested in the Hobbes–Buchanan analysis, then it would be possible to develop blueprints for social order.[13] But if such blueprints were possible, then socialist social theory would not confront any difficulties in operation. In fact, the very problem with the original model of Marxian socialism was the desire to develop a detailed blueprint of social organization that would coordinate economic life in an *ex ante* fashion.

In the rationalistic-constructivism of Hobbes man can design the good society by devising the institutions that govern human intercourse.[14] Society is a product of man's reason and not the result of an evolutionary history of trial and error. Institutions which are not consciously understood are to be rejected. The constructed order is the product of man's rational ability to draw up a social contract. The fundamental problem with the Hobbesian decision-maker is that he must be every man and thus no man. His reason is sufficient to ascertain the vast amount of information necessary to deduce the first principles of society yet he is blinded by the veil of ignorance as to his future status in that society.

Social order, in contrast to this rationalistic conception, is the product of human action, but not of human design.[15] This is an insight which the Hume–Hayek perspective of the liberal order highlights.[16] Constitutions simply codify rules that have evolved to govern human intercourse, rules that had previously been respected tacitly by individuals.[17] Rules emerge endogenously to a process of human interaction through time as individuals attempt to resolve conflicts.

The Hume–Hayek approach to understanding the nature of the liberal order offers an alternative to either an approach which emphasizes religious tradition or rationalist design. Rather than contrast reason with tradition, this approach to social theory can provide an analysis of reason within traditions. History is seen as a discovery procedure in which different group practices compete with one another. Practices which enhance the well-being of the group are maintained while those practices which prove detrimental to the well-being of the group are discarded. Through a process of rule innovation, imitation and evolution rule systems emerge to govern human interaction.

This Hume–Hayek approach also has the advantage of being capable of incorporating the strengths of both the Locke–Nozick approach and the Hobbes–Buchanan approach into its analysis of the liberal order. Rather than stress the morality of private property as derived from some conception of natural rights as is found in the Locke–Nozick perspective, we can now examine the consequentialist rationale for private property. Moreover, since private property can be shown to be a vital precondition for the social experimentation – especially in the economic realm – that is necessary for the progress and development of social order many of the libertarian implications that Nozick derives from the Lockean perspective can be maintained.[18] In addition, since codification of tacit rules is recognized as a fundamental part of social development, the Buchanan emphasis on the constitutional moment in political economy remains potent.

The key point of the Hume–Hayek approach is a complete rejection of the command and control approach to social order. This does not mean that social order is unorganized or chaotic. Instead, social interaction in a liberal society is characterized by a high degree of internal predictability. But it is an order that emerges as a by-product of activity that does not intend to produce any particular overall system by conscious design. Rather than command and control, the Hume–Hayek program emphasizes *cultivation* of a social order that allows great flexibility in alternative experiences of life.[19] Governance structures are to establish rules of the game which cultivate and encourage individuals to experiment in alternative social arrangements.[20]

Thus, besides enforcing respect for rules which serve as a precondition for experimentation there is little else that is left for governance structures to do with regard to detailed management of the social world. This should not be interpreted as an end to politics. Rather, the insights of the Hume–Hayek approach provide the basis for dealing with the politics and economics of the liberal order.

THE ROLE OF STATE ACTION

Beginning with a cultivation as opposed to a control mentality, we can start to provide statements concerning practical questions of public policy in the former communist countries. Under the former communist regimes the benefits of competition in politics and economics were explicitly disparaged. The defining characteristic of the real existing Soviet Union was *monopolization*. Conceptually, then, reform is a rather simple process of demonopolization. How to best do that, however, is not a simple matter. One thing we should know for sure, though, is that the policies advocated in the process of demonopolization cannot be policies which require vast amounts of government control and command.[21] In other words, policies which try to micromanage the transformation process will confront the same difficulties that the previous socialist policy regime faced.

This paradox of transition policy is the fundamental problem that must be addressed in issues ranging from the very nature of the role of government to concerns of monetary and fiscal policy. James Madison, over 200 years ago, addressed the fundamental paradox of liberal governance when he stated in *The Federalist Papers*, No. 51 that:

> If men were angels, no government would be necessary. If angels were to govern men, neither external nor internal controls on government would be necessary. In framing a government which is to be administered by men over men, the great difficulty lies in this: you must first enable the government to control the governed; and in the next place oblige it to control itself.[22]

At the same time that state action is empowered to promote the general welfare it must be constrained through constitutional rules which limit this power. Traditional economic justifications for state action depended on the theory of market failure. It seemed a reasonable assertion to state that in situations where the market fails to promote the general welfare the government should step in and act accordingly. But this argument was curiously myopic. The dichotomy between the examination of the logic of market and the logic of politics is best characterized by the ancient legend that has it that a Roman emperor, being asked to judge a singing contest between two contestants, heard only one contestant and gave the prize to the second under the assumption that the second singer could be no worse than the first. The problem, of course, is that this assumption is unwarranted.

It is by no means unambiguous that in situations of market imperfections government action will improve the situation. Government may actually make the situation worse. In fact, many perceived market imperfections at one moment may spur entrepreneurial discoveries which correct the situation in future periods.[23] Government action in this situation merely would distort the learning function of the market process by substituting a political solution to a problem that could be internalized through entrepreneurial creativity. Moreover, it can be demonstrated that many so-called market failures are actually a product of faulty rules which govern the economic game.

The current crisis in the US Savings and Loan industry provides a concrete example. Rather than blame the débâcle on speculative investment behavior of bankers, a more appropriate argument would be to find fault in the liability and insurance rules which produced a situation where bank directors could accrue all the profits from their activities but remain largely protected from losses. Such an environment produced what is known in economics literature as a moral hazard in which risky behavior becomes the norm. Economics per se cannot provide moral statements about whether profits are deserved or not, but it can provide statements about the consequences of alternative rules on human behavior. Traditional market failure theory drew the economists' attention away from examining the structure of alternative rules which governed decision-making processes.[24]

Arguments about market failure, therefore, must be conjoined with an appreciation of the strong possibilities of government failure in implementing the proposed solution. This would seem to suggest that each case should be treated separately and that no general rule could be established concerning state action. Of course, in dealing with public policies there is always the question of magnitudes. Government failure may indeed exist, but it may be less desirable than the existing market failure. Such a cost–benefit calculus, however, is severely limited in practice since economically meaningful costs and benefits are purely subjective in nature. Objectivistic notions of costs and benefits fail to produce an adequate understanding of economic processes and mislead analysts when addressing public policy questions.[25]

Again, the problems that the socialist policy-maker confronted in policy formation suggests how to establish criteria for public policy in the liberal order. The command and control mentality translates economic questions into engineering problems and offers technological solutions. Such an approach assumes a degree of objectivistic measurement of the variables which does not exist in the economic realm. Offering technological solutions for problems that can only be appropriately handled as economic, fails as viable public policy.

The information that is vital for economic questions is contextual. One of the chief sources of error in the engineering mentality is the assumption that economic data, such as 'costs,' are objectively given facts ascertained by observation, when in fact the data of economics can only be understood within the context of the chooser. The knowledge and judgement of the decision-maker will be wholly different when he acts in a competitive market from what it will be when he acts in a monopolistic one. Not only the nature of the incentives, but the nature of the knowledge generated and utilized, differs depending on the context of action.

The dynamics of economic processes require that viable policy discussion should be limited to an examination of the alternative rules. Even in situations when state action is deemed desirable it must be at the level of the rules and not particular market outcomes.[26] Given the experience of government failure in both the former socialist economies and Western democracies, the *presumption must go to the market*.

In addition, since the basic argument being offered here is that rules that govern social intercourse should cultivate experimentation, even in situations where the 'publicness' of the good requires state provision, private firms should not be excluded from attempting to provide the service on the open market.[27] Government may provide mail services, for example, but that should not mean that government can exclude competitors. And if technological innovations emerge which allow private provision of the service, then progress should not be deterred. Facsimile machines, for example, may one day eliminate mail carriers, but that would not be something to bemoan. The key ingredient to social development is free competition. Government too often is the source and protector of monopolistic practices. Competition, on the other hand, destroys monopoly and encourages experimentation. Not only does competition allow us to use already existing knowledge, but it is also the spur for the discovery of ever new and fresh knowledge. 'Competition,' Hayek writes, 'is not merely the only method which we know for utilizing the knowledge and skills that other people may possess, but it is also the method by which we all have been led to acquire much of the knowledge and skills we do possess.'[28]

One final point about state action must be made before we address more concrete questions of the policy of the transition. State action is by necessity non-neutral, i.e., intervention affects the underlying pattern and distribution of resources in society.[29] Intervention by definition changes the pattern of exchanges that would have voluntarily transpired on the market otherwise the intervention would not have been necessary – people would have already done what the intervention intends to compel them to do.

In a monetary economy the generally accepted medium of exchange represents a link in all exchanges. Money, in other words, is one half of all exchanges, i.e., it is the joint linking all transactions. This jointness aspect of money translates into the proposition that if policy alters the value of the monetary unit it also changes the pattern of exchanges in the economy.

The centrality of money in an economic system can be illustrated as follows. Imagine that the economy is like a well-shaped wheel, the spokes of the wheel represent the relative prices in the economy and the hub of the wheel represents the monetary unit. By either tightening or loosening the spokes we can change the shape of the wheel. The wheel may become distorted and not function as smoothly as before, but it can still roll. However, if for whatever reason the hub of the wheel was eliminated, then the wheel would collapse altogether and cease to function. Similarly, distorted relative prices disrupt economic forces, but destroying the currency would lead to the collapse of the entire economy.

Money cannot be viewed simply as a veil or tight joint, as is suggested in the classical dichotomy which stated that real variables only affect reals and nominal variables only affect nominals. The classical argument suggested that the real underlying distribution of resources would be unaffected by changes in the value of money. Changes in the value of money would be fully accommodated for by proportional changes in the price level. While the classical dichotomy contained an important argument against inflationists and monetary cranks who argued that by printing more monetary notes wealth could be achieved, it confused the nature in which changes in the value of money are transmitted in an economic system. This is not to suggest that Keynes's criticism of the classical dichotomy is to be accepted. On the contrary, Keynes failed to understand the workings of the monetary economy because in his system of thought money represented a broken joint.[30] Instead, the interesting questions in macroeconomics explore how monetary variables can alter the real distribution of capital resources in an economy by affecting the structure of relative prices. Recognition of this forces the economist to pay particular attention to systemic questions concerning the monetary regime itself and the rules under which it operates as opposed to particular pro- or counter-cyclical policies that are suggested by advocates of either demand-side or supply-side management of the economy.

Similarly, fiscal policy necessarily affects the pattern of exchanges. If you subsidize something you get more of it, if you tax something you get less. Of course, the magnitude of the effect varies, but the general point remains. Neither monetary or fiscal policy can be neutral, and therefore, when discussing policy rules for sustaining a liberal order this must always be kept in mind.

ESTABLISHING A LIBERAL REGIME IN THE FORMER COMMUNIST ECONOMY

The distorted world of the Soviet economy is best characterized by the gigantomania of the Stalinist system. In the 1930s the farming system was colonized in collectivization and through a practice of internal imperialism an industrialization drive was financed. On the backs of the peasant community industrial cities were built. Giant enterprise monopolies, in the strictest sense of establishing single producers of a particular good for the entire country, were created under the influence of the Marxian illusion about the infinite efficiency gains of economies of scale in order to industrialize the 'backward' Soviet economy. This industrialization drive left its permanent stamp on the industrial structure of the Soviet system and is evident to this day throughout the entire economy. It was estimated by Gosnab in 1990 that 80 per cent of the volume of output in the machine-building industry was manufactured by monopolists, and that 77 per cent of the enterprises in machine-building were monopoly producers of particular commodities. Locomotive cranes, tram rails, sewing machines, coking equipment, hoists for coal mines, and sucker-rod pumps, for example, were products produced by absolute monopolists in the Soviet economy. About 2,000 enterprises throughout the entire region of the former Soviet Union were the sole producers of specific products.[31]

In addition, the industrial cities attempted vertically to integrate entire industries. A survey by Goskomstat in 1987 reported that out of every 100 machine-building enterprises, 71 produced their own iron castings, 27 produced their own steel castings, 84 their own forging, 76 their own stamping and 65 their own hardware.[32] There was virtually no specialized production in the entire Soviet industrial structure.

The highly concentrated industrial structure combined with the absence of any kind of market signals produced chronic inefficiencies in production. Historically, the criterion for success was meeting the gross output targets set by the planning authorities. Success had little to do with quality of the product and nothing to do with satisfying consumer demand. The consequence of this economic environment is illustrated in the case of the Magnitogorsk steel manufacturing complex.[33] Founded in 1929, Magnitogorsk steelworks was considered the flagship of Soviet technology and industrial development. Magnitogorsk became an industrial city of 438,000 people by the late 1980s, and represented the largest steel complex in the world, producing about 16 million tons of steel each year. But, this industrial city has a severe housing shortage and has difficulty lifting its population above mere subsistence standards of living. It has destroyed the surrounding environment and overwhelmed its population with lung and other respiratory diseases. What was once held up as an international showcase of Soviet achievement has been revealed as simply another Soviet example of an industrial white elephant.

Of its reported 16 million tons of annual production, for example, no one really knows how much is actually Magnitogorsk's own defective steel being recycled through the production process. The quality of the steel produced is quite low even by the minimal standards set by the planners let alone world market standards. Nevertheless steel is produced and becomes the defective input in the machine-building industry, which in turn manufactures defective machines intended to produce more steel. Such production for production's sake is one of the most prevalent characteristics of all Soviet industry. Moreover, to produce 16 million tons of steel, the Magnitogorsk complex employs more than 60,000 workers. In contrast, the USX plant in Gary, Indiana, the most modern and integrated American steel plant, employs 7,000 workers and produces about 8 million tons annually. In addition to poor labor productivity, the difference in the size of the workforce between Magnitogorsk and USX can be attributed to lack of capital investment, the necessity of maintaining a large portion of the workforce simply to repair and build machines and tools required to operate the Magnitogorsk Works and the importance of keeping a padded labor force so that the plant has the ability to engage in the Soviet industrial phenomenon of 'storming' that occurs at the end of each production period in order to meet planned output targets.[34]

Magnitogorsk is just a microcosm of the entire Soviet industrial structure.[35] The simple fact of the matter is that throughout the Soviet system most people wake up to go to work in a factory that is in the wrong place to produce the wrong goods. Most of the enterprises are negative value added firms, that is the inputs that go into the production process are more valuable than the output produced.[36] The industrial structure of the former Soviet Union cannot be restructured, it must be rebuilt.

To complicate economic matters, in the Soviet-type system

microeconomic inefficiencies translated into macroeconomic imbalances. Negative value added firms required production subsidies which bloated the state budget which in turn led to increased pressure to finance expenditures by printing more rouble notes. In other words, state subsidization of production generated budget deficits and inflationary pressures, and these macroeconomic distortions in turn perpetuated the already existing maladjustments in the economic structure.[37] Moreover, since most state enterprises could not survive a market test, employment in these enterprises was simply a form of welfare payment to workers who in reality were either 'unemployed' or more accurately 'underemployed.' The implicit Soviet compact was: 'We pretend to work and they pretend to pay us.'

Labor was misallocated, capital was misallocated, macroeconomic policy was distorted and consumers were ignored. That is the real existing situation from which transition policy must begin its assessment of alternative policy paths. To realize just how structurally distorted the economy of the Soviet Union was, one need only remember that prior to the fall of the Berlin Wall East Germany was universally considered the shining example of socialist industrial efficiency. But, once exposed to the West German and world market it was revealed that the East German industrial power was nothing but a grand illusion. The Soviet economy begins from a much worse starting point than any of its former allies in the socialist bloc if for no other reason than that it existed under the perverted incentives and distorted information of socialist policies longer than any other country.

The connection between individual enterprise performance and macroeconomic policy must be severed for the economic transition to be accomplished. Moreover, the monetary system must be completely independent from the fiscal policy regime. In the West, there exists only the myth of independence between say the Federal Reserve System and the organs of fiscal policy in the US.[38] As research on political business cycles suggests, the Federal Reserve System was created by Congress and the Executive and acts as an agent of these bodies of government which helps to explain to a large degree the tremendous percentage of incumbency re-election. Budget deficits, spiraling public debt and bouts of inflationary distortions are not only a result of poor policy choice by leaders, but more fundamentally a consequence of the structural incentives of the institutional establishments of representative democracy and central banking. Monetary and fiscal policies, in other words, have become tools of political manipulation and not just tools for managing the economy. Of course, even if we could somehow constrain the political process so that monetary and fiscal policy was not subject to political manipulation but was instead limited to attempts to promote the general welfare, a serious problem would confront policy-makers. Best of intentions does not mean that the information necessary to accomplish appropriate management would be available to policy-makers in any readily assessable manner. Macromanagement, just like micromanagement, of the economy is a mistaken approach to public policy. Transition policy should not only steer clear of repeating the previous mistakes of the socialist regimes, but it should not repeat the same mistakes that Western governments have made.

Competition among enterprises must replace monopoly and subsidization, and competition introduced into the monetary and fiscal sphere will also produce desirable results in terms of economic growth and development. Introducing free competition into the system as fast as possible should be the major priority of transition policy. Transformation policy amounts to price liberalization, privatization, establishing a viable currency and controlling the state budget. These policies cannot be phased in over time because each particular policy has consequences for the others so they must be introduced simultaneously. Shock therapy possesses a logic which its critics too often miss.[39]

1. Price Liberalization

Price liberalization should not be confused with administrated price increases. Freeing of prices means eliminating government control completely. Raising prices by decree at the state stores is not a price liberalization. Prices need to be free to adjust to the forces of supply and demand. The function of free prices is to bring into coordination the most willing suppliers and the most willing demanders in a market. Prices ration goods and services through their ability to adjust constantly to changing market conditions. Under the previous policy regime, rationing was done either through political means, such as the special privileges that Party officials possessed, or through queuing for goods in short supply. Price liberalization will destroy the old way of allocating scarce resources.

Immediate price liberalization disturbs many individuals because of the fears of inflation, monopoly profits and income inequalities. The fear of inflation is largely unwarranted because individuals already exist in a situation of 'repressed inflation.' Long queues and persistent shortages of basic items characterize the socialist system. Freeing prices will simply eliminate the queues and shortages. Repressed inflation will become explicit as prices rise, but this will entice future competition which will lower prices. Inflation is not a matter of increases in prices, but rather everywhere and always a monetary phenomenon. Inflation is a consequence of the monetary regime reducing the value of the monetary unit. Free pricing is not the problem, the problem lies in the monetary regime.

The rouble overhang problem (i.e., the supply of notes held idle by consumers) is also largely a figment of planners' imagination. It is true that an overhang exists, but in an excess demand economy where black markets have flourished such as the former Soviet Union, it cannot be said that individuals are being 'forced to save.'[40] Instead, since goods can be readily had at the black market rate around the corner, individuals must be voluntarily saving under the expectation that they will eventually be able to acquire the goods at the artificially lower state price in the future. The rouble overhang problem emerged from the voluntary choices of Soviet citizens. In addition, the monetary authority had so destroyed the value of the rouble, that for many citizens the rouble was no longer convertible into goods. Barter became the predominant mode of trading with its corresponding problems for coordinating the plans of economic agents. Price liberalization is a necessary precondition for eliminating these distortions in the economic system.

The monopoly structure of the former socialist economies also creates a problem for many would-be reformers because it suggests that once prices are freed they will gravitate to monopolistic prices and not competitive ones.[41] It is argued, therefore, that privatization must occur before price liberalization.[42] But this misses a fundamental point about the introduction of market discipline. In order for markets to work they only require the lure of pure profit, the penalty of losses, free pricing and freedom of entry. The existing market structure does not matter as long as these preconditions for market operation are established. If so, then the current market structure will give way to a new order even if price liberalization brings monopolistic profits to the current enterprises in the short run.

Finally, the concern over basic equity is also a consequence of suspect reasoning. First, large discrepancies in income existed in the old regime. The Party elite lived an elaborate life-style compared to the average citizen.[43] In fact, these discrepancies were far more acute than those that exist in the West. While the average citizen struggled for the very minimum standards of existence in terms of housing, medical care and other basic services, the Party elite lived like kings. Introducing market forces into this situation destroys the old regime, it does not lead to gross inequities, it corrects them by eliminating the privileged position of state officials. Also, many argue that essential products, such as basic foodstuffs, should be exempt from price liberalization. But this gets the argument completely backward. Essential products are now in short supply in the official sector. Price liberalization is necessary to alleviate this situation. If anything, price liberalization should come to essential products first.

2. Privatization

How best to privatize the bloated behemoth of state enterprises in the former socialist countries is a subject of wide debate. Proposals range from voucher systems to controlled restructuring of state enterprises by Western institutions such as the International Monetary Fund, and public auction. Since I do not believe one can address past wrongs in any economically meaningful manner, and since in the absence of market signals the valuation of the assets of state enterprises is troublesome, I would suggest that ownership rights simply be given to the *de facto* owners, i.e., the state enterprise managers.[44]

Eliminating all subsidization of state enterprises and turning ownership over to the existing management, along with the introduction of price and trade liberalization will accomplish the goals of privatization without establishing a new bureaucracy – such as a Ministry of Ownership Transfer – to get in the way of the discovery procedure of competitive forces. Trade liberalization will import the price structure and discipline of the world market.[45] Price liberalization will force enterprise managers to pay attention to costs of production and other market signals.

In other words, privatize the economy – both small and large scale – as follows. The *de facto* property rights in the state enterprises that are held by current management be recognized as *de jure* rights. All consumer and producers' subsidies are abolished and state orders and price limitations are eliminated. Bankruptcy and liquidation of firm assets must be allowed. This has to be coupled with trade liberalization to eliminate the monopoly structure problem and import a market price structure. In this fashion, the fundamental industrial restructuring and reallocation of capital resources that is necessary to get the morbid Soviet economy untracked will be accomplished.

3. Monetary Reform

Liberalization policy demands a convertible currency. One of the main problems of the transition of the former Soviet economy to a market economy lies in the inconvertibility of the currency. A market economy requires a widely accepted medium of exchange that can purchase goods and services on the domestic market (internal convertibility), and that is easily converted into foreign currency (external convertibility) at free market rates. The reality of the Soviet economy under Gorbachev was that the rouble was neither an internally or externally convertible currency. Despite the wide variety of proposals for rouble convertibility, most have in common the reliance of a central banking system to institute the reform.

Ronald McKinnon, for example, argues that Western and Soviet economists who press for price liberalization, floating exchange rates, privatization and decentralized decision-making are mistaken because they have got the order of liberalization wrong. Before any liberalization proceeds, McKinnon argues, proper fiscal and monetary control over the Soviet economy must be secured.[46] An alternative, non-central bank approach, to currency reform has been proposed by Steve Hanke and Kurt Schuler. Hanke and Schuler argue that the best way to achieve and maintain currency convertibility would be through a currency board system as opposed to central bank management.[47] Robert Hetzel, however, has pointed out that while the currency board system is a substitute for central banking a government currency board has the disadvantage in that there is no binding way to assure that government officials will not force the board to devalue for domestic political reasons.[48] Successful monetary reform can be nothing short of complete depolitization of the monetary system.

The reasons for depolitization of the monetary system are straightforward. Government can only finance its affairs in one of three ways: tax, borrow or inflate. Inflation represents a hidden tax to the citizens. Depolitization of the monetary system eliminates the inflationary ability of the government and forces government to either borrow in the capital market or raise revenues through taxation to finance its affairs. Also by eliminating the ability to finance its expenditures through inflation, depolitization makes government more interest sensitive to its borrowing behavior, and so forces government policy-makers to be more disciplined in their financial borrowing.

The logic of the depolitization of money is also fairly straightforward.[49] The market for monetary services is no different than the market for other commodities. There is no need for government to 'manage' money. Rather than a regulated banking system based on central bank monopoly note issue, a more viable alternative can be found in an unregulated banking system of competitive note issue.

The fundamental problem with central banking, however, is not the problem of political manipulation of the monetary unit. The real problem is that central banking presupposes the capability of state authorities to access information that is neither in their interest nor ability to gather.[50] For central banking authorities to manage the supply of money accurately they would have to possess knowledge of the conditions of supply and demand which is not available to any one mind or group of minds. Both the political and economic problems of central banking are inherent to the institution itself. As with other centralized planning institutions, the attempt to manage monetary resources through administrative methods produces economic and political irrationalities.

On the other hand, competitive note issue will set in motion an entrepreneurial process which will adjust supply decisions of bank managers to meet the public's demand for monetary notes. The clearing mechanism under free banking will assure that managers will receive the appropriate signals for effective resource administration. The clearing mechanism provides signals concerning debit and credit that follow from the bank's under- or over-issue of notes. This information will cause bank managers to adjust their liabilities accordingly. Moreover, in a free banking system of competitive note issue, the return of notes and checks for redemption in base money will also provide incentives and information that is vital for the proper administration of the money supply. Monopoly note issue by a central bank simply cannot generate the incentives or information required to manage the money supply adequately. Central banks are not well equipped to know whether an adjustment in the supply of money is needed, nor are they well equipped to assess changes in the demand for notes.

Competition in note issue, however, promises all the same benefits that competition in any commodity does. The availability of substitutes will force bank managers to act prudently in forming their business decisions. Brand names will be important in the competitive process as some bank notes will become more respected than others. But as long as freedom of competition persists, then an effective administration of the money supply will result.

In the current situation of the former Soviet Union, the rouble has become basically worthless. Some reported exchange rates value the rouble at more than 100 roubles to one dollar in currency auctions at the end of 1991 and the beginning of 1992.[51] In the Russian Republic the printing presses have been running twenty-four hours a day. Free banking offers an alternative to this monetary chaos.[52]

Banks could offer notes backed by hard currency or some bundle of commodities or gold. The banks would offer deals on rouble exchanges to attract customers to their bank. Individuals would gravitate to bank notes that were most widely accepted for market transactions. Central bank roubles would disappear, as would the institutional organs of central banking, but monetary order would emerge and the money supply would be free of the manipulation of the political process.

One final note, free banking also offers an answer to the policy dilemma highlighted in Chapter 6 concerning commitment conveyance. Eliminating government control over the money supply not only pre-commits the regime, it also signals to market participants that the government is sincere in establishing restraints on its leading role in the economy. It will take such a drastic step that establishes binding constraints on government action and signals a firm commitment to structural reform to get economic liberalization policies on the right track. Allowing competitive note issue under a regime of free banking offers the best chance for achieving the simultaneity required for conveying a credible pre-commitment to liberal economic reform.

4. Fiscal Policy

If the political control of the money supply has been eliminated, then the government will not be able to finance its expenditures through the hidden tax of inflation. Without the ability to inflate, and thus pay debts back with cheaper money, government officials will in theory be more interest rate sensitive in their borrowing decisions. Of course, this reasoning is somewhat questionable because government officials are not in the same *context* as businessmen. They are not committing their own financial resources, nor do they face the discipline of market forces. In addition, given the changing fortunes of elected officials, those who borrow today most likely will not be in office when the bill is due in the future. Nevertheless, the elimination of the ability to inflate takes away one way in which political actors are able to hide the effects of their policies.

Political leaders will instead have to raise most revenues through taxation, which is directly felt by the electorate. Still the electorate may be rationally ignorant of a preponderance of legislative initiatives and the vote motive may be lacking, but making it more difficult to hide the costs of policies will reduce the ability of politicians to engage in special interest politics. Tax limitations along with balance budget requirements will also build in desirable constraints on government's ability to finance its affairs outside the consent of the governed.

The justification for activist fiscal policy derives mainly from Abba Lerner's concept of 'functional finance.' Lerner argued that economists should use the budget to balance the economy rather than worry about balancing the budget. During times of recession, when aggregate demand fell short of the level required to maintain full employment budget deficits could correct for the economic downturn. And, at times when aggregate demand exceeded full employment levels and produced inflationary pressures, budget surpluses could bring the economy into balance.[53]

This approach to fiscal policy belies a pretense of knowledge. In order to fine tune the economy with the tools of fiscal policy, government officials need to know not only what the current level of aggregate demand is, but also what the appropriate level of aggregate demand would be to maintain full employment. In addition, it is assumed that policy-makers can ascertain the precise effects of the multiplier so that full employment levels could be maintained. Without these crucial assumptions, government policy would not only be ineffective, it may actually be damaging to the economic order.

Budget deficits crowd out private investment activity and public debt erodes a country's capital stock. The problem with fiscal policy is an expenditure problem. A balanced budget with high levels of taxation and high levels of government expenditure would do little to promote the development of economic forces. The development of the economy requires reductions in the size and scope of government.

Government expenditures are largely justified in order to supply public goods. While few economists would question the public goods argument per se, there are severe problems that confront government provision of public goods.[54] Most fundamentally, there is a problem of the demand revelation for public goods. Under the situation of monopoly provision it is difficult, if not impossible, to ascertain the demand for public goods. Individuals do not face high-powered incentives within the political process to reveal accurately their demand for public goods.

What is missing from the political process is a competitive discovery process which motivates demand revelation. This situation can be improved on, however, by introducing as much competition as possible into the political provision of goods. First, it is one thing to establish that a good is public, it is another thing to grant government a monopoly in its provision. Private firms should be allowed to compete with government in the provision of public goods. Second, individuals must be free to move among localities. By allowing free migration of the population, localities will compete with one another for a tax base and will have an incentive to offer the demanded bundle of public services at reasonable prices (taxes). High tax areas will lose residents unless they provide an appropriate level of public services for the taxes paid. Technological advances, for example, have increased the ability of businesses to move capital quickly and this in turn has the potential of increasing the competitive pressures on government policy-makers to pursue desirable public policy at the local, national and international level.[55]

Competitive pressures will do their job most effectively as the locus of decision-making authority is reduced. The break-up of the Soviet empire, for example, might actually have been a necessary precondition for introducing the competitive forces which will aid in discovering the appropriate levels of tax and expenditure by regional governments in the former Soviet Union. The unintended consequence of ethnic strife and nationalistic awakening, may be the establishment of more manageable governance structures. Of course, the rhetoric of some of the nationalistic leaders is ugly and upsetting to liberal sensitivities (especially the rise of anti-semitism or the ethnic conflict between Armenia and Azerbaijan), but in a liberal environment these conflicts will give way to harmonious and mutually beneficial economic ties. The argument for the liberal free trade order was not limited to the gains in economic efficiency that followed from individuals pursuing their comparative advantage. Rather, liberal trade also promised peaceful social relations between individuals and nations as exchange came to dominate political conflict.[56]

During the communist period, the unique cultural and ethnic differences between the republics was officially suppressed. The first thing that occurred when the communist imposed order was lifted was that old sentiments of conflict arose again between republics. This is a natural reaction to the previous system of politically imposed order.

The old Soviet empire was doomed to collapse for structural reasons. In addition to the failed economic system, politically the empire simply overstepped the bounds of feasible control. Once Gorbachev unleashed the forces of *glasnost* and *demokratizatsiya* it was like squeezing a tube of toothpaste – the toothpaste cannot be put back in. The drive for independence by the republics was a necessary first step toward establishing a more liberal order.

Only independent states can decide that it is to their benefit to develop relationships with other states and enter into mutually beneficial agreements. There are potential dangers along this path of building a new liberal order, but there is in a fundamental sense no alternative.

The key ingredient in building successful bonds between the states is to guarantee free mobility of people, goods and services. The most effective check and balance to any political system is for the population to have the ability to vote with their feet. By allowing people and resources to flow freely, governments will be constrained in their activities.

Political competition in an environment where government's ability to hide the costs of its policies is constrained will generate a discovery procedure which will result in a close approximation to the desired bundle of public services and the level of taxation. The existence of readily available alternatives, rather than some a priori justification, will define the scope and size of the state. The basic precondition for this process to work is simply the elimination of any claims to monopolistic exclusion.

The fact that the ideal pattern of society cannot be arrived at in any a priori fashion does not mean that we must start from scratch. Historical experience and the insights of the social sciences provides us with some knowledge of which alternatives to avoid. Communism, fascism and other forms of authoritarian regimes which claim an exclusive right to truth are to be avoided. The fact that 'no utopia has ever been described in which any sane man would on any conditions consent to live, if he could possibly escape' tells us something.[57] Historically, most analysis of the ideal society concerns itself with the particular design of communities. It is not that designing communities is unimportant, rather as I have suggested, it is in the competition between communities that knowledge will be revealed concerning the appropriate relation between the citizen and the state. But, the real emphasis for reconstruction of the post-communist world must lie in developing the *framework* for society within which competition among the communities transpires.[58]

THE LOGIC OF SHOCK THERAPY

Price liberalization, privatization, monetary reform and fiscal policy constraints cannot be phased in over time for various reasons. The interconnectedness of each demands that they be introduced simultaneously.[59] In addition to this interconnection, there are also other logical reasons for adopting shock therapy as a method of transformation.

First, in order to signal a complete break with the old regime and establish credibility, the reforming government must make a drastic gesture. Gradualism translates into capitulation to the old structures of economic management.

Second, the economic situation in the former Soviet Union is so maladjusted that only a radical and systemic restructuring will get the economy on the path to prosperity. Just as the heroine addict must go through cold-turkey in order to cure his addiction, the malformed economy of the former Soviet Union must go through a similar process of healing. The bloated bureaucracy and the inefficient enterprises must be subjected to harsh economic realities which will provide incentives to adjust the social structure in a manner more consistent with the demands of the public. Capital resources are both heterogeneous and specific to certain production processes. Military plants cannot be turned into beer barrel plants overnight. Capital must be created and reallocated. This kind of realignment of the structure of production in society takes a drastic introduction of market forces.

Moreover, it must be recognized that extensive public welfare must be financed through a sustainable economic base. The public sector lives parasitically off the private sector through its power to tax. Without a developed economic base, extensive public services will simply thwart economic progress, and drain the productive energy of the private sector. Shock therapy represents the decision to get on the highway of high growth. A decision to exit for equity may be made later, but for the present it is necessary to stay on this road.

As I said earlier, the situation in the former Soviet economy is one where labor is misallocated, capital is misallocated and consumers are ignored. The only way to change this situation is through a drastic and complete introduction of market forces.[60] This requires that transition policy:

a. abolish enterprise subsidies and allow the liquidation of unprofitable enterprises;
b. eliminate government's ability to engage in inflationary practices;
c. eliminate all wage and price controls;
d. refrain from attempts to stimulate consumption;
e. abolish unemployment subsidies.

The most important thing government can do is not to interfere in the adjustment process, and to establish binding constraints on its activities so that future maladjustments are not generated by public policy choices. Rather than a cruel punishment, shock therapy is the only viable cure to the sickness that communism wrought.

IS DEMOCRACY NECESSARY?

The great advantage of democratic politics lies in the peaceful transition of power it engenders. Democracy, however, unless constrained, can lead to the tyranny of the majority over the minority. Liberalism is a theoretical doctrine which suggests what the law should be, democracy is simply a theoretical doctrine concerning the method by which law will be determined in a society.[61] Democratic politics may generate laws consistent with liberal values, but it also may not. The precondition for unleashing the competitive discovery procedures in economic and political life advocated above is a framework of law consistent with liberalism independent of the establishment of democracy. In other words, democracy is neither a necessary nor sufficient condition for establishing the liberal order.

The extension of democratic methods into areas where it is unwarranted can generate not only gross inefficiencies, but also illiberal public policy. There is a definite limit to the kind of questions that democratic politics can answer. The inability to arrive at a consensus concerning the use of the coercive powers of the state should mean that nobody has the right to exercise those powers. The power of the majority must ultimately derive from, and be limited by, the principles of conduct which the minority also accepts. Democracy is simply a means and not an end, and as such it must be constrained by the end for which it is to serve.

CONCLUSION

Conceptually the road from serfdom is not that difficult to figure out. Socialism failed because of its structural weaknesses. It could not generate the incentives and information necessary for economic progress. What is needed, therefore, to get the former socialist economy on the path of economic progress is to introduce as fast as possible the institutional structure which provides high-powered incentives to discover better ways of administering scarce resources. Free competitive markets provide the best institutional structure for this task.

Free markets, however, exist within a framework of liberal society. The main dynamic ingredient in a liberal society is the cultivation of experimentation with alternative social arrangements. Competition truly is the spice of life.

8

CONCLUSION

The fundamental attitude of true individualism is one of humility toward the processes by which mankind has achieved things which have not been designed or understood by any individual and are indeed greater than individual minds. The great question at this moment is whether man's mind will be allowed to continue to grow as part of this process or whether human reason is to place itself in chains of its own making.

F. A. Hayek[1]

INTRODUCTION

Vera Wollenberger is a proto-typical intellectual in the former communist bloc. She believed in the promise of communism, but was compelled to pursue a dissident path because of the ugliness of the East German regime. Her activism cost her a normal life. She was spied on and harassed by the Stasi (the East German Secret Police), fired from her job and even imprisoned because of her political activities with groups like the Church from Below, a human rights group she helped to organize. But Wollenberger persevered and today she is a Member of Parliament.

Unfortunately, her life in the post-communist world is still irrevocably scarred by the past. She helped shape a law intended to give victims of Stasi abuse a chance at justice. Since 2 January 1992 each victim has been allowed to read the file that the police had collected on them and discover who had betrayed them. Rather than achieving justice, opening the 125 miles of files that the Stasi had collected has shattered lives. The Stasi, it turns out, developed an extensive information network that went far beyond anyone's expectations and permeated deep into the social fabric of East German society. In addition to secret police agents, the Stasi relied heavily on the reports of friends, neighbors and family members to gather information on those under surveillance. In Wollenberger's case, her husband, Knud, provided the most detailed information on her activities to the Stasi.[2] It is estimated that the Stasi relied on the testimony of some 500,000 informers.[3] Purity from communist collaboration has proven to be a rare commodity.

How are the untainted members of society to pass judgement on the rest? For most of the communist era, dissident activity in Eastern Europe was rare. Tacit consent to communist power was the rule. Citizens had to go along to get along. Communist Party membership in the countries of Eastern Europe represented between 10 to 20 per cent of the population.[4] The revolutions of 1989 have literally thrust some individuals from prison to power.[5] Lech Walesa, for example, in the span of a decade rose to prominence as the opposition leader of Solidarity in 1980, was harshly put down by General Jaruzelski's imposition of martial law in 1981, eventually formed a coalition government with Jaruzelski in 1989 and emerged as the President of Poland in 1990.

The Polish government, however, has not sought revenge for past oppression. Most of the government apparatus is populated by the same individuals who were there under Jaruzelski's rule. Some Members of Parliament tried to pass legislation that would ban ex-communist officials from public office for ten years. This legislation has so far been successfully blocked by a strange coalition – former communists and the liberal intellectual leaders of Solidarity, who find the legislation unjust and unnecessary.

The puzzles in Walesa's Poland are not just political. Walesa's moral and political power derives from his base – the Solidarity labor union. But Walesa is the President of a government supposedly introducing capitalism as quickly as possible.[6] Catering to the demands of labor for higher pay, greater security and decision-making control over production does not accord well with tested notions of efficient capitalist production.

The surreal situation of post-communism was most evident in Czechoslovakia, where a dissident poet and playwright, Vaclav Havel, became the President. Havel and his Charter 77 group were the conscience of Central and Eastern European political dissent under the old regime.[7] Imprisoned and blacklisted in his work, Havel continued to struggle to stop the abuse of human rights under the communist regime throughout the 1970s and 1980s. After the revolution of 1989, Havel found himself in charge of a government that had to transform society and prevent the degeneration of Czechoslovakia into civil war.

Havel reports that on the day he assumed the presidency he was given a list of fellow writers who had informed on him. Havel states, however, that on that day he 'lost' that list and completely forgot the names of those on it. Personally, he leaned toward letting sleeping dogs lie, but as president, he could not make that choice for the people. People, whose lives were destroyed by the old regime, would feel that the revolution remained unfinished unless justice was served.[8]

But the delicate balance that must be struck between justice and revenge in creating a civil society is not at all an easy one to achieve. The punish and purge mentality that many reformers believe is necessary to accomplish a 'debolshevization' of these societies leads to witch hunts and character assassinations. In other words, many of the same vices that the old regime is pronounced guilty of are simultaneously advocated by the new regime as necessary to root out and punish communist collaborators.[9]

The National Assembly of the Czech and Slovak Federal Republic, for example, passed legislation preventing former secret police agents, informers, senior communist officials and other former members of Communist Party organs from holding public jobs for a five-year period. Suspect individuals are not allowed to hold high-level administrative posts in government ministries, the military, intelligence offices, police, communication industry and state-owned enterprises involved with foreign trade, rail transportation and banking. The 'lustration' law also precludes impure individuals from obtaining high academic posts, and working within the legal system as judges, prosecutors and investigators. It is estimated that the law could adversely affect over a million people.

The understandable anger that people possess concerning their former life under communism is expressed in the demand for revenge. But at the same time their fear of the future is expressed in the demand for the social stability of subsidized prices and guarantees against unemployment. The psychological trauma of transformation is born of both the despair of realizing how much of life was wasted under communism, and the apprehensiveness of having to take full responsibility for one's choices in the post-communist society.[10] As the former regime breaks up, entrenched ways of life break down. The old sources of prestige are now reasons to be despised, whereas the new paths to success, such as accumulating capital and turning a profit, were considered mortal sins under the old regime.

THE POLITICS AND ECONOMICS OF ERROR

The situation in Russia is more acute than any other transforming country. The Communist Party's rule was much longer and its penetration into the social fabric was much deeper. In January 1990, the Communist Party still claimed a membership of around 19 million.[11] And, even though in the year preceding the August coup attempt about 20 per cent (4 million) of the membership quit the Party, its influence continued to permeate Soviet society.[12] Before the election of Boris Yeltsin as President of Russia, for example, Party cells existed in all state-run places of work. Yeltsin's move to dissolve Party cells was a direct and major challenge to the Party's grip on the everyday lives of the people of Russia.

Still, and in spite of the fact that the Party has been officially divested of power, its effective power remains alive. This survival is largely due to the fact that communist apparatus was endowed with a political monopoly, and, therefore, its members alone were able to acquire the administrative skills necessary to govern. Communism has been abolished and the Russian government seems committed to democratic rule, but civil service offices are largely run, and the military command is exclusively run, by former communists.[13] Moreover, the effect of the Communist monopolistic position in society was not only in limiting administrative experience to those that loyally served the Party, but the entire realm of public life was abdicated by the population.

The use of political terror, right from the founding of the Soviet state by Lenin, subdued the population into compliance and reinforced the monopolistic situation. The Russian people understood, as Richard Pipes has argued, that 'under a regime that felt no hesitation in executing innocents, innocence was no guarantee of survival. The best hope of surviving lay in making oneself as inconspicuous as possible, which meant abandoning any thought of independent public activity, indeed any concern with public affairs, and withdrawing into one's private world. Once society disintegrated into an agglomeration of human atoms, each fearful of being noticed and concerned exclusively with physical survival, then it ceased to matter what society thought, for the government had the entire sphere of public activity to itself.'[14]

The former Soviet Union was the exemplar of the modern totalitarian state. Russia has not yet opened the files of the KGB to mass inspection.[15] But, if the East Germans are shattered by the extent to which the Stasi employed friends, neighbors and family to gather information, then it is probably safe to assume that revelations of the KGB's activities would destroy any hope for civil society in Russia. Betrayal may have simply been the price one paid for getting along. Sometimes, it is better to get on with the future rather than focus on redressing past wrongs. Bygones are bygones and, however unpleasant, nothing can be done to change what has happened. The present and future must not be sacrificed to the past.

This is not to suggest that historical conscience is not fundamental to civil society. On the contrary, I believe that Gorbachev's great contribution was allowing the Russian people the chance to regain their own history – blemishes and all. But the activities of the German Parliament and the Czech and Slovac National Assembly are counter-productive. What happened happened, nothing can be done to change it. If it is understood that the ugliness that occurred was due to institutional failings, then institutions can be established to guard against it ever happening again. The real problem with much of the demand for purification is that it seems to stress the 'bad people' explanation. 'If we guard against bad people, then all will be well.' Unfortunately, that advice achieves nothing on the path to a civil society.

Moreover, focusing on the past and attempting to purify the population simply bogs down the process of transformation. In the political realm, purification rituals involving the 'naming of the namers' requires the new leaders to resort to the same unpleasant tactics that their oppressors relied on before. In addition, on the economic front, resentment on the part of the people against former members of the *nomenklatura* underlies arguments against 'spontaneous privatization' and the capitalization of former Communist Party assets. In Russia, for example, *privatisatsia* (privatization) is commonly referred to as *prikhvatisatsia* (piratization).[16] Both the politics and economics of purification undermine any attempt to transform quickly into a market economy with a limited government.

A successful political economy strategy for the transformation requires an understanding of the past, but a focus on the future. A romantic view of the politics of transformation may suggest that enlightened leaders can simultaneously punish and purge those that deserve it without tainting the rest of the civil order. But realism in politics questions that ability.

Political choice, as choice in general, is susceptible to two kinds of errors: (1) errors of omission and (2) errors of commission. In other words, political choice may entail rejecting a policy that should have been accepted or accepting a policy that should have been rejected. Either way, inefficiency and waste occur. But basic principles of decency demand that the civil order of law be structured in a way that guards against errors of commission even if that biases the system in the direction of committing errors of omission. Letting a guilty party go free, in other words, is strongly preferred to convicting an innocent party. The witch hunts and character assassinations associated with purification drives flaunt that basic principle of civil society.

The most fundamental function of free markets, moreover, is their role in error detection. The social institutions of competitive markets, most notably monetary prices, provide signals to economic actors concerning errors and motivate the learning that leads to the mutual adjustments among market participants to eliminate the previous errors of omission (profit opportunities hitherto unrecognized) and commission (losses suffered as a result of failed projects).

A realist vision of political economy must recognize that errors are omnipresent in social life. The normative focus must be on political and economic institutions that cope well with error and motivate individuals to adjust their actions to eliminate most of the errors that are committed. Communism was a political and economic system that in practice possessed no weapons to eliminate errors of the kind being discussed here. Political and legal institutions of communism were not biased against errors of commission as liberal institutions are supposed to be. And, the economic institutions of communism simply did not provide any signal to economic actors concerning errors of either omission or commission. As a result, the real existing social, political and economic life under communism was one of perpetual error.

What I have tried to demonstrate throughout this book is that the reform efforts under Gorbachev failed to introduce anything that would correct the error-prone situation in the former Soviet Union. The problems of political and economic organization, as well as the issue of credibility, were never addressed by Gorbachev. Moreover, in Chapter 7, I tried to suggest what I thought would be necessary to correct the situation. Those suggestions were introduced without regard to the political feasibility of any proposal I offered. What is considered politically feasible at any point in time changes too quickly to be an issue of concern. Instead, the policy suggestions sought to provide an institutional framework which would be able to tolerate and encourage experimentation and learning among diverse peoples

137

in a manner which addresses the problems of political economy that I have raised throughout the book. If such a system is coherent, then it may serve as a useful benchmark from which to compare reform efforts.

THE YELTSIN REFORMS

Boris Yeltsin's unlikely ascendancy has brought the promise of a new freedom to Russia. Unlike Gorbachev, Yeltsin rose to political power through the industrial management ranks, rather than strictly through Communist Party activity.[17] A graduate of the Polytechnic Institute of Sverdlovsk, Yeltsin went to work at the Urals Machinery Plant (Uralmash). He only joined the Communist Party at the age of 30, and did so mainly for professional career advancement reasons. Yeltsin became the manager of Uralmash at 32. Later he was named First Secretary of Sverdlovsk in 1976 and was finally brought to Moscow by Gorbachev in 1986. But, in October 1987 he attacked Yegor Ligachev for his efforts in resisting reform and Gorbachev for his timid support of reform against conservative forces. As a result, Yeltsin was purged and ridiculed as uncouth, drunken and mentally incompetent. But unlike previous Communist Party officials who had fallen from grace throughout Soviet history, Yeltsin rose again as a leader of the democratic opposition. In 1991 he became the first democratically elected President in Russian history. His courageous stance in the face of the August 1991 coup attempt solidified his position as the future hope of Russia.

In January 1992, the Yeltsin government began a new stage of radical economic reform in Russia. The reforms go much further toward establishing a market economy than any of the proposed plans introduced during the Gorbachev era.[18] Whereas Gorbachev remained throughout his reign emotionally and intellectually committed to some form of socialist economic planning, Yeltsin has rejected socialism and emotionally, if not intellectually, embraced the necessity of capitalist markets for bringing prosperity to Russia. He has surrounded himself with a team of young economists, such as Yegor Gaidar and Anatoly Chubais, who supposedly possess a strong commitment to reforming the Russian economy and joining the international economic community. But there remain fundamental problems with even Yeltsin's shock therapy.

Gorbachev's piecemeal reforms neither improved the apparatus of central economic administration (the rhetoric of the first stage, 1985–7) nor introduced market discipline (the rhetoric of the second stage, 1987–91). As a result, the economic situation actually grew worse under Gorbachev. Budget deficits soared as subsidies to both enterprises and consumers continued to accelerate. The deficits, in turn, were covered by printing more roubles. The combined budget deficit for the central and republic governments in 1990 was an estimated 20 per cent of GNP, and by the fall of 1991 the exchange rate on the rouble was over 100 roubles to the dollar. Gorbachev's hesitations and reversals eventually destroyed any credibility the reform efforts possessed with Western financial institutions by the winter of 1990–1.

Yeltsin, therefore, inherited not only an abject economic failure, but an entire social system of production in absolute ruins. On 28 October 1991, Boris Yeltsin announced his economic reform package. The Yeltsin program eschewed gradualism. 'The period of moving in small steps,' Yeltsin stated,

> is over. The field for reforms has been cleared of mines. There is a unique opportunity to stabilize the economic situation over several months and to begin the process of improving the situation. Under conditions of political freedom, we must provide economic freedom, lift all barriers to the freedom of enterprises and entrepreneurship, and give people the opportunity to work and to receive as much as they can earn, casting off bureaucratic constraints.[19]

Yeltsin's broad program consisted of: (1) macroeconomic stabilization, including the 'unfreezing' of prices, (2) privatization and the creation of a healthy 'mixed economy' with a strong private sector and (3) foreign trade liberalization.

Yeltsin followed up this promise of radical reform with ten presidential decrees and resolutions on 15 November 1991 which placed full economic power in his hands. Russia, he decreed, would take control of all financial agencies in its territory. Russia would also completely control oil, diamond and precious metal output in its territory. In essence, Yeltsin delivered the crushing final blow to the old structures of Union power.[20]

Then, on 2 January 1992, Yeltsin's government acted unilaterally and freed most consumer-goods and producer-goods prices from administrative regulation. But the Yeltsin economic program has been attacked from all directions.

Conservatives, like Russian Vice-President Aleksandr Rutskoi, accuse Yeltsin of 'seeking to conduct yet another experiment on the Russian people.'[21] Moreover, much of the opposition that the Yeltsin's reform program faced at the Congress of People's Deputies in April 1992 was due to the fact that many in the Congress still represent the old guard, including state enterprise managers who are unsure of where the reforms will leave them.[22]

On the other hand, liberal reformers like Larisa Piyasheva, argue that the Yeltsin program for economic stabilization lacks a foundation in basic free market economics. 'The stabilization of the economy,' she states, 'should begin with the privatization of property, not with setting extortionate taxes and the introduction of inordinately high prices.' Both the 28 per cent value added tax and the implementation of price liberalization without first privatizing make no sense to her. All that will result from these efforts is a discrediting of economic liberalization. Piyasheva concluded that 95 per cent of what the Russian government is implementing represents 'economic exercises devoid of common sense.'[23]

Nikolai Petrakov has argued that the Yeltsin price reform has 'nothing in common with market-based setting of prices.'[24] And, Mikhail Leontyev criticizes the program in even more biting terms, referring to Yeltsin's price liberalization as the 'Pavlovization' of liberal reform. The price liberalization of January 1992 amounts to nothing more than another administrative price increase. The basic institutions of regulated distribution of goods remain intact. 'Free' prices are not preventing limits from being placed on the quantity of goods that can be sold to individual consumers. Even worse, the government has reinforced the practice of trade restrictions by limiting the ability of individuals to buy low and sell high in the market-place by placing a 25 per cent mark-up ceiling on retail prices.[25]

The main adversary of the Yeltsin reforms, however, may in fact be Yeltsin's own populist posture. He has already backed away from some of the harsh short-term realities of economic liberalization. Yeltsin has criticized political opponents and the members of the media who have attacked his program for reform as engaging in blasphemous political profiteering. But Yeltsin is not just a critic of political profiteering, he has also expressed outrage at monopolistic profiteering on the part of producers.[26] In addition, he has already made some significant concessions to appease segments of the population and privatization has not advanced at a rapid pace.[27] But without rapid privatization, price liberalization will not solicit the supply response desired.

The Gaidar reform team has decided to pursue the public auction method of privatization. Nizhni Novgorod, Russia's third largest city, has been chosen as the testing ground for selling off government-owned shops, which if proven to be a successful model could be copied throughout Russia. Even under these most favorable conditions, though, only three dozen shops have been sold in the first two months. At that rate, it would take 8 years to sell the shops in Nizhni Novgorod alone. The government intended to sell 100,000 shops within a year.[28] The auction method does not work quickly enough in privatizing even small shops.

Given the industrial structure of the economy, the most important component of reform is the quick privatization of economic entities. Agricultural reforms are moving quickly along the lines of a 'give away' scheme. At the beginning of 1991, 97 per cent of Russia's farm land was comprised of 26,000 state-owned farms, whereas 3 per cent represented 38 million private plots. Russia, however, has started to eliminate the large state-owned farms by simply giving away the farm land to the farmers. Since January 1992, farmers on state-owned farms have been allowed to vote on whether to remain state-owned, or to be operated under various alternative property arrangements. Only 10 per cent have voted to remain state-owned. 90 per cent have voted to experiment with alternative arrangements. 50 per cent have chosen to divide their giant farms into family farms or private farm associations where farm land is owned and managed privately, but the farm equipment is commonly shared. The other 40 per cent have voted to remain a single unit, but be operated as a privately held cooperative.[29] This agricultural reform model should be copied for the industrial sector as well.

The main concern of reformers should be to transfer resources as quickly as possible to private hands and establish a rule of law that protects private property and the freedom of entry.[30] Once resources are in private hands and property rights are well-defined and strictly enforced, resources will tend to flow in the direction where they are valued most by economic actors. Small shops and large industrial enterprises should simply be transferred to the previous *de facto* owners. As I argued in Chapter 7, the managers of existing enterprises would be in the best position to take over control of the state-owned firms. But, in a fundamental sense it does not matter if ownership is transferred to managers or workers. As long as subsidies to enterprises are eliminated, freedom of entry is permitted and liquidation of assets is allowed, resources will be channeled in a manner consistent with their effective use. Privatization coupled with comprehensive foreign trade liberalization will demonopolize the industrial system in one step. Normal market forces of profit and loss will guide resource use from that moment on.

In addition, rather than engage in endless debate, perhaps the public/private question could be solved by simply copying a Western model, say the US, with an added proviso.[31] Services that have traditionally received an economic justification for public provision and/or regulation on market failure grounds could remain as state-run enterprises – public utilities, courts and legal system, schools, national defense and so on. But, all other services need to be turned over to the market. Moreover, even in those areas where it is thought that government provision must remain, responsibility for that provision must be decentralized to the most local level and exclusivity must be denied. Competition from alternative producers, as well as from other local and regional governments, will assure that a public/private mix will emerge that corresponds in a reasonable manner with the desire of the populace.

This type of program, however, is far removed from the IMF-type of reform that the Yeltsin team is following. On 28 February 1992, the Russian government released a memorandum on economic policy reconfirming the commitment to economic reform and their integration into the world economy. This memorandum was sent to the Board of Directors of the IMF to be considered in deliberations on whether Russia would be offered full-membership in the IMF.[32] The Russian government, along with most of the other republics of the former Soviet Union, was offered full-membership on 27 April 1992.[33]

Unlike the received wisdom, I do not see this as an unequivocally desirable invitation. Certainly, IMF and World Bank membership grants a degree of credibility in the international market-place to the reforming countries. But, how successful has the advice of these institutions been in helping other countries reform their economies? The IMF's standard policy calls for an economic austerity program that is questionable on theoretical and empirical grounds. Even Jeffrey Sachs has admitted that the critics have a point when they argue that 'there are almost no success stories of countries that have pursued IMF austerity measures and World Bank structural adjustments to reestablish creditworthiness and restore economic growth.'[34]

The basic problem is the IMF's preoccupation with managed macroeconomic stabilization policy which biases analysis in a direction away from the microeconomic structural reform required. A tax system that rewards saving and that encourages investment, abolition of tariffs and other trade restrictions and elimination of burdensome regulations on industry would go a long way toward restructuring the system. Successful monetary reforms, moreover, have traditionally been accomplished by either redeeming the currency for a more credible foreign currency or a precious metal, rather than through the devaluation programs sponsored by the IMF and financed by a monetary stabilization fund.

Foreign loan and credit programs do not lead to the needed structural changes. The 'Grand Bargain' idea is neither grand nor a bargain.[35] And while Grigory Yavlinsky's 'Grand Bargain' proposal is no longer on the table, the appeals for Western aid from the Gaidar reform team possess the same implicit logic: provide aid for the peaceful transition or else ugly Russian nationalism and militarism will most likely resurface. But foreign aid will not lead to the fundamental structural changes in the political economy that are necessary. Instead, the funds provided in the name of stabilization will unfortunately send Russia down the same failed path that Latin America and Africa have gone in the past few decades at the urging of international lending institutions. Yeltsin, like Gorbachev before him, will find himself at the helm of an economy descending further and further into an abyss of despair and deprivation.

Prosperity, on the other hand, will come from creating opportunities for investment of capital, both foreign and domestic, to turn a profit. Government (or government agency) to government aid is not the source of economic development. The flow of private financial resources into an economy is the important signal to receive indicating that reforms are moving in the right direction. Stability of law and the ability to repatriate profits will attract business investment from afar and stimulate economic development. The development of a nation's economy is the consequence of an open-ended process of the discovery of opportunities for mutual gain among actors. Not only must the institutional environment generate incentives so economic actors use existing resources in an efficient manner, but the institutional climate must also provide incentives that stimulate the perception of new possibilities among economic actors for effective resource use that had remained unexploited until their discovery. In other words, economic development flourishes whenever an institutional framework is established within which spontaneous processes of unpredictable mutual discovery of opportunities are encouraged.[36] With its rich abundance of natural resources, Russia could develop into the thriving world economy of the twenty-first century under the right institutional conditions.[37] Unfortunately, Yeltsin's Russia is still a long way from establishing the requisite market and legal institutions for that development to happen.

THE SPIRIT OF THE AGE

Whatever happens in Russia, the collapse of communism possesses a meaning that goes well beyond the immediate problems of the day – no matter how profound those problems are. Whether Yeltsin fails or succeeds, the political and intellectual world will never be the same. The twentieth century was the age of socialism, and that era is now over.[38] In an even more fundamental sense the collapse of communism has signalled the end of modernism and all that entails.[39]

'The end of Communism,' Vaclav Havel writes, 'is, first and foremost, a message to the human race.' We have not yet fully deciphered its meaning. But, in its deepest sense, 'the end of Communism has brought a major era in human history to an end. It has brought an end not just to the 19th and 20th centuries, but to the modern age as a whole.'[40] Marxism was the quintessential modernist movement. Through rational design man's emancipation from the oppressive bonds of nature and other men would be accomplished. Lenin was the guardian, and then deliverer of this emancipation project to Russia. Lenin, in addition to Russian Marxism, was influenced by the fanatical rationalist Nikolai Chernyshevsky, and especially his novel, *What is to be Done?*, from which Lenin drew the title, and much of the spirit behind, the basic charter of the Bolshevik movement. 'The result,' Martin Malia points out, 'was a fantasy of Reason-in-Power that mesmerized the entire twentieth century, both East and West.'[41]

With the socialist movement the Enlightenment turned against mankind and enslaved him in chains made of his own Reason. The death of the political economy of socialism does not mean the end of ideological dispute nor the rejection of reason. History has not ended, even in the narrow sense that Francis Fukuyama intended.[42] The substitution of technocratic problem solving for passionate discussion of ideas and values is not the intellectual curse that follows the death of communism as a legitimating power, but rather the logical consequence of modernistic scientism.

The post-communist era, if anything, will require that ideological visions of what is good and just be articulated by new spokesmen. Imagination, idealism and the purely abstract goal of a free society must replace the scientistic notions of the past era in which the desire to order society in strict accordance to a rational plan ended in political arbitrariness and economic poverty. Just because the ideas that fuel the imagination may not be brand new does not necessarily mean that they are old.[43]

The liberalism of the nineteenth century failed because of its inability to protect against opportunistic invasion (namely, interest group factions within representative democracy), and the socialism of the twentieth century failed because it was an incoherent utopia (unable to engage in rational economic calculation, and, thus, to progress economically). What is required for the twenty-first century is a vision of a new, but workable, utopia. A post-modern vision of politics and economics if you will. Such a vision of political economy must combine the humility toward the power of reason to control social processes found in the Scottish Enlightenment, with the wealth of theoretical and empirical information that is to be gleaned from the twentieth-century experience with economic planning in both East and West.

CONCLUSION

We have the good fortune to live in exciting times. A world that had appeared to settle into a nice equilibrium since the 1970s was suddenly sent spinning in the mid- to late-1980s. New questions concerning international relations, economics, politics, law, ethnic tranquility and nationhood are now up in the air. Most of these questions are far from being answered, and probably will not be in the foreseeable future. And, even if we come to a consensus on some of the issues, each generation must ask them anew. But, universal principles of social interaction do exist for us to discover and those we find must be incorporated into the social wisdom if we are to avoid destroying civilization.

If the Soviet experience can teach us anything, it is that we must, as Richard Ericson has put it, 'abandon the Faustian urge to control, to know in advance, and thus, to allow economic outcomes to arise naturally as the unpredictable consequences of market interaction.'[44]

The processes of market interaction fundamentally lay beyond our control. Rather than attempt to design optimal plans and control social forces, our intellectual efforts must be devoted to asking questions about the institutional framework within which activities beyond our control will take place. Raising and providing useful answers to such questions, however, requires an array of disciplines.

Economics is an important, in fact essential, component in this inquiry. But, economics cannot provide all the answers. Politics, philosophy, history and cultural theory, along with other intellectual disciplines and common sense, must also be employed.

Most importantly, though, moral reasoning must be allowed to regain a legitimate place in scholarly endeavors. Perhaps the most fundamental reason why Sovietologists were so surprised by the events of the late 1980s was the hegemony of a scientistic methodology which disregarded evidence from the humanities (such as literature and personal testimony) and dismissed questions of human meaning as metaphysical nonsense. Reasoned debate about such fundamental issues can, and must, take place if we are to think in an effective way about the politics and history of our times.

NOTES

1 INTRODUCTION

1 John Stuart Mill, 'The claims of labour' [1845], in *Essays on Economics and Society*, vol. 4, *Collected Works of John Stuart Mill* (Toronto: University of Toronto Press, 1967), p. 370.

2 See Stanislav Shatalin, N. Petrakov and G. Yavlinsky, *Transition to the Market* (Moscow: Cultural Initiative Foundation, 1990), republished as *500 Days* (New York: St Martin's Press, 1991). See also '500 Days to Shake the World,' *The Economist* (15 September 1990): 93–4, and David Remnick, 'Gorbachev shifts on economy,' *The Washington Post* (13 September 1990): A30–A31.

3 See Ed Hewett, 'The new Soviet plan,' *Foreign Affairs* (Winter 1990/91): 146–67. Hewett argues that the major strength and stumbling block to the 500-Day Plan was the issue of confederation which correctly recognized the collapse of the union, but was a position which Gorbachev simply could not endorse in the fall of 1990. The Ryzhkov Plan, on the other hand, while retaining central power, granted some increased autonomy to the republics. Gorbachev enlisted the services of Abel Aganbegyan to draft a compromise plan of the Shatalin and Ryzhkov Plans, which eventually became the Presidential Plan.

4 See the reports by Quentin Peel, 'Reformers despair of 500-day plan as Soviet prices soar,' *Financial Times* (12 October 1990): 20, 'Gorbachev's economic program,' *New York Times* (17 October 1990): A8, Bill Keller, 'Gorbachev offers his plan to remake Soviet economy, but includes no timetable,' *New York Times* (17 October 1990): A1 and A8, 'Soviet plan in the middle,' *New York Times* (18 October 1990): A1 and A14, 'Gorbachev's economic plan approved,' *New York Times* (20 October 1990): A6 and Peter Passell, 'Gorbachev counsels a prudent revolution,' *New York Times* (21 October 1990): E3.

5 Boris Pinkser, a leading pro-market Soviet intellectual and the husband of Larissa Popkova-Piyasheva, holds the opinion that Reagan's military build-up was the major contributory factor responsible for the breakdown of the Soviet empire. (Personal conversation with Pinkser on his visit to New York in 1991.) A sample of Pinkser and Piyasheva's views can be found in Lev Timofeyev (ed.) *The Anti-Communist Manifesto*

(Bellevue, WA: Free Enterprise Press, 1990). Piyasheva created a polemical stir in the market debate in the Soviet Union when she published her short paper, 'Where are the *Pirogi* Meatier?,' *Novy Mir*, no. 5 (1987), translated in Anthony Jones and William Moskoff (eds) *Perestroika and the Economy* (New York: M. E. Sharpe, 1989), pp. 99–103. See also her, 'Why is the plan incompatible with the market?,' *Annals* (January 1990): 80–90.

6 The idea of Gorbachev as a benevolent liberal reformer became the dominant Western perspective after the events of 1989. See, for example, the discussion of Gorbachev in Joshua Muravchik, 'Gorbachev's intellectual odyssey,' *New Republic* (5 March 1990): 20–5. Muravchik argued that Gorbachev 'may yet complete his odyssey by sailing the Soviet ship of state safely beyond the grotesque clutches of Leninism and Marxism to the friendly port of democracy and freedom.' For the events of 1989, Gorbachev was awarded Man of the Decade by *Time* and won the Nobel Peace Prize.

7 See *New York Times* (1 January 1989): A1.

8 See the discussion of the economics of German unification in Leslie Lipschitz and Donogh McDonald (eds) *German Unification: Economic Issues* (Washington, DC: International Monetary Fund, 1990). On the importance of the collapse of the East German model for Soviet reformers see Marshall Goldman, *What Went Wrong With Perestroika* (New York: Norton, 1991), pp. 56–7.

9 Aggregate measurements of well-being, such as per capita GNP, place the former Soviet Union at about 25 per cent of the corresponding figure in the US economy. See *PlanEcon Report*, 6 (52) (28 December 1990): 17. However, since many goods are not available in the state stores at the official price, such calculations overstate the purchasing power of citizens in a shortage economy.

10 See George Orwell, *Animal Farm* (New York: Harcourt Brace Jovanovich, 1946). Orwell's book was a parable of the corruption of the Soviet revolution by Stalin and the consequences of collectivization and industrialization. The ideological dictum that all animals were equal gave way to the reality that though all animals were equal some animals were more equal than others. In the end, one could not tell the difference between the pigs (the leaders of the animals) and the humans outside of the farm – the pigs had become just like their previous oppressors.

11 See David Levy, 'The bias in centrally planned prices,' *Public Choice*, 67 (1990): 213–26. Also see Konstantin Simis, *USSR: The Corrupt Society* (New York: Simon and Schuster, 1982), and Olimpiad Ioffe, *Gorbachev's Economic Dilemma* (St Paul: Merrill/Magnus Publishing, 1989) for a discussion of the monopolistic and rent-seeking behavior of individuals within the Soviet economy.

12 See the pioneering studies on non-market decision-making under non-democratic regimes by Gordon Tullock, *The Social Dilemma* (Blacksburg, VA: Center for Study of Public Choice, 1974) and *Autocracy* (Boston: Kluwer, 1987).

13 See Mancur Olson, *Rise and Decline of Nations* (New Haven: Yale University Press, 1983).

NOTES

2 THE ROAD TO NOWHERE

1 Arthur Koestler, *Darkness at Noon* (New York: Macmillan, 1941), p. 58.
2 See the reports in *The New York Times* (2 May 1990): A1, *The Financial Times* (2 May 1990): 1 and the report by Quentin Peel, 'Revolt against Moscow gathers pace across Union,' *The Financial Times* (3 May 1990): 2.
3 See the reports of the Revolution Day Parade in *The New York Times* (8 November 1990): A1 and A12, and *Wall Street Journal* (8 November, 1990): A21.
4 See Robert Kaiser, *Why Gorbachev Happened?* (New York: Simon & Schuster, 1991), p. 247, and Hedrick Smith, *The New Russians* (New York: Random House, 1990), p. 132.
5 See Robert Conquest, *The Great Terror: A Reassessment* (New York: Oxford University Press, 1990) and *The Harvest of Sorrow* (New York: Oxford University Press, 1986), and G. Warren Nutter, *The Growth of Industrial Production in the Soviet Union* (Princeton: Princeton University Press, 1962) and *Political Economy and Freedom* (Indianapolis: Liberty Press, 1983). Also see Gary Becker's discussion of Nutter in 'Capitalism vs. communism: why it's still no contest,' *Business Week* (2 May 1988): 20. For a discussion of Conquest see Tatyana Tolstaya, 'In cannibalistic times,' *New York Review of Books* (11 April 1991): 3–6. As she points out, when Conquest's *The Great Terror* was published in the Russian journal *Neva* in 1990 many readers exclaimed that they knew all this already. But where had they learned it? From Conquest. When the *Great Terror* was first published in English twenty years ago, Tolstaya informs us, it quickly became an underground classic in the Soviet Union with which all thinking people were acquainted. For an interpretative essay on the rise of historical conscience under Gorbachev see David Remnick, 'Dead souls,' *New York Review of Books* (19 December 1991): 72–81. Also see Thomas Sherlock, 'Politics and history under Gorbachev,' *Problems of Communism* (May–August 1988): 16–42.
6 See Roy Medvedev, *Let History Judge*, revised edition (New York: Columbia University Press, 1989), Alexander Tsipko, *Is Stalinism Really Dead?* (New York: Harper Collins, 1990); and Nikolai Shmelev and Vladimir Popov, *The Turning Point: Revitalizing the Soviet Economy* (New York: Doubleday, 1989). Shmelev created a stir with his article, 'Advances and debts,' *Novy Mir*, no. 6 (1987), as did Vasily Selyunin with 'Sources,' *Novy Mir*, no. 5 (1988); both articles fundamentally challenged Soviet claims to economic success.
7 *Pravda* (9 November 1991): 1, translated in *The Current Digest of the Soviet Press*, 43 (45) (11 December 1991): 1–2. Though no official government parade occurred, two demonstrations did take place. At one demonstration, in fact, several pro-communists set flowers at the foot of the Lenin monument and carried signs denouncing Gorbachev and Yeltsin. In the other demonstration at Lubyanka (formerly Dzerzhinsky Square), pro-democracy groups held signs that included one that read: 'Lenin – the national disgrace of Russia! Forgive us, Russia, for this

disgrace that we suffered from 1917 until Aug. 19, 1991.' Another read: 'November 7, 1917 – a day of national tragedy.'

8 See Serge Schmemann, 'A Russian is swept aside by forces he unleashed,' *The New York Times* (15 December 1991): 1, 12–13, for a report of Gorbachev's rise and fall from power. On Gorbachev's resignation see *The New York Times* (26 December 1991): A1; *The Wall Street Journal* (26 December 1991): A3. See *The Current Digest of the Soviet Press*, 43 (52) (29 January 1992): 1–6 for domestic reports on Gorbachev's resignation. Also see Robert Tucker, 'The last Leninist,' *The New York Times* (29 December 1991): 9.

9 Douglas North, *Structure and Change in Economic History* (New York: Norton, 1981), p. x.

10 See Mary O. Furner, 'Knowing capitalism: public investigation and the labor question in the long progressive era,' in Mary O. Furner and Barry Supple (eds) *The State and Economic Knowledge* (New York: Cambridge University Press, 1990), p. 241–86. Furner argues that with industrial maturity, economic gains in productivity and wealth were offset by rising social conflict, economic waste in terms of manpower and uncertainty due to business cycles. The private contractual relationships mediated on the market gave way to market failure, collective action and class conflict. *Laissez-faire* policy necessarily ended and was replaced by a multifaceted corporate liberalism, social activism and egalitarian democratic collectivism, which marked the boundaries of modern liberal discourse from the Progressive Era to the New Deal and beyond.

11 The drastic change in the climate of opinion during the end of the nineteenth and beginning of the twentieth centuries put a 'fear of socialism' in the hearts and minds of businessmen. Woodrow Wilson challenged leading businessmen, in an address to the Economic Club in New York on 23 May 1912, to develop an alternative vision of the future:

> What is the alternative, gentlemen? You have heard the rising tide of socialism . . . Socialism is not growing in influence in this country as a programme . . . If it becomes a programme, then we shall have to be very careful how we propose a competing programme . . . If you want to oust socialism you have got to propose something better. It is a case, if you will allow me to fall into the language of the vulgar, of 'put up or shut up.' . . . It is by constructive purpose that you are going to govern and save the United States . . . Very well, then, let us get together and form a constructive programme [that posterity will say that after America had passed through a simple age] . . . when the forces of society had come into hot contact . . . there were men of serene enough intelligence . . . of will and purpose to stand up once again . . . [and who found out] how to translate power into freedom, how to make men glad that they were rich, how to take envy out of men's hearts that others were rich and they for a little while poor, by opening the gates of opportunity to every man . . .

As quoted in Martin Sklar, 'Woodrow Wilson and the political economy of modern United States liberalism,' in Ronald Randosh and Murray Rothbard (eds) *A New History of Leviathan* (New York: E. P. Dutton 1972), pp. 56–7, fn. 84.

The alternative program put forward by the leading businessmen of the day was government regulation of the economy. This drive to regulate their own industry expressed the desire to 'help shape the right kind of regulation before the wrong kind [was] forced upon [them].' See the letter from Ralph Easley to George Perkins, 9 June 1909, as quoted in James Weinstein, *The Corporate Ideal in the Liberal State* (Boston: Beacon Press, 1968), p. 33. Perkins, who was a partner in the banking house J. P. Morgan and Co., argued that a business court was needed. Ruthless competition led to waste, the sweatshop, child labor and panic and failure. A court comprised of leading businessmen of honorable reputation would ensure the control of competition and promote cooperation between business, labor and government. Thus, such a program would correct the flaws of capitalism without rejecting the system as a whole. Perkins, 'Wanted – a national business court,' *The Independent* (30 November 1911): 1173–7. Gabriel Kolko, *The Triumph of Conservativism* (New York: Free Press, 1963), presents the classic discussion of the rise of political capitalism between the end of the nineteenth century and the First World War.

12 On the effect that this has had on modern economic education see Arjo Klamer and David Colander, *The Making of an Economist* (Boulder: Westview Press, 1990). Also see Don Lavoie, 'The present status of interpretation in economics,' Center for the Study of Market Processes, George Mason University, unpublished paper, 1986.

13 The metaphor of a frictionless machine was borrowed from physics. On the nature of 'physics envy' in economics see, Philip Mirowski, *More Heat than Light* (New York: Cambridge University Press, 1989). One of the most fundamental problems with the friction metaphor in economics is that as it is usually employed it overlooks the fundamental fact that market institutions to a large degree operate only because of frictions. Just like the friction between the sole of our shoes and the road enables us to walk (on a perfectly smooth surface we could find no grip and therefore would not be able to walk), the existence of frictions in the market are the spur for entrepreneurial discovery in competitive capitalism. Israel Kirzner has persistently stressed this point in his work on the theoretical nature of competitive markets. See Kirzner, *Competition and Entrepreneurship* (Chicago: University of Chicago Press, 1973), *Perception, Opportunity and Profit* (Chicago: University of Chicago Press, 1979) and *Discovery and the Capitalist Process* (Chicago: University of Chicago Press, 1985). Also see the interview with Kirzner by Stephan Boehm, 'Austrian economics and the theory of entrepreneurship,' *Review of Political Economy*, 4 (1) (1992): 95–110.

14 John Maynard Keynes, 'National self-sufficiency,' *The Yale Review* (1933): 761–2. In 1926, Keynes had argued 'that if Communism achieves a certain success, it will achieve it, not as an improved economic technique, but as a religion.' Keynes argued that the main problem with the conventional critique of communism was that 'We hate Communism

so much, regarded as a religion, that we exaggerate its economic inefficiency; and we are so much impressed by its economic inefficiency that we underestimate it as a religion.' A sound critique of communism, therefore, required the critic to neither exaggerate its economic inefficiency nor underestimate its power as a religion. Keynes, *Laissez-Faire and Communism* (New York: New Republic, 1926), pp. 129–30.

15 Keynes, *The General Theory of Employment, Interest and Money* (New York: Harcourt Brace Jovanovich, 1936(1964)), pp. 378–81.

16 See Frank Knight, 'The case for communism: from the standpoint of an ex-liberal' (1932), *Research in the History of Economic Thought and Methodology: Archival Supplement* 2 (1991): 57–108. Also see Warren Samuels, 'Introduction,' to Knight's article, 49–55. Knight was a deeply pessimistic person 'incapable of summoning up much enthusiasm for any human institution' and his concern at the time of writing 'The case for communism,' was that liberal society had failed to provide social order. If that was the case, Knight reasoned, then communism may regrettably provide the social order so desperately needed. Knight also argued that the problems of collectivism were not economic problems, but political problems, and as such, the economic theorist had little or nothing to say about the efficacy of collectivism. See Knight, 'The place of marginal economics in a collectivist system,' *American Economic Review*, 26 (1) (March 1936): 255–66. However, also see Knight, 'Socialism: the nature of the problem' (1940) in *Freedom and Reform: Essays in Economics and Social Philosophy* (Indianapolis: Liberty Classics, 1982), pp. 154–93, where he argued that the fundamental economic problem of socialism arises due to the dynamic nature of economic life which demands adjustment and adaptation on the part of economic decision-makers in response to ever-changing conditions.

17 See Paul Homan, 'Economic planning: proposals and the literature,' *Quarterly Journal of Economics*, 47 (1) (November 1932): 102–22.

18 William Loucks, 'Public works planning and economic control: federal, state, and municipal,' *Annals* (July 1932): 114.

19 See William J. Barber, 'Government as a laboratory for economic learning in the years of the Democrat Roosevelt,' in Mary O. Furner and Barry Supple (eds) *The State and Economic Knowledge* (New York: Cambridge University Press, 1990), pp. 103–37.

20 Rexford Tugwell and Howard Hill, *Our Economic Society and Its Problems* (New York: Harcourt, Brace and World, 1934), p. 527. Tugwell in numerous writings stressed the theme that laissez-faire was a bankrupt idea out of touch with the modern world. Tugwell's formula for solving the economic problems of the day was 'concentration and control' of the industrial sector. See, for example, Tugwell, 'The principle of planning and the institution of laissez-faire,' *American Economic Review* (March 1932): 75–92.

21 Julian Huxley, *A Scientist Among the Soviets* (New York: Harper & Brothers, 1932), p. 60.

22 A classic case of an apologist was the correspondent for *The New York Times*, Will Duranty.

23 The founding fathers, however, did not possess such a naive view of

democracy. Much of the analysis of modern public choice economics derives inspiration from the work of the founders on constitutional design. See, in particular, James Buchanan and Gordon Tullock, *The Calculus of Consent* (Ann Arbor: University of Michigan Press, 1962). One possible explanation of the loss of the basic wisdom of the founders may be due to changes in the intellectual landscape with the 'death of God' in the nineteenth century. Whereas before man was viewed as a fallen angel in need of constraint, now he was viewed as a risen ape capable of great accomplishments. Rather than constrained, this vision of man sought to unleash man's unlimited potential. See Peter Boettke, 'Constitutional erosion caused capitalist decay,' *The World and I* (November 1991): 540–2. Unleashing the powers of democracy was one method to tap into that potential. For an examination of the alternative perspectives on social theory that derive from a constrained versus unconstrained vision of man see Thomas Sowell, *A Conflict of Visions* (New York: William Morrow, 1987).

24 Letter from Keynes to F. A. Hayek dated 28 June 1944 in John Maynard Keynes, *Collected Works*, vol. 27 (New York: Cambridge University Press, 1980), p. 387.

25 Herman Finer, *Road to Reaction* (Chicago: Quadrangle Books, 1945), p. v. For a more even headed criticism of Hayek see, Barbara Wootton, *Freedom under Planning* (Chapel Hill: University of North Carolina Press, 1945).

26 See Peter Boettke, 'Analysis and vision in economic discourse,' *Journal of the History of Economic Thought*, 14 (Spring 1992): 84–95.

27 As Hayek wrote, 'The consequences of this is that in the statistical study of social phenomena the structures with which the theoretical social sciences are concerned actually disappear. Statistics may supply us with very interesting and important information about what is the raw material from which we have to reproduce these structures, but it can tell us nothing about these structures themselves. In some fields this is immediately obvious as soon as it is stated. That the statistics of words can tell us nothing about the structure of a language will hardly be denied. But although the contrary is sometimes suggested, the same holds no less true of other systematically connected wholes such as, for example, the price system.' See *The Counter-Revolution of Science* (Indianapolis: Liberty Classics, 1979(1952)), pp. 108–9.

28 See Richard Ericson, 'The Soviet statistical debate,' in Henry Rowen and Charles Wolf (eds) *The Impoverished Superpower* (San Francisco: ICS Press, 1990), p. 77.

29 Grigory Khanin and Vasily Selyunin, 'The elusive figure,' *Novy Mir*, no. 2 (February 1987), translated in *The Current Digest of the Soviet Press*, 39 (25) (1987): 10–12.

30 *CIA: Handbook of Economic Statistics, 1987* (Washington, DC: GPO, 1987): 24–5.

31 Soviet per capita GNP in 1990 was estimated to be $5,060 as compared to $21,000 for the US. See *PlanEcon Report*, 6 (52) (28 December 1990): 17. Even this figure overstates Soviet GNP because of the unavailability of many goods at official prices. Also see Andres Aslund,

'How small is Soviet national income?,' in Rowen and Wolf (eds) *The Impoverished Superpower* (see Note 28), pp. 13–61.

32 See Merton Peck and Thomos Richardson (eds) *What Is To Be Done?* (New Haven: Yale University Press, 1991), p. 4.

33 See Rowen and Wolf, 'Introduction,' *The Impoverished Superpower* (see Note 28), p. 7.

34 This is not meant to suggest that the former Soviet Union posed no threat to world peace. Clearly, the stock pile of nuclear weapons amassed by the Soviet government could destroy the world several times over, as could those collected in the West. But, two questions immediately emerge concerning Soviet military power when confronted with the revised data. How could the Soviet Union have accomplished its military build-up with such a backward economy, and could these military developments be sustained over time? To answer these questions, we must recognize the fundamental distinction between a technological problem – where there is only one unified end considered by decision-makers – and an economic problem – where there are multiple ends being pursued within society. By turning all economic problems into technological problems a social system eliminates the problem of competing ends for which scarce means must be allocated among alternative uses. However, the technological approach to social policy does not allow the experimentation, and the social learning of trial and error that generates the innovations and industrial progress that are vital for economic development. Without sustainable economic development, moreover, military power erodes. On the difference between a society which provides for the reconciliation of many ends and one in which only one end may be pursued see F. A. Hayek, *Law, Legislation and Liberty*, vol. 2 (Chicago: University of Chicago Press, 1978), pp. 107–32. Also see James Buchanan, 'Markets, states, and the extent of morals,' in *What Should Economists Do?* (Indianapolis: Liberty Press, 1979), pp. 219–29. On the relationship between economics and military power see Tyler Cowen, 'Economic effects of a conflict-prone world order,' *Public Choice*, 64 (February 1990): 121–34.

35 See Seymour Melman, *The Permanent War Economy* (New York: Simon and Schuster, 1974) and *Profits without Production* (New York: Alfred Knopf, 1983) for a critical discussion of the military economy.

36 Even if left-wing intellectuals opposed increased military expenditures, their arguments concerning the desirability of socialism as an economic system simply reinforced right-wing fears about the threat of communism.

37 As pointed out by V. Sirotkin,

> It has become a copybook maxim to assert that the policy of 'War Communism' was imposed on the Bolsheviks by the Civil War and the foreign intervention. This is completely untrue, if only for the reason that the first decrees on introducing the 'socialist ideal' exactly 'according to Marx' in Soviet Russia were issued long before the beginning of the Civil War (the decrees of Jan. 26 and Feb. 14, 1918, on the nationalization of the merchant fleet and of all banks),

while the last decree on the socialization of all small handicraftsmen and artisans was issued on Nov. 29, 1920, i.e., after the end of the Civil War in European Russia. Of course, the Civil War and the intervention left an imprint. But the main thing was something else – the immediate implementation of theory in strict accordance with Marx (from 'Critique of the Gotha Program') and Engels (from 'Anti-During').

See Sirotkin, 'Lessons of NEP,' *Izvestia* (9 March 1989), translated in *The Current Digest of the Soviet Press*, 41 (10) (5 April 1989): 6.

38 John Reed, *Ten Days that Shook the World* (New York: Penguin Books, 1985(1919)): 129. Also see Leon Trotsky, *The History of the Russian Revolution*, vol. 3 (London: Pathfinder, 1980(1932)), pp. 323–4.

39 'Program of the Communist Party of Soviet Russia,' in Nikolai Bukharin and E. A. Preobrazhensky, *The ABC of Communism* (Ann Arbor: University of Michigan Press, 1966(1919)), p. 390.

40 V. I. Lenin, *The Immediate Tasks of the Soviet Government* (1918), in *Collected Works*, vol. 27 (Moscow: Progress Publishing, 1977), p. 352.

41 *Program of the Communist Party of Soviet Russia*, 397. Also see the discussion of money and banking in Lenin's *Draft Programme of the RCP(B)* (1919), in *Collected Works*, vol. 29, p. 115 (see Note 40).

42 Bukharin and Preobrazhensky, *The ABC of Communism* (see Note 39), p. 77.

43 Stephen Cohen, *Bukharin and the Bolshevik Revolution* (New York: Oxford University Press, 1980(1973)), p. 123.

44 V. I. Lenin, *The New Economic Policy and the Tasks of the Political Education Departments* (1921), in *Collected Works*, vol. 33, pp. 63–4 (see Note 40).

45 The importance of the NEP is not limited to historical understanding, but is intimately connected to the Gorbachev reforms. Gorbachev described perestroika as a return to the NEP. As Theodore Draper wrote, 'This return to an NEP-type reform is particularly characteristic of the unfolding Gorbachev period; Gorbachev himself has invoked the precedent of the NEP, as if it gave him a license to do what he wants to do. Thus, we are not straying too far from the present in paying special attention to the NEP period. Nep-thinking is imbedded in the present.' Draper, 'Soviet reformers: from Lenin to Gorbachev,' *Dissent* (Summer 1987): 287.

46 V. I. Lenin, *Political Report of the Central Committee of the RCP(B)* (1922), in *Collected Works*, vol. 33, p. 289 (see Note 40).

47 V. I. Lenin, *Better Fewer, But Better* [1923], in *Collected Works*, vol. 33, p. 487 (see note 40).

48 Richard Day, *Leon Trotsky and the Economics of Isolation* (New York: Cambridge University Press, 1973), p. 69.

49 By 1938, Stalin had out-manipulated *all* of the original Bolshevik leaders. Of the original central committee of the Bolshevik Party in 1917, by 1938 only Stalin remained. See the dramatic picture detailing the fate of the Old Bolsheviks in *Spartacist*, 41–2 (Winter 1987–8): 38.

50 See, for example, Joseph Stalin, *Economic Problems of Socialism in the USSR*, 2nd edn (Moscow: Foreign Languages Publishing, 1953), pp. 104–

5, where he argued that the fact that since a considerable proportion of the collective farm output goes into the market and perpetuates the system of commodity circulation prevented the 'elevation of collective-farm property to the level of public property.' The goal of socialist policy, Stalin argued, must be to eliminate commodity production and institute a system of production for direct use. 'Such a system would require an immense increase in the goods allocated by the town to the country, and it would therefore have to be introduced without any particular hurry, and only as the products of the town multiply. But it must be introduced unswervingly and unhesitatingly, step by step contracting the sphere of operation of commodity circulation and widening the sphere of operation of products-exchange.'

51 See Michael Voslensky, *Nomenklatura* (New York: Doubleday, 1984), pp. 14–67.

52 Eugene Zaleski, *Stalinist Planning for Economic Growth, 1933–1952* (Chapel Hill: University of North Carolina Press, 1980), p. 484.

53 See Paul Craig Roberts, *Alienation and the Soviet Economy* (New York: Holmes and Meier, 1990(1971)), pp. 48–88, for the pioneering analytical study of the polycentric nature of the Soviet economy. Roberts derived and developed his ideas from the suggestive work of Michael Polanyi. See, in particular, Polanyi, *The Logic of Liberty* (Chicago: University of Chicago Press, 1980(1951)), pp. 111–37.

54 See Aleksander Bajt, 'Property in capital and in the means of production in socialist economies,' *Journal of Law and Economics*, 11 (April 1968): 1–4. Also see Svetozar Pejovich, *The Economics of Property Rights* (Boston: Kluwer, 1990), pp. 97–103, 115–20. In addition, see Jack Wiseman, 'Property rights and East European liberalisation,' *The Financial Times* (3 April 1990).

55 Selyunin, 'Sources,' *Novy Mir*, no. 5 (May 1988), translated in *The Current Digest of the Soviet Press*, 40 (40) (1988).

56 See Gregory Grossman, 'The "second economy" of the USSR,' *Problems of Communism* (1977), reprinted in Morris Bornstein (ed.) *The Soviet Economy: Continuity and Change* (Boulder, CO: Westview Press, 1981). Also see Grossman, 'Roots of Gorbachev's problems: private income and outlay in the late 1970s,' *Gorbachev's Economics Plans*, vol. 1 (Washington, DC: GPO, 1987), pp. 213–29. In addition, see F. J. M. Feldbrugge, 'The Soviet second economy in political and legal perspective,' in Edgar Feige (ed.) *The Underground Economies* (New York: Cambridge University Press, 1989) and G. Belikova and A. Shokhin, 'The black market: people, things and facts,' *Ogonek* (September 1987), translated in *Soviet Review*, 30 (3) (May–June 1989): 26–39.

57 W. H. Chamberlin, *The Russian Revolution*, vol. 2 (Princeton: Princeton University Press, 1987(1935)), p. 105.

58 See Gary Anderson, 'Profits from power: the Soviet economy as a mercantilist state,' *The Freeman*, 38 (12) (December 1988): 483–92.

59 Leonid Abalkin, 'Relying on the lessons of the past,' *Kommunist*, 16 (1987), translated in *Problems of Economics* (June 1988): 7, 11, 15.

60 See the classic discussion of the distinction in John Stuart Mill, *Principles of Political Economy* (New York: Augustus M. Kelley, 1848(1976)),

pp. 199ff. Mill argued that while the laws of production are governed by nature, the laws of distribution are solely a matter of human institutions.

61 See the analysis of Joseph Schumpeter, 'The crisis of the tax state,' in Richard Swedberg (ed.) *The Economics and Sociology of Capitalism* (Princeton: Princeton University Press, 1990(1918)), pp. 99–140. Also see David Prychitko, 'The welfare state: what is left?,' *Critical Review*, 4 (4) (Fall 1990): 623–5.

62 Alain Besancon, 'Anatomy of a spectre,' *Survey*, 25 (4) (Autumn 1980): 156–8.

63 Mikhail Gorbachev, *Political Report of the CPSU Central Committee to the 27th Party Congress* (Moscow: Novosti Press Agency, 1986), p. 6.

64 Mikhail Gorbachev, *Perestroika* (New York: Harper & Row, 1987), p. 17.

65 See Tatyana Zaslavskaya, 'The Novosibirsk Report,' *Survey*, 28 (1) (Spring 1984): 106.

66 See Abel Aganbegyan, *The Economic Challenge of Perestroika* (Bloomington: Indiana University Press, 1988), pp. 1–44.

67 See Abel Aganbegyan, 'Acceleration and perestroika,' in Aganbegyan and Timofeyev, *The New Stage of Perestroika* (New York: Institute for East–West Security Studies, 1988), p. 26.

68 See Zbigniew Brzezinski, *The Grand Failure* (New York: Simon & Schuster, 1988), pp. 263ff.

69 Gertrude Schroeder, *The System Versus Progress* (London: Centre for Research into Communist Economies, 1986), p. 75.

70 See Paul Craig Roberts and Karen LaFollet, *Meltdown: Inside the Soviet Economy* (Washington, DC: CATO Institute, 1990), pp. 39–74, for a discussion of the plight of Soviet consumers.

71 Nick Eberstadt, *The Poverty of Communism* (New Brunswick: Transaction Publishers, 1988), p. 50.

72 Francine du Plessix Gray, *Soviet Women: Walking the Tightrope* (New York: Doubleday, 1989), pp. 13–27.

73 Marshall Goldman, *USSR in Crisis* (New York: Norton, 1983), p. 99.

74 David Willis, *Klass: How Russians Really Live* (New York: Avon Books, 1985), p. 59.

75 Konstantin Simis, *The Corrupt Society* (New York: Simon & Schuster, 1982), p. 299.

76 Gorbachev, *Perestroika*, p. 51 (see Note 64).

77 Gorbachev, *Perestroika*, pp. 51–2 (see Note 64).

78 Selyunin, 'Sources,' p. 17 (see Note 55).

79 Nikolai Shmelev, 'Economics and common sense,' *Znamia* (July 1988), translated in *Problems of Economics* (March 1989): 58.

80 Vasily Selyunin, 'A profound reform or the revenge of the bureaucracy?,' *Znamia* (July 1988), translated in *Problems of Economics* (March 1989): 31.

81 For a 'conservative' defense of the Soviet regime see Nina Andreyeva, 'Polemics: I cannot waive principles,' in Isaac Tarasulo (ed.) *Gorbachev and Glasnost* (Wilmington: Scholarly Resources, 1989), pp. 277–90. Andreyeva's letter generated much controversy when it was published in *Sovetskaya Rossiya* on 13 March 1988 and solicited responses from

Gorbachev and his supporters in the pages of *Pravda* on 5 April 1988. In addition, in a poll conducted in the Soviet Union in November of 1989 40 per cent of those polled stated that they wished to see a return of a 'strong hand' and to the old system of economic management. See *The New York Times* (5 November 1989). However, there have been some important questions raised concerning the validity of the poll. See Aleksandras Shtromas, 'Russia on the road to political and economic freedom,' in Richard Ebeling (ed.) *Austrian Economics: Perspectives on the Past and Prospects for the Future* (Hillsdale: Hillsdale College Press, 1991), p. 236.

82 'Perhaps the most painful legacy of all,' Gertrude Schroeder argued, 'rests in the inherited values, attitudes, and habits of the work force. For decades, people have been taught that private property means exploitation and that socialism means a welfare state, an egalitarian distribution of income, permanent job security, and low prices for the basic necessities of life. In other words, people have learned to let the government take care of them. But successful perestroika requires a virtual renunciation of such attitudes and values; it requires "new thinking" and a "new psychology" as Gorbachev often puts it.' See Gertrude Schroeder, 'The Soviet economy: is perestroika possible?,' *The World and I* (November 1989): 55.

83 See Marshall Goldman, *What Went Wrong with Perestroika* (New York: Norton, 1991), p. 116, for a discussion of the 'envy' effect toward private farmers during the Gorbachev regime. Goldman, however, argues that the hostility toward private trade is not solely a legacy of communist indoctrination, but is deeply rooted in the Russian culture. While undoubtedly cultural factors matter, one of the main propositions that will emerge from my argument in this book is that institutional rules are a much greater force in determining economic performance than either the endowment of natural resources or the cultural heritage of a country.

84 See Mikhail Gorbachev's interview in *Komsomolskaya Pravda* (24 December 1991), translated in *The Current Digest of the Soviet Press*, 43 (51) (22 January 1992): 7–8.

85 See Mikhail Gorbachev's formal response to the ethnic unrest in response to the fiftieth anniversary of the Stalin–Hitler Pact in *The Current Digest of the Soviet Press*, 41 (34): 1–9, (38): 5–10. Also consider the 'Tbilisi crackdown' on 8 April 1989 where Soviet troops were sent in using sharpened shovels and lethal gas to restore order and ended up killing 20 and poisoning 1,000 people. See Peter Reddaway, 'The threat to Gorbachev,' *New York Review of Books* (17 August 1989): 21. Also the events following the Lithuania declaration of independence in March 1990 demonstrated the ambiguity within Gorbachev's domestic political policy.

86 See, for example, the report by Bill Keller in *The New York Times* (25 April 1990): A7, on the decision by the Gorbachev regime not to follow Poland's example of 'shock therapy' and to postpone fundamental economic reform. Also see *The Financial Times* (23 May 1990): 2, 4.

87 Alice Gorlin, 'The Soviet economy,' *Current History*, 85 (October 1986): 325–8; 343–5.

88 Gorbachev, *Perestroika*, p. 86 (see Note 64). The complete text of the Law on the State Enterprises was published in *Pravda* (1 July 1987) and translated in *The Current Digest of the Soviet Press*, 39 (30) (1987): 8–13, 24, and 39 (31) (1989): 10–27, 28. Also see the analysis of the law by Richard Ericson, 'The New Enterprise Law,' *The Harriman Institute Forum*, 1 (2) (February 1988).

89 See the report by John Lloyd in *The Financial Times* (25 April 1990) that Nikolai Petrakov, Gorbachev's personal economic advisor at that time, blamed communism for the decision to delay market reforms.

90 See David Lascelles, 'After the great lie, the ghastly truth,' *The Financial Times* (9 March 1990): 19, for a description of economic life inside the Soviet Union five years after the rise of Gorbachev.

91 Aganbegyan, *The Economic Challenge of Perestroika*, pp. 133–5 (see Note 66).

92 Anders Aslund, *Gorbachev's Struggle for Economic Reform* (Ithaca: Cornell University Press, 1989), p. 185, argues that it would be inappropriate to refer to the reforms as Gorbachev's reforms because all reform laws emerge as a compromise package. 'The overall conclusion,' Aslund states, 'is that Gorbachev pushes energetically for reform, but does not control its design. The Soviet Union is actually governed by a truly collective leadership. Therefore it is not very accurate to talk about "Gorbachev's economic reforms." '

93 See Abalkin, 'The radical economic reform: top priority, tasks and long-term measures,' *Ekonomicheskaya Gazeta*, 43 (October 1989), translated in *The Current Digest of the Soviet Press*, 41 (46) (13 December 1989): 10–15, 39–40.

94 Earlier Ryzhkov had proposed a program which would have slashed state ownership from 85 per cent to 30 per cent. See *The New York Times* (17 November 1989): A16. But on Wednesday 13 December 1989, Prime Minister Ryzhkov delivered a speech, that represented the official position on perestroika, which undermined the earlier movement toward a market economy and was seen as a clear victory for GOSPLAN. See Ryzhkov, 'Efficiency, consolidation, and reform are the path to a healthy economy,' *Pravda* (14 December 1989), translated in *The Current Digest of the Soviet Press*, 41 (51) (17 January 1990): 1–9. Also see *The Financial Times* (15 December 1989): 18.

95 See *The Financial Times* (20 March 1990): 18 and Ed Hewett, 'Prognosis for Soviet economy is grave, but improving,' *New York Times* (25 March 1990) for a discussion of the promise of radical market reforms.

96 See the *Investor's Daily* (2 April 1990): 10, for a report of Vyacheslav Senchagov, chief of the State Price Committee, speech to the deputies of the Supreme Soviet. He suggested that the Soviet Union would follow Poland's 'shock therapy' approach, but added that such a plan may be blocked by angry consumers. Therefore, while a radical approach would be preferred, a more moderate approach may be pursued during the transition to maintain the population's confidence.

97 See Ed Hewett and Richard Hornik, 'Hurry, doctor,' *Time* (7 May 1990): 84–7, for a criticism of Gorbachev's decision to back off from radical reform in the spring of 1990.

98 Abel Aganbegyan, *Inside Perestroika* (New York: Harper & Row, 1989).

99 See *The Current Digest of the Soviet Press*, 41 (40) (1 November 1989).

100 See Alfred Kahn and Merton Peck, 'Price deregulation, corporatization, competition,' in Merton Peck and Thomas Richardson (eds) *What Is To Be Done?*, p. 43 (see Note 32).

101 See Goldman, *What Went Wrong with Perestroika*, p. 110 (see Note 83). The adverse reputational effect of Gorbachev's indecision and inconsistency will be discussed at length in Chapter 6.

102 See Padma Desai, *Perestroika in Perspective* (Princeton: Princeton University Press, 1989), p. 53.

103 This argument is more fully developed in Gary Anderson and Peter Boettke, 'Perestroika and public choice: the economics of autocratic succession in a rent-seeking society,' *Public Choice* (1992), forthcoming.

104 See William Odom, 'How far can economic and social change go in the Soviet Union?,' in Ronald Liebowitz (ed.) *Gorbachev's New Thinking* (Cambridge, MA: Ballinger Publishing, 1988), p. 86.

105 See Marjorie Brady, 'The Fascist element in perestroika,' *The Wall Street Journal* (31 October 1989).

106 *Izvestia* (17 October 1990), for example, reported that with an official poverty line set at 78 roubles/month, 40 million lived in poverty. If the poverty line was raised to 100 roubles/month, it estimated that the figure would be 70.9 million.

107 Yuri Maltsev, 'Foreword,' in Peter Boettke, *The Political Economy of Soviet Socialism: The Formative Years, 1918–1928* (Boston: Kluwer, 1990).

108 See F. A. Lutz, 'The German currency reform and the revival of the German economy,' *Economica*, 16 (May 1949): 122–42, Henry Wallich, *Mainsprings of the German Revival* (New Haven, CT: Yale University Press, 1955) and Egon Sohmen, 'Competition and growth: the lesson of West Germany,' *American Economic Review* (1959): 986–1003. An interesting note, however, is that the majority of the economics profession viewed the Erhard reforms with great caution. See, for example, Horst Mendershausen, 'Prices, money and the distribution of goods in postwar Germany,' *American Economic Review*, 39 (June 1949): 646–72, and Walter Heller, 'The role of fiscal-monetary policy in German economic recovery,' *American Economic Review*, 40 (May 1950): 531–47. Also see the discussion in T. W. Hutchison, *The Politics and Philosophy of Economics* (New York: New York University Press, 1981): 155–75.

109 Alvin Rabushka, *The New China* (Boulder, CO: Westview Press, 1987).

110 Hernando DeSoto, *The Other Path* (New York: Harper & Row, 1989).

111 See Walter Laqueur, *The Long Road to Freedom* (New York: Charles Scribner's, 1989), p. 203.

112 As quoted in Hedrick Smith, *The New Russians* (New York: Random House, 1990), p. 185.

3 THE THEORETICAL PROBLEMS OF SOCIALISM

1 Alexander Tsipko, *Is Stalinism Really Dead?* (New York: Harper Collins, 1990), p. 12.

2 Ludwig von Mises, *Socialism* (Indianapolis: Liberty Classics, 1981(1922)) p. 41.

3 Mikhail Gorbachev, for example, has even recently reiterated the standard socialist and Western Marxist argument that the Soviet collapse had nothing to do with socialist ideas, but rather represented the collapse of Stalinism. See Gorbachev, 'No time for stereotypes,' *New York Times* (24 February 1992): A19. On the intellectual staying power of Marxism in the face of recent events see Henry F. Myers, '*Das Kapital*, his statues topple, his shadow persists: Marx can't be ignored,' *The Wall Street Journal* (25 November 1991): A1 and A4.

4 Tspiko, *Is Stalinism Really Dead?*, p. 12 (see Note 1).

5 For an extensive history of Marxism see Leszek Zolakowski, *Main Currents of Marxism*, 3 vols (New York: Oxford University Press, 1985(1978)). On Marx's project see Andrzej Walicki, 'Karl Marx as philosopher of freedom,' *Critical Review*, 2 (4) (Fall 1988): 10–58.

6 See Don Lavoie, *Rivalry and Central Planning* (New York: Cambridge University Press, 1985), pp. 29–30.

7 Karl Marx, *Capital* (New York: Modern Library, 1906(1867)), p. 92.

8 Alan Ryan, 'Socialism for the nineties,' *Dissent* (Fall 1990): 441–2, (emphasis added).

9 David L. Prychitko has argued that the organizational logic of even the most decentralized and democratic socialism leads to centralization during the process of resolving the conflicts of alternative requests for resource use. See Prychitko, 'Marxism and decentralized socialism,' *Critical Review*, 2 (4) (Fall 1988). Also see Prychitko, *Marxism and Workers' Self-Management: the Essential Tension* (Westport, CT: Greenwood Press, 1991), pp. 83–100.

10 For this reason it has been forcefully argued that the Lange–Lerner theoretical system did not provide an answer to Mises's critique of socialism. See Paul Craig Roberts, 'Oskar Lange's theory of socialist planning,' *Journal of Political Economy*, 79 (3) (May/June 1971): 562–77; Karen Vaughn, 'Economic calculation under socialism: the Austrian contribution,' *Economic Inquiry*, 18 (1980): 535–54; Peter Murrell, 'Did the theory of market socialism answer the challenge of Ludwig von Mises?,' *History of Political Economy*, 15 (1) (Spring 1983): 92–105; and Lavoie, *Rivalry and Central Planning*. Also see Larissa Popkova-Pijasheva, 'Why is the Plan incompatible with the market?,' *Annals*, 507 (January 1990): 80–90, and Anthony deJasay, *Market Socialism* (London: IEA, 1990), for criticisms of the logical coherence of market socialism.

11 Kornai, *The Road to a Free Economy* (New York: Norton, 1990), p. 58.

12 Adam Smith did possess a germ of the argument when he stated that:

> What is species of domestic industry which his capital can employ, and of which the produce is likely to be of the greatest value, every individual, it is evident can, in his local situation, judge much better

than any statesman, or lawgiver can do for him. The statesman, who should attempt to direct private people in what manner they ought to employ their capitals, would not only load himself with a most unnecessary attention, but assume an authority which could safely be trusted, not only to no single person, but to no council or senate whatever, and which would nowhere be so dangerous as in the hands of a man who had folly and presumption enough to fancy himself fit to exercise it.

See *The Wealth of Nations* (New York: Modern Library, 1937), p. 423. Also see his discussion of how the coordination of the number of individuals that must act in concert with one another even to produce common products 'exceeds all computation' (Ibid., p. 11).

13 Mises, *Socialism*, p. 186 (see Note 2).
14 Mises, *The Theory of Money and Credit* (Indianapolis: Liberty Classics, 1980(1912)), p. 153.
15 Mises, *Socialism*, p. 101 (see Note 2).
16 Mises, *The Theory o, Money and Credit*, p. 62 (see Note 14).
17 Mises, *Socialism*, p. 187 (see Note 2).
18 Mises, *Socialism*, p. 191 (see Note 2).
19 See F. A. Hayek, *Individualism and Economic Order* (Chicago: University of Chicago Press, 1980(1948)) for his classic papers on this issue, and *The Fatal Conceit* (Chicago: University of Chicago Press, 1988) for his most recent statement on the issue.
20 Hayek, *The Road to Serfdom* (Chicago: University of Chicago Press, 1976(1944)), pp. 134–52.
21 Don Lavoie, *National Economic Planning: What is Left?* (Cambridge, MA: Ballinger Publishing, 1985), p. 201.
22 Aristotle, *The Politics*, Stephen Everson (ed.) (New York: Cambridge University Press, 1988), p. 26. Also see Svetozar Pejovich, *The Economics of Property Rights: Towards a Theory of Comparative Systems* (Boston: Kluwer, 1990).
23 V. Pareto, *Manual of Political Economy* (New York: Augustus M. Kelley, 1971(1927)), p. 171. Also see Michael Polanyi, 'The span of central control,' in *The Logic of Liberty* (Chicago: University of Chicago Press, 1980(1951)), p. 111, where he argues that:

I affirm that the central planning of production – in the rigorous and historically not unwarranted sense of the term – is strictly impossible; the reason being that the number of relations requiring adjustment per unit of time for the functioning of an economic system of n productive units is n-times greater than can be adjusted by subordinating the units to a central authority.

24 This was basically Oskar Lange's last argument in the calculation debate. As he wrote:

Were I to rewrite my essay today, my task would be much simpler. My answer to Hayek and Robbins would be: so what's the trouble? Let us put the simultaneous equations on an electronic computer and we shall obtain the solution in less than a second. The market process with its cumbersome tatonnements appears old-fashioned. Indeed, it may be considered as a computing device of the pre-electronic age.

See Lange, 'The computer and the market,' in C. H. Feinstein (ed.) *Socialism, Capitalism and Economic Growth: Essays Presented to Maurice Dobb* (New York: Cambridge University Press, 1967), p. 158. See Don Lavoie, 'Computation, incentives, and discovery: the cognitive function of markets in market socialism,' *Annals*, 507 (January 1990), pp. 72–9, for a rebuttal of Lange's argument.

25 As Mises pointed out: 'The attributes of the business man cannot be divorced from the position of the entrepreneur in the capitalist order. . . . An entrepreneur deprived of his characteristic role in economic life ceases to be a business man. However much experience and routine he may bring to his new task he will still only be an official in it.' (Refer *Socialism*, pp. 190–1, see Note 2.)

26 The problems of time inconsistency and credible commitments will be addressed in Chapter 6.

27 This does not mean that economists must model political actors as *homo economicus* or wealth maximizing agents. Rather, a loose form of self-interest and rationality is all that is needed to discuss the logic of the situation. Agents have ends and they arrange their means to attain those ends. The ends could include ideological pursuits, high ideals or monetary reward. What matters for economic analysis is the implications for the analysis of market and political processes that follow from viewing individuals as purposive actors. In addition, this position also aids policy debate because the economist can treat ends as given and simply examine whether the means chosen to attain the end were effective or not. Such a position of value freedom may prove helpful in overcoming conflicts of ultimate values in analyzing alternative policies.

28 Not only is there a logic behind the totalitarian tendency of socialist planning, David Levy has also raised an interesting question concerning the socialist planners' incentives in setting 'prices' to allocate scarce resources. 'If the central planner,' Levy argues, 'has the legal right both to set prices, and to allocate whatever shortages might exist from time to time, then perhaps the rational economic planner will set prices below market clearing.' In other words, the centrally planned price will be a biased estimator of the value of the marginal product of any resource for the simple reason that since the wealth created by planners can be appropriated by planners we should expect them to set the official price below the market clearing level and artificially restrict output – in effect, raising the implicit price to the monopoly level and reaping the scarcity rent. See Levy, 'The bias in centrally planned prices,' *Public Choice*, 67 (3) (December 1990), pp. 216–17.

29 Very interesting discussions of the growth of government intervention and its effect on the US political economy can be found in Robert Higgs, *Crisis and Leviathan* (New York: Oxford University Press, 1987) and Richard Wagner, *To Promote the General Welfare* (San Francisco: Pacific Institute, 1989).

30 Hayek, 'Foreword,' in Boris Brutzkus, *Economic Planning in Soviet Russia* (Westport, CT: Hyperion Press, 1981(1935)), pp. viii–ix.

4 THE NATURE OF THE SOVIET-TYPE SYSTEM

1 H. L. Mencken, 'Capitalism' (1935), in *A Mencken Chrestomathy* (New York: Vintage Books, 1982), pp. 296–7.
2 See, for example, H. H. Ticktin, 'Towards a political economy of the USSR,' *Critique*, 1 (Spring 1973): 20–41, and 'The class structure of the USSR and the elite,' *Critique*, 9 (Spring/Summer 1978): 37–61.
3 See Paul Gregory and Robert Stuart, *Soviet Economic Structure and Performance*, 3rd edn (New York: Harper and Row, 1986), pp. 155–214. In the leading textbook on the Soviet economic system discussion of the second economy is limited to less than two pages (pp. 203–4). And, in the discussion of price setting, reliance on world market prices is limited to one line (p. 195).
4 For a discussion of the debate concerning the conceptualization of the Soviet system as centrally planned see Igor Birman, 'From the achieved level,' *Soviet Studies*, 30 (2) (April 1978): 153–72, J. Wilhelm, 'Does the Soviet Union have a planned economy? A comment on "From the achieved level",' *Soviet Studies*, 31 (2) (April 1979): 268–74, Alec Nove, 'Does the Soviet Union have a planned economy? A comment,' *Soviet Studies*, 32 (1) (January 1980): 135–7 and John Wilhelm, 'The Soviet Union has an administered, not a planned economy,' *Soviet Studies*, 37 (1) (January 1985): 118–30.
5 See Ludwig von Mises, *Planned Chaos* (1947), reprinted as epilogue in *Socialism: An Economic and Sociological Analysis* (Indianapolis: Liberty Classics, 1981(1922)), pp. 479–540; *Omnipotent Government: The Rise of the Total State and Total War* (Spring Mills, PA: Libertarian Press, 1985(1944)), pp. 55–8; *Human Action*, 3rd rev. edn (Chicago: Henry Regnery, 1966), pp. 717–19.
6 The most important notable exception to this was Ed Hewett, *Reforming the Soviet Economy* (Washington, DC: Brookings Institution, 1988), pp. 94–220, where he contrasts how the system was designed to operate with how it actually operated in practice. As Hewett states: 'An analysis of the potential effect of reforms on the system must rest on an understanding of how those reforms will interact with the system as it actually functions, rather than as it is supposed to function' (p. 153).
7 For a detailed discussion of the institutions of Soviet planning implemented in the first years following the revolution see Silvana Malle, *The Economic Organization of War Communism, 1918–1921* (New York: Cambridge University Press, 1985) and Thomas Remington, *Building Socialism in Bolshevik Russia: Ideology and Industrial Organization, 1917–1921* (Pittsburgh: University of Pittsburgh Press, 1984). For an interpretative examination of the formation of the Soviet political economy see Peter Boettke, *The Political Economy of Soviet Socialism: The Formative Years, 1918–1928* (Boston: Kluwer, 1990).
8 See J. M. Montias, 'Planning with material balances in Soviet-type economies,' *American Economic Review*, 49 (4) (1959): 963–85. Montias argued that while some, such as the German economist Walter Eucken, had challenged the efficacy of centralized economic planning, analysts should not forget that static efficiency is not the be-all and end-all of planning. 'The Soviet system with all its compulsion and waste is a vehicle for high

rates of growth. To some extent, a higher rate of growth than might otherwise be feasible makes up for short-run inefficiencies' (p. 982). As was argued in Chapter 2, however, the higher rate of growth was only an illusion.

9 See Peter Rutland, *The Myth of the Plan: Lessons of the Soviet Planning Experience* (LaSalle, IL: Open Court, 1985), pp. 101–67.

10 See Alain Besancon, *The Soviet Syndrome* (New York: Harcourt Brace Jovanovich, 1978), pp. 87–103.

11 See Israel Kirzner, *The Meaning of Market Process* (London: Routledge, 1992), pp. 139–62. Kirzner argues that one cannot solve the problem of dispersed information by postulating equilibrium prices. The ability of the price system to coordinate the plans of participants, in fact, does not lie in the hypothetical system of equilibrium, nor in the accuracy of the information conveyed by equilibrium prices. Rather, the price system coordinates economic plans through the ability of disequilibrium prices to offer opportunities for pure profit to economic actors. When market participants experience plan failure this is expressed in an array of prices that alerts economic actors to the possibilities of pure profit. The price system, through a process of error detection and the lure of pure profit, motivates economic actors to learn how better to coordinate their plans with those of other market participants.

12 For a discussion of the problems that 'shirking' presents to economic organizations see Armen Alchian and Harold Demsetz, 'Production, information costs and economic organization' (1972), in Armen Alchian, *Economic Forces at Work* (Indianapolis: Liberty Press, 1977), pp. 73–110.

13 On the problems that superiors face in coordinating the activities of subordinates within and between bureaus within the bureaucratic hierarchy see Gordon Tullock, *The Politics of Bureaucracy* (Lanham, MD: University Press of America, 1987(1965)), pp. 120–220.

14 See Paul Gregory, *Restructuring the Soviet Economic Bureaucracy* (New York: Cambridge University Press, 1990), pp. 13–24, for a discussion of the principal/agent problem applied to the Soviet situation. My analysis differs from Gregory because despite his employment of the principal/agent literature he maintains a 'public interest' view of the Soviet leadership by claiming that the leadership was concerned with the obtainment of economic goals at the least cost of society's resources, whereas I want to jettison the public interest view of the Soviet leadership. Ed Hewett also implicitly maintains a public interest view when he states that he 'assumes that Soviet leaders are most interested in the growth rate of national income, of labor productivity (which is closely related), and of living standards.' However, this assumption prevents him from satisfying one of the main goals in his study – to develop a successful explanation of the reform process which is built on 'a good theory of the politics of economic reform.' See Hewett, *Reforming the Soviet Economy*, pp. 10 and 238 (see Note 6).

15 See John H. More, 'Agency costs, technological change and Soviet central planning,' *Journal of Law and Economics*, 24 (2) (October 1981): 189–214. Also see Arye Hillman and Adi Schnytzer, 'Illegal economic activities and purges in a Soviet-type economy: a rent-seeking perspective,' *Interna-*

tional Review of Law and Economics, 6 (1986): 87–99, Jan Winiecki, 'Large industrial enterprises in Soviet-type economies: the ruling stratum's main rent-seeking area,' *Communist Economies*, 1 (4) (1989): 363–83, Gary Anderson and Peter Boettke, 'Perestroika and public choice: autocratic succession in a rent-seeking society,' *Public Choice* (1992), forthcoming and Gary Anderson and Peter Boettke, 'Socialist venality: a rent-seeking model of the Soviet-style economy,' mimeo (1992).

16 On the importance of the economic monopoly to Soviet power see Olimpiad Ioffe, *Gorbachev's Economic Dilemma* (St Paul: Merril/Magnus Publishing, 1989), p. 4. 'The Soviet system,' Ioffe argues, 'consists of two essential ingredients: unlimited political power of the ruling elite and economic monopoly by the same elite as the source of its unlimited power. If either of these elements is eliminated, the Soviet system will have been replaced by another system.'

17 Though universally accepted, the idea that centralization during wartime or emergency is unequivocally desirable is also questionable. Take the example of labor mobilization in wartime. Undoubtedly the military draft allocates labor quickly, but it does so in a very costly manner. Certainly the draft hides the cost of fighting the war to the taxpayer, but the opportunity cost associated with the draft is quite high. In other words, the military draft does not reduce the cost of mobilizing labor for the war. The draft simply transfers the cost burden of maintaining the military from taxpayers to draftees. For a discussion of the argument for centralization in emergency situations see Patrick Bolton and Joseph Farrell, 'Decentralization, duplication and delay,' *Journal of Political Economy*, 98 (4) (1990). Bolton and Farrell, however, do not address the question from an opportunity cost perspective. For an examination of the implications for economic reasoning of consistently pursuing the opportunity cost logic see Philip Wicksteed, 'The scope and method of political economy in light of the "marginal" theory of value and distribution' (1914), in *The Common Sense of Political Economy*, vol. 2 (London: Routledge, 1938), pp. 772–96; James Buchanan, *Cost and Choice: An Inquiry in Economic Theory* (Chicago: University of Chicago Press, 1978(1969)); and James Buchanan and G. F. Thirlby (eds) *LSE Essays on Cost* (New York: New York University Press, 1981(1973)).

18 The Soviet system represented an institutional innovation which provided the ruling elite with a high degree of security against the competition of political entrants at the cost of reduced economic efficiency. The system proved to be one of the great political successes (in terms of protecting the rulers from competition) at the same time that it was perhaps the greatest economic failure of the twentieth century.

19 Soviet economic history is in some sense the history of economic reform attempts. While the leaders claimed great achievements, they constantly sought to reform the system in a manner which corrected the failure, but maintained the illusion. 'War communism' (1918–21) sought to establish the Marxist utopia overnight, but led instead to the utter collapse of the Russian economy. The Bolsheviks were forced to retreat from their original ideological position concerning the transition to socialism and introduce market liberalizations in order to maintain political power. The

New Economic Policy of the 1920s, however, gave way to the collectivization and industrialization of the 1930s. The Second World War was followed by a post-war reconstruction. The late 1950s and early 1960s were characterized by Khrushchev's attempts at political liberalization and economic reform. The much discussed Liberman reforms of the mid-1960s attempted to introduce profit incentives in state enterprises. In the 1970s, Brezhnev introduced industrial reforms to no avail. Finally, with the Gorbachev reforms the myth of Soviet industrial strength was challenged by the leadership. But, even with Gorbachev's reforms the idea was never to reject the 'socialist choice' of October 1917. The original Gorbachev reforms were conceived as improvements in the administrative procedures of economic planning – to enforce strict labor discipline and accelerate industrial development. Superministries and superagencies were created to improve the techniques and efficiency of state economic planning and an anti-alcohol campaign was pursued to eliminate drunkenness and sloth among workers. Leonid Abalkin, *The Strategy of Economic Development in the USSR* (Moscow: Progress Publishers, 1987) and Abel Aganbegyan, *The Economic Challenge of Perestroika* (Bloomington, IN: Indiana University Press, 1988) give a pretty clear account of the original economic philosophy behind the Gorbachev reforms.

20 The classic paper on the *de facto* Soviet economy is Gregory Grossman, 'The "second economy" of the USSR' (1977), in Morris Bornstein (ed.) *The Soviet Economy: Continuity and Change* (Boulder, CO: Westview Press, 1981), pp. 71–93. Also see the discussion of the different 'colored markets' that were in operation in the former Soviet Union in Aron Katsenelinboigen and Herbert Levine, 'Market and plan, plan and market: the Soviet case,' in Moris Bornstein (ed.) *The Soviet Economy*, pp. 61–70.

21 See Hewett, *Reforming the Soviet Economy*, p. 155 (see Note 6). Also see Joseph Berliner, *Factory and Manager in the USSR* (Cambridge: Harvard University Press, 1957), pp. 207–30.

22 See Hedrick Smith, *The Russians* (New York: Quadrangle, 1976). One of the most important features of Smith's book was his insistence on exploring the *sub-rosa* existence of Soviet counter-society. Soviet citizens, Smith points out, were masters at lying low. The scientific ban on genetics under Stalin and Khrushchev did not stamp out research in genetics, rather scientists secretly keep their science alive. Cybernetics had a similar history. Rock and jazz music, while publicly condemned, nevertheless flourished in underground clubs and music studios. Many of the most interesting cultural and intellectual developments were going on in a private and secret world hidden from officials and foreigners.

23 See Ludmilla Alexeyeva, *Soviet Dissent: Contemporary Movements for National, Religious, and Human Rights* (Middletown, CT: Wesleyan University Press, 1985).

24 See Boris Yeltsin, *Against the Grain* (New York: Summit Books, 1990), pp. 157–68, for a discussion of some of the privileges accorded to those on the top of the political pyramid. Also see David Willis, *Klass: How Russians Really Live* (New York: Avon Books, 1985).

25 Ferenc Feher, Agnes Heller and Gyorgy Markus, *Dictatorship over Needs: An Analysis of Soviet Societies* (New York: Basil Blackwell, 1983),

pp. 98–105, argue that there were 'three economies' in operation. The first economy was the official planned economy. The second economy was the unofficial economy on the consumption side, and the third economy was the unofficial economy on the production side. The second and third economies, however, existed only to fill in the gaps of the first economy. Moreover, these economies were interconnected with the second linking up to the first through the third.

26 Perhaps the most prevalent alternative method of rationing goods and service in the former Soviet Union was *blat*. The word implies the use of personal influence to obtain goods and service that one is not formally entitled. The prevalence of *blat* in Soviet economic life was expressed in common sayings. In the 1950s, for example, a common expression was: 'Blat is higher than Stalin.' (Refer Berliner, *Factory and Management in the USSR*, pp. 182–206, see Note 21.)

27 See Mark Thorton, *The Economics of Prohibition* (Salt Lake City: University of Utah Press, 1992). The Gorbachev anti-alcohol campaign produced the same undesirable effects as did other periods of prohibition. No sooner had state controls on the production and sale of alcohol been imposed, than a *samogon* (moonshine) industry arose to meet consumer demand. For a discussion of some of the unintended consequences of the anti-alcohol campaign see Anders Aslund, *Gorbachev's Struggle for Economic Reform* (Ithaca, NY: Cornell University Press, 1989), pp. 75–6, and Marshall Goldman, *What Went Wrong With Perestroika* (New York: Norton, 1991), pp. 137–8.

28 Milton and Rose Friedman, *Tyranny of the Status Quo* (New York: Harcourt Brace Jovanovich, 1984), pp. 137–41, extend the argument to argue against current drug laws in the US.

29 The lack of a well-established alternative supply network for scarce resources meant that 'theft' from the state sector was the major supply system for the unofficial economy. Diverting resources from the state sector into the market system also continued with the development of cooperatives under Gorbachev. In fact, the lack of a viable alternative supply network made the cooperatives simultaneously dependent on the official supply system and vulnerable to the criminal element in order to protect those supplies accrued through 'illegal' diversion of goods from the state sector.

30 See, for example, Lenin, *Political Report of the Central Committee of the R.C.P.(B.)* (27 March 1922), *Collected Works*, vol. 33 (Moscow: Progress Publishers, 1980), pp. 263–309. Lenin's basic argument was that communists in the socialist sector had yet to learn how to manage the economy correctly. They had everything at their disposal in terms of power and resources, but they lacked ability. Responsible communists must learn the ABCs of business and management. If they fail to learn how to manage the economy properly, then they will fail in their test against private capital. The 'last and decisive battle' must be won in the competition between the socialist sector and private capital. Nikolai Bukharin argued that 'if the tendencies of capitalist growth gain the upper hand over the tendencies to improve large industry, then we are doomed.' See Bukharin, 'The New Economic Policy of Soviet Russia,' in Lenin, Bukharin and

Rutgers, *The New Policies of Soviet Russia* (Chicago: Charles H. Kerr, 1921), p. 60. Trotsky represented the Bolshevik attitude on this question most clearly. He may have accepted the NEP as a necessary policy shift for the time, but he accepted market principles only tentatively. His firm conviction was that the superiority of industrial planning would eventually eliminate the anarchy of capitalist production within socialist competition. The success of the planning principle would spread to the entire market, swallowing and eliminating it. The success of large-scale planning under the NEP would lead to the liquidation of the NEP as an economic policy and its replacement with a full socialist policy. See Trotsky, 'Thesis on industry' (6 March 1923), in Robert V. Daniels (ed.) *A Documentary History of Communism*, vol. 1 (New York: Vintage, 1962), pp. 234–7. Also see Richard Day, *Leon Trotsky and the Economics of Isolation* (New York: Cambridge University Press, 1973), p. 82.

31 As Michael Polanyi argued, the Soviet central 'plan' was simply the meaningless aggregate of all the individual plans of enterprises. In other words, the Soviet plan was analogous to a chess captain announcing the aggregate moves of his players. But outside of the particular context of the game each individual player was engaged in such an aggregate statement of moves is meaningless and does not constitute a 'move in chess.' Similarly, stating the sum of output of two plants is no more meaningful than announcing the move of two castles in two separate games of chess. See Polanyi, 'The span of central direction,' in *The Logic of Liberty* (Chicago: University of Chicago Press, 1980(1951)), pp. 134–5.

32 See Don Lavoie, 'Political and economic illusions of socialism,' *Critical Review*, 1 (1) (1986–7): 1–35. Lavoie argues that a strict distinction must be drawn between power and control in political economy. The Soviet government possessed tremendous political power, but it did not control the Soviet economy. What really went on in the Soviet economy was a vast amount of government intervention into a polycentric order that economic officials did not (and could not) understand in the concrete detail necessary to plan the system. The economic system remained, fundamentally, out of their control despite the existence of almost unlimited political power. In some sense, then, the Soviet economy was not categorically different from the economies in the West. The difference was one of degree, not kind. The Western politician's claim to be steering the economy with fiscal, regulatory and monetary policy is no less of a façade covering up blind interventionism and justifying political power, than the Soviet façade of planning. The main difference between the West and the Soviet Union was the pervasiveness of Soviet interventionism.

33 Milovan Djilas, *The New Class: An Analysis of the Communist System* (New York: Praeger, 1957) and *The Unperfect Society: Beyond the New Class* (New York: Harcourt, Brace & World, 1969).

34 Ideology played a dominant role in the founding of the Soviet industrial structure, but after the purge of the old Bolsheviks by Stalin in the 1930s, the ideological influence waned considerably. The ideology led to the establishment of centralized institutions of economic planning, but the ideology was utopian, and, as such, could not be realized. The institutions of central planning were captured by the guardians of the new order who

directly benefited from their possession of instruments of political power over the economy.

35 For a historical treatment of the leading role of the Party in industrial planning see William Conyngham, *Industrial Management in the Soviet Union: The Role of the CPSU in Industrial Decision-Making, 1917-1970* (Stanford: Hoover Institution Press, 1973).

36 See, for example, the discussion in Vladimir Andrle, *Managerial Power in the Soviet Union* (Lexington, Mass.: Lexington Books, 1976), pp. 39-66.

37 See Michael Voslensky, *Nomenklatura: The Soviet Ruling Class, An Insider's Report* (New York: Doubleday, 1984), pp. 68-111.

38 Voslensky, *Nomenklatura*, pp. 127-8 (see Note 37).

39 I do not have space to establish the argument here, but I would assert that the entire equity/efficiency trade-off is mistaken. Income distribution over time tends to spread as individuals from different generations move within different income groups, provided they are not legally prevented from doing so by a rigid caste system. Socialist societies were both inequitable and inefficient. Competition in the free market tends to compel suppliers to increase the quality of their product and offer it at a lower price. Economic competition makes available to average citizens products that only the most wealthy individuals in the previous generation could afford. There simply is no inherent 'economic law' in the operation of competitive capitalism that leads to greater discrepancies in income. Efficiency gains bring with them the cheaper production of goods and services that otherwise would be more costly to produce.

40 For an examination of some of the related issues to recontracting see Paul Hauslohner, 'Gorbachev's social contract,' *Soviet Economy*, 3 (1) (1987): 54-89.

5 THE LOGIC OF POLITICS AND THE LOGIC OF REFORM

1 Alexis de Tocqueville, *The Old Regime and the French Revolution* (New York: Doubleday, 1955(1856)), p. 167.

2 For example, Adam Michnik has argued that:

If, after the dogmatic faith in the benefits of the planned economy, there comes an equally dogmatic faith in the benefits of the market, then we are in trouble ... [T]he market is not a self-activated mechanism that can replace the economic policy of the state . . . We know the difference between the market as it is seen by Milton Friedman and the market with a human face.

See Michnik, 'The two faces of Eastern Europe,' *The New Republic* (12 November 1990): 24.

3 As Ed Hewett points out, the problem that confronted GOSPLAN within the bureaucratic planning system of the Soviet Union was analogous to the bureaucratic problems within US Bureau of Budget. Both bureaucracies attempted to arrive at a consensus by mediating among the

competing claims of various interest groups. See Hewett, *Reforming the Soviet Economy* (Washington, DC: Brookings Institution, 1988), p. 121.

4 See James Buchanan and Richard Wagner, *Democracy in Deficit* (New York: Academic Press, 1977) for an analysis of the legacy of the Keynesian system of activist policy. Also see Charles Murray, *Losing Ground* (New York: Basic Books, 1984) for a discussion of the failure of social policy, James Bennett and Thomas DiLorenzo, *Underground Government: The Off-Budget Public Sector* (Washington, DC: Cato Institute, 1983) and *Destroying Democracy: How Government Funds Partisan Politics* (Washington, DC: Cato Institute, 1985) for an examination of fiscal policy and tax-funded politics. Also see Jeffrey Friedman, 'The new consensus: I. The Fukuyama thesis,' *Critical Review*, 3 (3–4) (Summer/Fall 1989): 373–410, and 'The new consensus: II. The democratic welfare state,' *Critical Review*, 4 (4) (Fall 1990): 633–708, for a discussion of the implications for political philosophy of continuities between 'first world' and 'second world' interventionism.

5 John Kenneth Galbraith, 'The rush to capitalism,' *The New York Review of Books* (25 October 1990): 51–2. Also see John Kenneth Galbraith, *The Culture of Contentment* (New York: Houghton Mifflin, 1992), where he argues that despite the myth of a *laissez-faire* revolution with Reagan, non-intervention has been highly selective. While government spending and activism has decreased in some areas, it has increased in others. Galbraith is quite accurate in his assessment of the situation with regard to the leading role of government in the US economy. The US economy is far from *laissez-faire* capitalism. In fact, the impact of government intervention is felt throughout the entire economic system.

6 For a theoretical explanation of the growth of government see Sam Peltzman, 'The growth of government,' *Journal of Law and Economics*, 23 (October 1980): 209–87. Peltzman explains the growth of government as the outcome of the incentive to use the political process to redistribute wealth. Counter-intuitively, he concludes, with empirical evidence across nations to support his claim, that with the greater equality of private income, the demand for political redistribution increases. In other words, the growth of the 'middle class' in the twentieth century, has been a major factor in the growth of government as this group became more capable of perceiving and articulating their interest in political redistribution. Also see George Stigler, 'Director's law of public income redistribution,' *Journal of Law and Economics*, 13 (April 1970): 1–10, for a discussion of the 'middle class' thesis. In addition, see Robert Higgs, *Crisis and Leviathan* (New York: Oxford University Press, 1987) for a discussion of the erosion of constitutional constraints in the twentieth century and the corresponding loss in economic freedom, and Richard Wagner, *To Promote the General Welfare* (San Francisco: Pacific Research Institute, 1989). Also see F. A. Hayek, *The Constitution of Liberty* (Chicago: University of Chicago Press, 1960) and *Law, Legislation and Liberty*, 3 vols (Chicago: University of Chicago Press, 1973–9) for a philosophical, legal and economic analysis of the failed attempt at constitutional democracy and suggestive proposals to correct the situation.

7 The classic work in the economic analysis of politics is James Buchanan

and Gordon Tullock, *The Calculus of Consent* (Ann Arbor: University of Michigan Press, 1962). Also see the discussion of the operation of democratic politics found in Murray Rothbard, *Man, Economy and State*, vol. 2 (Los Angeles: Nash Publishing, 1970(1962)), pp. 775-6 and *Power and Market* (Kansas City: Sheed, Andrews & McMeel, 1977), pp. 189-99.

8　See Alexander Hamilton, James Madison and John Jay, *Federalist Papers* (New York: New American Library, 1961(1788)), nos 10, 47-51. Also see the papers discussing this issue in James Gwartney and Richard Wagner (eds) *Public Choice and Constitutional Political Economy* (Greenwich, CT: JAI Press, 1988).

9　On the history of the Federal Reserve System see Murray Rothbard, 'The Federal Reserve as a cartelization device: the early years, 1913-1930,' in Barry Siegel (ed.) *Money in Crisis* (Cambridge, MA: Ballinger Publishing, 1984), pp. 89-136, and Gabriel Kolko, *The Triumph of Conservatism* (New York: The Free Press, 1963), pp. 139-58, 217-54. With regard to antitrust policy see Kolko, *The Triumph of Conservatism*, pp. 255-78, James Weinstein, *The Corporate Ideal in the Liberal State, 1900-1918* (Boston: Beacon Press, 1968), pp. 62-91 and Martin Sklar, *The Corporate Reconstruction of American Capitalism, 1890-1916* (New York: Cambridge University Press, 1988). Also see Dominick Armentano, *Antitrust and Monopoly* (New York: Wiley & Sons, 1982) and *Antitrust Policy* (Washington, DC: Cato Institute, 1986) and Thomas DiLorenzo, 'The origin of antitrust: an interest group perspective,' *International Review of Law and Economics*, 5 (1985): 73-90.

10　But, since these *de facto* owners did not have *de jure* ownership they could not reap capital gains from efficient resource use. As a result, they faced the same incentives that government and non-profit bureaucracies face in the West. For a discussion of the behavior of bureaus within a representative democracy see William Niskanen, *Bureaucracy and Representative Government* (Chicago: Aldine, 1971). Because of the principal/agent problem discussed in Chapter 4, bureaucratic inefficiencies can easily result. Bureaucracies exist in order to supply goods and services to the public, but they do not report directly to the consuming public of those services. Rather, bureaus report to elected officials, who in a frictionless political environment would represent the true preferences of the citizens. But, because of the existence of political 'failures,' such as rational abstention and rational ignorance, voter preferences are not conveyed in an unambiguous manner. The distortion allows bureaus to escape close monitoring by the citizens. Since bureaucrats cannot usually benefit monetarily from their bureaus' monopoly position as the sole supplier of some public service, they tend to reap those benefits in many other indirect ways. Perquisites at the office is one manifestation, but perhaps the main source of inefficiency is the incentive to maximize the bureaus' budget. In other words, bureau heads face an incentive to expand the size of their bureau well beyond what would be its optimal size, because the larger the bureau the more prestige, power, influence, reputation and opportunity for promotion.

11　For an analysis of these failures see James Buchanan, 'Our times: past, present and future,' in Martin J. Anderson (ed.) *The Unfinished Agenda:*

Essays on the Political Economy of Government Policy in Honour of Arthur Seldon (London: Institute for Economic Affairs, 1986), pp. 29–38, and 'Post-Reagan political economy,' in Alan Peacock (ed.) *Reaganomics and After* (London: Institute for Economic Affairs, 1989), pp. 1–16.

12 Anthony deJasay, *The State* (Oxford: Basil Blackwell, 1985), p. 232.

13 See Milton and Rose Friedman, *Tyranny of the Status Quo* (New York: Harcourt Brace Jovanovich, 1984), pp. 41–51.

14 See Racquel Fernandez and Dani Rodrik, 'Resistance to reform: status quo bias in the presence of individual-specific uncertainty,' *American Economic Review*, 81 (5) (December 1991): 1146–55.

15 John Kenneth Galbraith ('The rush to capitalism,' see Note 5) is certainly concerned, but so are many other economists, such as Alec Nove. Nove has published his concerns *within* the Soviet Union. See Nove, 'The limits of full economic accountability,' *Problems of Economics*, 32 (2) (July 1989): 25–35. This article was originally published in *Ekonomika i Organizatsia Promyshlennogo Provizvodstva*, no. 9 (1988).

16 See, for example, Stanley Fischer and Alan Gelb, 'The process of socialist economic transformation,' *Journal of Economic Perspectives*, 5 (4) (Fall 1991): 91–105.

17 See, for example, Senator Bill Bradley, 'We can't afford not to help East Europe,' *Washington Post* (30 March 1990): A23. Former President Richard Nixon burst back on to the intellectual and political scene in 1992 with his plan for aid to Russia. See Richard Nixon, 'The challenge we face in Russia,' *Wall Street Journal* (11 March 1992): A14. Nixon chided the presidential candidates for ignoring the most important issue since the end of the Second World War. He argued that a 'new despotism' of Russian nationalists would emerge unless Yeltsin succeeded. Nixon argued that his plan did not amount to charity, but was in the self-interest of the US. If Russia successfully transformed into a market economy, then the US would gain billions in trade and millions of jobs for its citizens. Also see the editorial, 'Russia acts, US slumbers,' in *The New York Times* (25 March 1992): A22, for the general sentiment of the intellectual establishment. But see Doug Bandow, 'Why waste aid on Russia?,' *New York Times* (26 March 1992): A23 for a counter-argument which suggests that we re-examine the IMF's record. For an analysis of the economic consequences of the Marshall Plan see Tyler Cowen, 'The Marshall Plan: myths and realities,' in Doug Bandow (ed.) *US Aid to the Developing World* (Washington, DC: Heritage Foundation, 1985): 61–74.

18 See *The New York Times* (2 April 1992): A1, A10–11. But see the reports of conflict and confusion over the package in *The New York Times* (9 April 1992): A1, A10. Also *The New York Times* (13 April 1992): A12, reports that developments at the Congress of People's Deputies concerning backtracking by the Russian government on economic reform could delay Western aid. But, as reported in *The New York Times* (15 April 1992): A1, the reform government reached a compromise with the Congress. The Congress adopted a declaration that accepted 'in principle' the economic reforms of the Yeltsin government. Also see *The New York Times* (16 April 1992): A9.

19 See P. T. Bauer, *Dissent on Development* (Cambridge: Harvard

University Press, 1976) for a critique of development planning. Also see Peter Boettke (ed.) *The Collapse of Development Planning* (New York: New York University Press, forthcoming).

20 The conviction is already evident in some reform economists, such as Larisa Piyasheva, who has stated that perestroika was nothing but a search for Western credit to give socialism a shot in the arm. 'Our economic system,' she argued at a Moscow conference, 'is wrong. The principles of socialist economics are wrong . . . "No compromise" is the new slogan.' As quoted in Paul Craig Roberts, 'Seven days that shook the world,' *National Review* (15 October 1990). Also see the profile on Piyasheva by Cathy Young, 'Russia's real radicals: creating a Moscow market,' *Reason* (April 1992): 37–41.

21 See the discussion of the political problems with economic reform under Gorbachev in Timothy Colton, 'The politics of systemic economic reform,' *Soviet Economy*, 3 (2) (1987): 145–70. Colton argues that Gorbachev's efforts should be held up against three yardsticks: (1) Brezhnev's record, (2) reform efforts in other communist countries, such as Hungary and China and (3) Gorbachev's own rhetoric. Only in comparison to Brezhnev does Gorbachev's record of reform appear to do reasonably well. Both Hungary under Janos Kadar and China under Deng Xiaoping, as well as Gorbachev's own rhetoric, out-perform to a considerable degree the reform efforts that were actually adopted under Gorbachev.

22 Vasily Selyunin, 'Sources,' *Novy Mir*, no. 5 (May 1988), translated in *The Current Digest of the Soviet Press*, 40 (40) (2 November 1988): 17.

23 The events in Peru with President Alberto Fujimori announcing a self-coup on 5 April 1992 are a contemporary case of an authoritarian coup in the name of liberalization. His stated intention is to push through economic reforms, stop terrorism, write a new democracy and establish in Peru a vibrant democracy. See *The Economist* (11 April 1992): 41.

24 See A. J. Polan, *Lenin and the End of Politics* (Berkeley, CA: University of California Press, 1984) for a discussion of Lenin's political thought and its imprint on the Soviet system. Also see Jerry Hough and Merle Fainsod, *How the Soviet Union is Governed* (Cambridge: Harvard University Press, 1979) and Richard Sakwa, *Soviet Politics: An Introduction* (London: Routledge, 1989).

25 See Lenin's 'Testament' (December 1922), in Robert V. Daniels, *A Documentary History of Communism*, vol. 1 (New York: Vintage Books, 1960), pp. 223–5.

26 M. Voslensky, *Nomenklatura: The Soviet Ruling Class* (New York: Doubleday, 1984), p. 61.

27 See Gordon Tullock, *Autocracy* (Boston: Kluwer, 1987), pp. 158–9, for a discussion of this third route.

28 See Paul Gregory, *Restructuring the Soviet Economic Bureaucracy* (New York: Cambridge University Press, 1990), pp. 1–8.

29 See, for example, John Gooding, 'Perestroika as a revolution from within: an interpretation,' *The Russian Review*, vol. 51 (January 1992): 36–57.

30 See Ed Hewett, *Reforming the Soviet Economy* (Washington, DC: Brookings Institution, 1988), p. 326.

NOTES

31 See the criticism of Gorbachev's economic plan in Gertrude Schroeder, 'Gorbachev: "radically" implementing Brezhnev's reforms,' *Soviet Economy*, 2 (4) (1986): 289–301.

32 This thesis is developed in Gary Anderson and Peter Boettke, 'Perestroika and public choice: the economics of autocratic succession in a rent-seeking society,' *Public Choice* (1992), forthcoming.

33 Edgar Kiser and Yoram Barzel argue that the protodemocratic institutions of England, such as the Magna Carta, Parliament and an independent judiciary evolved as the unintended consequence of the self-interested wealth-maximizing behavior of the rulers and some of their subjects. See Kiser and Barzel, 'The origins of democracy in England,' *Rationality and Society*, 3 (4) (October 1991): 396–422.

34 There is abundant evidence of a massive turnover in Soviet officials during the Gorbachev era. By 1985–6, the average age of Politburo members dropped by six years. Sharp drops in age were also recorded in the Party Secretariat and on the Presidium of the Council of Ministers. Middle-level positions within the Soviet government also experienced drastic personnel changes. The number of changes in offices recorded were 'the most sweeping of the entire post-Stalin period.' See Timothy Colton, *The Dilemma of Reform in the Soviet Union* (New York: Council on Foreign Relations, 1986), pp. 89, 114–15.

35 For an informative journalistic account of the problems that the nascent private market 'cooperators' confronted in dealing with and outmaneuvering the Soviet bureaucracy see A. Craig Copetas, *Bear Hunting with the Politburo* (New York: Simon and Schuster, 1991). The debate over perestroika, Copetas states, at times appeared as if individuals were 'debating whether or not to invent the wheel while airplanes buzzed overhead' (p. 70).

36 For an analysis of the devolution of the Soviet system see Peter Murrell and Mancur Olson, 'The devolution of centrally planned economies,' *Journal of Comparative Economics*, 15 (2) (June 1991): 239–65. Murrell and Olson argue that the decline of the former socialist economies resulted because of an institutional sclerosis that evolved as the encompassing interest of the leader for economic growth was muted by the narrow interest of subordinates.

37 The most visible 'liberal' democratic leaders were Boris Yeltsin, Gavril Popov and Anatoly Sobchak. If these three were the political voice, Andrei Sakharov was the soul of the liberal opposition. One outgrowth of the emergence of a liberal intellectual and political movement was the writing of political memoirs by Soviet politicians. See, for example, Boris Yeltsin, *Against the Grain* (New York: Summit Books, 1990), Eduard Shevardnadze, *The Future Belongs to Freedom* (New York: The Free Press, 1991) and Anatoly Sobchak, *For a New Russia* (New York: The Free Press, 1992).

38 Mancur Olson, *The Rise and Decline of Nations* (New Haven: Yale University Press, 1982). Olson applies his theoretical argument concerning the logic of collective action to the Soviet-type system in 'The logic of collective action in Soviet-type societies,' *Journal of Soviet Nationalities*, 1 (2) (Summer 1990): 8–27.

NOTES

39 See F. A. Hayek, *Law, Legislation and Liberty*, vol. 1, pp. 56–65 (see Note 6). The value of freedom of choice, Hayek argued, lies in the opportunities it provides for the discovery of unforeseen and unpredictable possibilities. As such, the loss suffered from restrictions on freedom of choice is not known. Therefore, freedom of choice must be held as a principle that must not be sacrificed for particular pragmatic concerns of a given time. If freedom of choice, instead, is treated as a matter of expediency, then it will lose out to coercive interference since we hardly know what concrete benefit freedom of choice will provide in any particular instance.

40 See the roundtable discussion between Andrei Sakharov, Yelena Bonner, Stephen Cohen, Ed Hewett and Victor Winston, 'Interpretations and perceptions of perestroyka,' in Ed Hewett and Victor Winston (eds) *Milestones in Glasnost and Perestroyka* (Washington, DC: Brookings Institution, 1991), p. 145.

41 See Yelena Bonner, 'Five years of perestroika: "bloodless revolution" or revolting development?,' *Glasnost* (July–September 1990): 4–8.

42 See E. Iasin, 'Destatization and privatization,' *Kommunist*, no. 5 (1991), translated in *Problems of Economics*, 34 (8) (December 1991): 5–22. estatization meant that the transition to a mixed economy would be accomplished through decentralized management without changing the ownership structure. State enterprises, for example, would be leased. The owner of fixed capital – the state – would remain the same, but the output of working capital would belong to the leasee. Privatization, on the other hand, represented destatization envisaged as the transfer of state property to other owners.

6 CREDIBILITY IN SOVIET REFORMS

1 William Shakespeare, *The Merchant of Venice* in *The Complete Works of William Shakespeare*, vol. 2 (New York: Bantam Books, 1988), Scene 4.1.

2 Andres Aslund, for example, even before the August coup concluded that 'Looking back at Soviet economic policy during the second half of the 1980s, it is difficult to avoid the impression that virtually every possible mistake has been made. Perestroika has proved to be an utter economic failure.' Aslund, *Gorbachev's Struggle for Economic Reform*, 2nd edn (Ithaca, NY: Cornell University Press, 1991), p. 225.

3 For interesting interpretative essays on the events in the former Soviet Union see Martin Malia, 'A new Russian revolution?,' *New York Review of Books* (18 July 1991), and 'The August revolution,' *New York Review of Books* (26 September 1991).

4 Mikhail Gorbachev, *Perestroika* (New York: Harper & Row, 1987), p. 33.

5 See Mark Harrison, 'Why did NEP fail?,' in K. Smith (ed.) *Soviet Industrialization and Soviet Maturity* (London: Routledge, 1986), p. 26, where he argues that the rejection of the NEP simply reflects 'the needs of a state committed to a rapid, large-scale industrialization to reduce the commitment of resources to agriculture and to enforce reduced living standards on both town and country.'

6 Alec Nove, 'The logic and cost of collectivization,' *Problems of Commu-*

176

nism (July–August 1976): 59.

7 See, for example, Stephen Cohen, *Bukharin and the Bolshevik Revolution* (New York: Oxford University Press, 1981(1973)), and Nikolai Shmelev and Vladimir Popov, *The Turning Point* (New York: Doubleday, 1989).

8 An attempt at developing the revisionist interpretation is made in Peter Boettke, *The Political Economy of Soviet Socialism: The Formative Years, 1918-1928* (Boston: Kluwer, 1990), pp. 34–8, 113–46.

9 See, for example, Israel Kirzner, 'The perils of regulation,' in *Discovery and the Capitalist Process* (Chicago: University of Chicago Press, 1985).

10 The classic statement of this problem is F. A. Hayek, 'The use of knowledge in society,' in *Individualism and Economic Order* (Chicago: University of Chicago, 1980(1948)). Also see Don Lavoie, *Rivalry and Central Planning* (New York: Cambridge University Press, 1985) and *National Economic Planning: What is Left?* (Cambridge: Ballinger Publishing, 1985), pp. 51–92.

11 See Mitton Friedman, 'A monetary and fiscal framework for economic stability,' in *Essays in Positive Economics* (Chicago: University of Chicago Press, 1953), p. 145.

12 The argument for rules rather than discretion can also be linked to the discussion of competitive market processes above. Since economic processes are in a constant state of flux, public policy that would also be in a discretionary state of flux would simply compound the instability and uncertainty of social arrangements. Fixed policy rules ground the constant flux of economic activity with some certainty. A variation of this argument with regard to the law is developed by Mario Rizzo, 'Law amid flux,' *Journal of Legal Studies*, 9 (2) (March 1980): 291–318.

13 See Geoffrey Brennan and James Buchanan, *The Reason of Rules* (New York: Cambridge University Press, 1985), pp. 82–96.

14 See Tyler Cowen, 'Self-constraint versus self-liberation,' *Ethics*, 101 (January 1991): 360–73, for a discussion of these issues associated with individual choice.

15 Clear presentations of this problem for public policy are presented in Herb Taylor, 'Time inconsistency: a potential problem for policymakers,' *Business Review (Federal Reserve Bank of Philadelphia)* (March–April 1985): 3–12, and 'Rules v. discretion,' *The Economist* (2 March, 1991): 71–2.

16 A classic defense of discretionary policy can be found in Abba Lerner, *The Economics of Control* (London: Macmillan, 1944).

17 See F. Kydland and E. Prescott, 'Rules rather than discretion: the inconsistency of optimal plans,' *Journal of Political Economy*, 85 (3) (1977): 473–91.

18 Mikhail Heller and Aleksandr Neckrich, *Utopia in Power* (New York: Summit Books, 1986), p. 217.

19 Boris Pasternak, *Doctor Zhivago* (New York: Signet Books, 1958), p. 387.

20 One exception to this is John Litwack, who has stressed that within the institutional arrangement of perestroika the leadership was unable to establish a credible commitment to liberalization policies. See Litwack, 'Discretionary behavior and Soviet economic reform,' *Soviet Studies*, 43 (2) (1991): 255–79.

21 Marshall Goldman, *What Went Wrong With Perestroika* (New York: Norton, 1991), pp. 37–8, for example, emphasizes the point that all previous efforts at reform within the Soviet Union were viewed as a 'big lie' by the citizens of the former Soviet Union. The suppression of the kulaks in the 1920s and 1930s and Khrushchev's agricultural policies in the early 1960s had not been forgotten by the population and explain why individuals were reluctant to invest private income on economic ventures. Hardly a family in the former Soviet Union did not have a member that was directly affected by Stalin's terror, and this served as part of a historical memory which each citizen possessed concerning the nature of the CPSU. (See also Goldman, p. 116).

22 Henry Hazlitt discusses this particular problem of trust and strategic interaction in reforming a communist political and economic system in his novel, *Time Will Run Back* (Lanham, MD: University Press of America, 1986(1951)), pp. 126ff.

23 I recognize that several issues are bundled here. The reforms of the NEP and perestroika did not fail simply because of credibility problems. For example, many of the policies were simply incentive incompatible. And, it is also questionable to what extent the objective of liberalization was ever part of the agenda in either case. However, in attempting to tease out the different problems with Soviet reform history the credibility aspect provides fundamental insights into questions of policy design.

24 For an examination of the policies of 'war communism' see, Peter Boettke, *The Political Economy of Soviet Socialism*, pp. 63–111 (see Note 8). Also see Peter Boettke, 'The political economy of utopia,' *Journal des Economistes et des Etudes Humaines*, 1 (2) (1990): 91–138. For a discussion of the debate over the meaning of these events in Western historiography see Peter Boettke, 'The Soviet experiment with pure communism,' *Critical Review*, 2 (4) (1988): 149–82; Alec Nove, 'The Soviet experiment with pure communism: a comment,' and my rejoinder in *Critical Review*, 5 (1) (1991): 121–8.

25 Alan Ball, *Russia's Last Capitalists: The Nepmen, 1921–1929* (Berkeley, CA: University of California Press, 1987), p. 23. Also see N. Gubsky, 'Economic law in Soviet Russia,' *Economic Journal*, 37 (June 1927): 226–36, for a contemporary account of the Civil Code.

26 Ball, *Russia's Last Capitalists*, p. 30 (see Note 25).

27 Ball, *Russia's Last Capitalists*, p. 75 (see Note 25).

28 The Soviet constitution barred from voting or holding office:

1. people using hired labor to make profits;
2. people living on 'unearned income,' which included income from private enterprises and property;
3. private traders and middlemen.

Lishentsy could not have careers in the military, or join cooperatives and trade unions, or publish newspapers or organize gatherings. In addition, they had to pay higher fees for utilities, rent, medical care, schools and all public services.

29 Aleksandr Solzhenitsyn, *The Gulag Archipelago*, vol. 1 (New York:

Harper and Row, 1973), p. 52.

30 See Nikolai Bukharin, 'Concerning the new economic policy and our tasks' (1925) in *Selected Economic Writings on the State and the Transition to Socialism*, Richard Day (ed.) (New York: M. E. Sharpe, 1982), pp. 196-7. Ambiguity in the rules, Bukharin argued, would produce nothing but contradictory expectations, which would deter economic progress. Sizing up the situation, he stated, 'Consider the fact that the well-to-do upper stratum of the peasantry, along with the middle peasant, who is also striving to join the well-to-do, are both afraid at present to accumulate. A situation has been created in which the peasant is afraid to buy an iron roof and apprehensive that he will be declared a kulak; if he buys a machine, he makes certain that the communists are not watching. Advanced technology has become a conspiracy. . . . The result is that the middle peasant is afraid to improve his farm and lay himself open to forceful administrative pressure; and the poor peasant complains that we are preventing him from selling his labor power to the wealthy peasants, etc.' In response, Bukharin argued that 'In general and on the whole, we must say to the entire peasantry, to all its different strata: enrich yourselves, accumulate, develop your farms.' This statement, of course, later became a bludgeon in Stalin's hands to demonstrate Bukharin's rightist deviation.

31 E. H. Carr, *Socialism in One Country: 1924-1926*, vol. 1 (Baltimore: Penguin Books, 1958), pp. 208-9.

32 See E. H. Carr, *The Bolshevik Revolution, 1917-1923*, vol. 3 (New York: Norton, 1981(1953)), p. 377.

33 See G. I. Khanin, 'Why and when did NEP die?,' *Eko*, no. 10 (1989), translated in *Problems of Economics*, 33 (4) (August 1990): 21, 24.

34 As Robert Conquest explains: 'When the market mechanism had failed to give satisfaction, requisition made up the shortfall, and the government then went back to the market. *But from the peasant point of view, the market was no longer a reasonably secure outlet, but one that might be superseded at any moment by requisition.* And in the further deterioration of market relations thus produced, the government remembered the success it had had with forced requisition, and did not reflect that it was the requisition of grain produced with the incentive of the market, and that in the new circumstances this was certain to shrink in quantity.' See Conquest, *The Harvest of Sorrow* (New York: Oxford University Press, 1986), p. 93.

35 See 'The law on individual enterprise,' *Pravda* (21 November 1986), translated in *The Current Digest of the Soviet Press*, 38 (46) (17 December 1986); 'The law on State enterprises,' *Pravda* (1 July 1987), translated in *The Current Digest of the Soviet Press*, 39 (30-1) (1987); 'The law on cooperatives,' in J. L. Black (ed.) *USSR Documents Annual* (Gulf Breeze, FL: Academic International Press, 1988), 7: pp. 122-51.

36 See Goldman, *What Went Wrong With Perestroika*, p. 140 (see Note 21).

37 On the concept of 'hard' and 'soft' budget constraints see Janos Kornai, 'The soft budget constraint,' *Kyklos*, 39 (1) (1986): 3-30; and *The Road to a Free Economy* (New York: Norton, 1990).

38 Litwack discusses the situation facing the Soviet manager in his paper

'Discretionary behavior and Soviet economic reform,' 257 (see Note 20). As he states:

> A Soviet manager . . . is often averse to expending resources for improving the performance of his or her firm. But this is not because of a well-defined progressive tax scheme that requires sharing future benefits with the government. The problem is that the tax scheme tomorrow is at the discretion of superiors in the hierarchy. They will determine conditions only after observing the performance of the firm today. In the absence of long-run commitment, these superiors naturally attempt to extract surpluses from those subordinate organizations that reveal themselves to be more productive. In addition, poorly performing enterprises are typically 'bailed out'. . . The expectation of discretionary extraction and bailouts creates an incentive problem at lower levels.

39 Goldman, *What Went Wrong With Perestroika*, pp. 141–2 (see Note 21).
40 See Hewett, *Reforming the Soviet Economy* (Washington, DC: Brookings Institution, 1988), p. 340, fn. 60.
41 William Taubman and Jane Taubman, *Moscow Spring* (New York: Summit, 1989), p. 46.
42 See Misha Belkindas, 'Privatization of the Soviet economy under Gorbachev II,' *Berkeley-Duke Occasional Papers on the Second Economy of the USSR*, no. 14 (April 1989): 1–35.
43 As Belkindas, 'Privatization of the Soviet economy,' points out opportunities for unearned income originate because of the shortage economy. Illegal housing transactions, medical care, admission to an institution of higher education, etc., are just some examples of how illicit transactions can 'correct' for the failings of the official economy.
44 See Belkindas, 'Privatizing the Soviet economy,' 37–97 for an overview of the development of private cooperatives in the Soviet Union. In addition, see Anthony Jones and William Moskoff, *Ko-ops: The Rebirth of Entrepreneurship in the Soviet Union* (Bloomington, IN: Indiana University Press, 1991). Also see David Prychitko, *Marxism and Worker Self-Management: The Essential Tension* (Westport, CT: Greenwood, 1991), for an examination of the theoretical and historical issues associated with the cooperative movement in general and its relationship to the main debates in comparative economic systems.
45 See Anthony Jones and William Moskoff, 'New cooperatives in the USSR,' *Problems of Communism* (November–December 1989): 27–39. With regard to the hostility toward the emerging cooperatives they state that 'cooperative activity has . . . engendered a great deal of hostility from two groups: the consuming public, which it is supposed to serve, and the bureaucracy, which it threatens' (p. 32). Also see the discussion of the economic environment within which cooperatives had to operate and the array of official responses in terms of restrictions, interference and taxation which stifled the development of cooperatives in Jones and Moskoff, *Ko-ops*, pp. 34–77 (see Note 44). In addition, see Goldman, *What Went Wrong With Perestroika*, p. 113 (see Note 21). 'The

halfhearted toleration of cooperative and private trade,' Goldman states, 'was guaranteed to sabotage the whole effort.'

46 The evolution of working capital markets, for example, depends crucially on the ability of the state to be bound by commitments that it will not confiscate assets. 'The shackling of arbitrary behavior of rulers and the development of impersonal rules' that successfully bind the state is a key component of institutional transformation. See Douglas North, *Institutions, Institutional Change and Economic Performance* (New York: Cambridge University Press, 1990), p. 129.

47 See Gertrude Schroeder, 'The Soviet economy on a treadmill of perestroika: Gorbachev's first five years,' in Harley D. Balzer (ed.) *Five Years That Shook the World* (Boulder, CO: Westview Press, 1991), pp. 31–48. Specifically on the consumer crisis, see James Noren, 'The economic crisis: another perspective,' and Gertrude Schroeder, ' "Crisis" in the consumer sector: a comment,' in Ed Hewett and Victor Winston (ed.) *Milestones in Glasnost and Perestroika: The Economy* (Washington, DC: Brookings Institution, 1991), pp. 360–414.

48 'As Gorbachev moved back and forth from one comprehensive reform to another,' Marshall Goldman argues, 'he became more and more uncertain about subjecting the Soviet Union to the type of shock therapy such reforms would inevitably necessitate. He also concluded that unless reined in, the reform process would ultimately shrink his powers and those of the Soviet Union over central economic control, thus reducing the Soviet Union to an ineffective economic entity.' See Goldman, *What Went Wrong With Perestroika*, p. 222 (see Note 21). Gorbachev's economic zigging and zagging was not the only credibility issue at hand. The politics of discretionary power were also an issue of concern with liberal intellectuals. Individuals were not certain that the zigs permitted today would not be superseded by repressive zags tomorrow. 'Today,' Andrei Sakharov warned, 'it is Gorbachev, but tomorrow it could be somebody else. There are no guarantees that some Stalinist will not succeed him.' As quoted in Robert Kaiser, *Why Gorbachev Happened?* (New York: Simon & Schuster, 1991), p. 245.

49 Dani Rodrik has addressed the issue of commitment signalling with regard to policy reform in a game-theoretic framework. As he sums up his argument: 'At the outset of any reform, the public will typically be unable to fathom the true motivations of the government undertaking the reform. Since the distorting policies in question have been put in place by those in power to begin with, what reason is there to believe that the authorities now "see the light"? . . . Signalling via policy-overshooting can then help reduce the confusion. . . The more severe are the credibility problem and its consequences, the more likely it is that a sharp break with the past will be viewed as attractive.' Therefore, if the credibility gap is particulary important, as it is in the Soviet situation, then for the appropriate signal to be conveyed all notions of gradualism must be put aside. Policy overshooting can distinguish a sincere reform government from its insincere counterpart. Thus, policy overshooting will have the effect of rendering the policy reform more credible than it otherwise would be, and alleviate the problems associated with lack of credibility.

See Rodrik, 'Promises, promises: credible policy reform via signalling,' *Economic Journal*, 99 (September 1989): 771.

7 CHARTING A NEW COURSE

1 Robert Kaiser, *Why Gorbachev Happened?* (New York: Simon & Schuster, 1991), p. 314.
2 See Paul Craig Roberts, ' "Property owners" are rising from Russia's economic rubble,' *Business Week* (13 May 1991): 16. As Roberts pointed out, though Gorbachev's reforms failed to produce results in the official sector, they unofficially succeeded by spurring the emergence of a *de facto* propertied class within whose hands the economic future of Russia rests.
3 See, for example, Jean Baechler, *The Origin of Capitalism* (Oxford: Blackwell, 1975), and Harold Berman, *Law and Revolution* (Cambridge: Harvard University Press, 1983). Also see Fernand Braudel, *Civilization and Capitalism*, 3 vols (New York: Harper & Row, 1982).
4 See Ludwig von Mises's discussion of the basis of human society in *Human Action: A Treatise on Economics*, 3rd rev. edn (Chicago: Henry Regnery, 1966), pp. 143–76. Also see Henry Hazlitt, *Foundations of Morality* (Los Angeles: Nash Publishing, 1972), and Murray Rothbard, *Man, Economy and State*, vol. 1 (Los Angeles: Nash Publishing, 1970), pp. 85–6.
5 The classic paper on this aspect of competition is Charles Tiebout, 'A pure theory of local expenditures,' *Journal of Political Economy* (October 1956), reprinted in Tyler Cowen (ed.) *The Theory of Market Failure* (Fairfax, VA: George Mason University Press, 1988), pp. 179–91. Also see David Friedman, 'An economic theory of the size and shape of nations,' *Journal of Political Economy*, 85 (February 1977): 59–77.
6 See Bruno Leoni, *Freedom and the Law* (Los Angeles: Nash Publishing, 1972), p. 177.
7 Leoni makes the compelling argument that the problem of economic calculation under socialism is simply one case of the more general problem confronting complex human interaction; the discovery and use of knowledge that is dispersed throughout the society in order to accommodate the constantly changing conditions of human life. Leoni contrasts the evolution of judge-made common law which emerges out of an historical process with legislative law and argues that legislative law is vulnerable to the same problems that socialism confronts. See Leoni, *Freedom and the Law*, pp. 18–19, 90–1 (see Note 6). This is also a theme repeated forcefully in Hayek's writings. Also see the discussion in Bruce Benson, *The Enterprise of Law* (San Francisco: Pacific Research Institute for Public Policy, 1990), chaps 2–7, for a contrast between customary legal systems and authoritarian law. Chapters 4–7, in particular, discuss the public choice dimensions of authoritarian law under representative democracy. For a discussion of the contradictions of democracy see Murray Rothbard, *Power and Market* (Kansas City: Sheed Andrews and McMeel, 1977(1970)), pp. 189–99.
8 See Don Herzog, *Without Foundations* (Ithaca, NY: Cornell University

NOTES

Press, 1985) for a criticism of foundationalist justifications of political theory found in Hobbes, Locke and the utilitarians, and an argument for the adoption of the contextual justification for political theory found in David Hume and Adam Smith.

9 See John Locke, *Two Treatises on Government* (New York: Cambridge University Press, 1991(1690)) and Robert Nozick, *Anarchy, State and Utopia* (New York: Basic Books, 1974).

10 See Thomas Hobbes, *Leviathan* (New York: Collier Books, 1962(1651)) and James Buchanan, *The Limits of Liberty* (Chicago: University of Chicago Press, 1975). Also see John Rawls, *A Theory of Justice* (Cambridge: Harvard University Press, 1971).

11 See Israel Kirzner, *Competition and Entrepreneurship* (Chicago: University of Chicago Press, 1973) for a discussion of the limits of equilibrium as opposed to market process theory in exploring the properties of competitive markets.

12 See James Buchanan, 'Ethical rules, expected values and large numbers,' *Ethics* (October 1965), reprinted in *Freedom in Constitutional Contract* (College Station: Texas A&M Press, 1977), pp. 151-68.

13 Ironically, it is also the case that if in the Hobbesian state of anarchy individuals could come voluntarily to agree to form a social compact and establish a government, then there would be no need to form a government since voluntary action could solve the public goods problem. Either government represents the ultimate public good and therefore cannot emerge out of the voluntary actions of individuals within the Hobbesian jungle, or it can be established through agreement and therefore is not necessary. See Joseph Kalt, 'Public goods and the theory of government,' *Cato Journal*, 1 (Fall 1981): 565-84.

14 See, for example, Hobbes's discussion of language and science in *Leviathan*, part 1, chaps 4-5. For a criticism of conventionalist views of social institutions, and money and language in particular, see Steve Horwitz, *Monetary Evolution, Free Banking and Economic Order* (Boulder, CO: Westview Press, 1992).

15 While rule-making may be the product of rational design, the processes of rule selection are spontaneous. Thus, in principle rule constructivism is not as flawed an approach to social theory as the preceding paragraphs may suggest. The problem with the approach, however, is that it does not pay sufficient attention to the evolutionary feedback mechanism in rule selection. The approach I advocate to discuss the first principles of the liberal order seeks to explore both the reason of rules and the evolutionary processes by which rules are selected over time.

16 See David Hume, *A Treatise on Human Nature* (Oxford: Oxford University Press, 1978(1740)), Book III, and Hume, *Essays Moral, Political and Literary* (Indianapolis: Liberty Classics, 1985), and F. A. Hayek, *The Constitution of Liberty* (Chicago: University of Chicago Press, 1960), *Law, Legislation and Liberty*, 3 vols (Chicago: University of Chicago Press, 1973, 1976, 1979), and *The Fatal Conceit* (Chicago: University of Chicago Press, 1988).

17 Hume argues that it cannot be denied that combinations of men were founded on a contract, but that this contract 'was not written on

183

parchment, nor yet on leaves or barks of trees. It preceded the use of writing and all the other civilized arts of life. But we trace it plainly in the nature of man, and in the equality, or something approaching equality, which we find in all the individuals of that species. . . . Nothing but their own consent, and their sense of the advantages resulting from peace and order, could have had that influence.' Hume, 'Of the original contract,' in *Essays*, p. 468 (see Note 16).

18 Israel Kirzner, *Discovery, Capitalism and Distributive Justice* (Oxford: Basil Blackwell, 1989) argues that standard ethical assessments of capitalism have failed not because of flaws in the ethical arguments themselves, but because they misperceive the nature of market processes; namely, the discovery function of market competition. The lure of pure profit sets in motion an entrepreneurial discovery procedure in which individuals tend to learn how to arrange resources in a more effective manner to satisfy the demands of others. Private property is an essential precondition for the learning process of competition to be enacted.

19 Hayek argues that:

> Activities in which we are guided by a knowledge merely of the principle of the thing should perhaps better be described by the term *cultivation* than by the familiar term 'control' – cultivation in the sense in which the farmer or gardener cultivates his plants, where he knows and can control only some of the determining circumstances, and in which the wise legislature or statesman will probably attempt to cultivate rather than control the forces of the social process.

Hayek, 'Degrees of explanation,' *British Journal for the Philosophy of Science* (1955), reprinted in *Studies in Philosophy, Politics and Economics* (Chicago: University of Chicago Press, 1967), p. 19.

20 'Life in a pluralistic liberal society,' Stephen Macedo writes, 'is a smorgasbord confronting us with an exciting array of possibilities. Society is open to change and diversity: less of a stigma attaches to unconventional lifestyles and to changes in lifestyle. The combination of diversity and openness to change constitutes an incitement to self-examination and invitation to experiment.' But as Macedo further points out:

> If all the world became liberal, all the world would become the same in certain important respects. Individuality, constrained by liberal norms, would flourish everywhere, but the diversity of forms of political organization would be eliminated, the differences between forms of social life would be reduced, and every sphere of social life would bear the peculiar tint of liberal values. It would be wrong to identify the spread of liberalism with the maximization of diversity or the liberation of unlimited experimentation: liberal norms rule out many experiments in social organization, require a common subscription to liberal rights, and encourage a uniformity of tolerance, openness, and broad-mindedness. If the spread of liberalism eliminates certain forms of diversity, it also extends the liberal community and liberal peace.

See Macedo, *Liberal Virtues* (Oxford: Oxford University Press, 1990), pp. 278–9.

21 'It must be remembered,' Richard Ericson points out, 'that the ultimate configuration of institutions and interactions is unknowable, a largely unintended consequence of the growth of decentralized agent interaction. Thus, a final lesson for successful reform taught by the nature of the traditional Soviet-style system is to abandon the Faustian urge to control, to know in advance, and thus to allow economic outcomes to arise naturally as the unpredictable consequences of market interaction.' See Ericson, 'The classical Soviet-type economy: nature of the system and implications for reform,' *Journal of Economic Perspectives*, 5 (4) (Fall 1991): 26.

22 James Madison, *The Federalist Papers* (New York: New American Library, 1961), p. 322.

23 The public goods problem exists, for example, because in situations where goods are characterized by (1) jointness in consumption and (2) non-excludability of non-payers, firms in private markets cannot survive and provide the service. However, the very existence of these problems may entice entrepreneurs to discover new technologies in order to overcome these problems and successfully enter the particular market in question. Some computer software programs, for example, contain 'worms' so that successful copying of the program is precluded. Shopping malls and condominiums are examples of the use of tie-in arrangements for the private provision of public goods. Shopping malls provide streets and security that are paid for by the provision of private goods such as clothing, food and other items sold in the mall. For a discussion of these issues see Dan Klein, 'Tie-ins and the market provision of collective goods,' *Harvard Journal of Law and Public Policy*, 10 (Spring 1987): 451–74. See also David Schmidtz, *The Limits of Government: An Essay on the Public Goods Argument* (Boulder, CO: Westview Press, 1991), for a general examination of the public goods problem.

24 For a collection of articles of both traditional market failure theory and its critics see Tyler Cowen (ed.) *The Theory of Market Failure* (see Note 5).

25 See James Buchanan, *Cost and Choice* (Chicago: University of Chicago Press, 1969).

26 It must always be kept in mind that political choices are not among alternative distributions, but rather among alternative institutional arrangements that generate patterns of distribution and allocation. See Rutledge Vining, 'On two foundation concepts of the theory of political economy,' *Journal of Political Economy*, 77 (1969): 199–218. Also see Vining, *On Appraising the Performance of an Economic System* (New York: Cambridge University Press, 1984).

27 See F. A. Hayek, *Law, Legislation and Liberty*, 3: 41–64 (see Note 16).

28 F. A. Hayek, *Law, Legislation and Liberty*, 3: 75 (see Note 16).

29 For a discussion of some of the issues involved with this proposition see Christos Pitelis and Ioanna Giykoy-Pitelis, 'On the possibility of state neutrality,' *Review of Political Economy*, 3 (1) (1991): 15–24. For the argument with regard to monetary policy see Ludwig von Mises, 'The non-neutrality of money (1938), in Richard Ebeling (ed.) *Money, Method*

and the Market Process: Essay by Ludwig von Mises (Boston: Kluwer, 1990), pp. 69–77, and with regard to fiscal policy see Murray Rothbard, 'The myth of neutral taxation,' *Cato Journal*, 1 (2) (Fall 1981): 519–64.

30 These issues are discussed in Roger Garrison, 'Time and money: the universals of macroeconomic theorizing,' *Journal of Macroeconomics*, 6 (2) (Spring 1984): 197–213.

31 See Heidi Kroll, 'Monopoly and transition to the market,' *Soviet Economy*, 7 (2) (April–June 1991): 144–5. Also see *The Economist* (11 August 1990): 67.

32 See Heidi Kroll, 'Reform and monopoly in the Soviet economy,' Briefing Paper no. 4, Center for Foreign Policy Development, Brown University (September 1990), p. 7.

33 See Stephen Kotkin, *Steeltown, USSR* (Berkeley, CA: University of California Press, 1991).

34 See Kontkin, *Steeltown, USSR*, p. 17 (see Note 33).

35 See Bill Keller's discussion of the Uralmash Machine Tool Works. This article highlights persistence of interlocking monopolies and near-total reliance on centralized decision-making that characterized the industrial structure of the supposedly reformed Soviet economy under Gorbachev. Keller, 'Industrial colossus typifies the miseries of the Soviet economy,' *New York Times* (6 January 1991): 8.

36 See Ronald McKinnon, *The Order of Economic Liberalization* (Baltimore: Johns Hopkins University Press, 1991), pp. 162–86, for a discussion of the phenomenon of negative value-added firms. McKinnon's conclusions, however, about adopting a cautious trade policy until privatization is accomplished do not necessarily follow from his analysis of the distinction between firms that just make losses and firms that are value subtractors. See the discussion in *The Economist* (5 January 1991): 51, and the letter in response by Jeffrey Sachs, *The Economist* (19 January 1991): 61.

37 See Judy Shelton, *The Coming Soviet Crash* (New York: Free Press, 1989): chaps 1–3. Also see Gur Ofer, 'Budget deficit, market disequilibrium, and economic reforms,' *Soviet Economy*, 5 (1989): 107–61, reprinted in Ed Hewett and Victor Winston (ed.) *Milestones in Glasnost and Perestroyka: The Economy* (Washington, DC: Brookings Institution, 1991), pp. 263–307. Ofer, for example, reports that *PlanEcon* estimates that in 1988 the Soviet government ran a budget deficit of around 98.7 billion roubles or about 11 per cent of GDP. Shelton, building on the work of Soviet emigrant economist Igor Birman, challenges Soviet budget records pointing out that there is a gap between claimed revenue and identified sources of revenue in the budget revenue numbers in 1987, for example, of around 146.4 billion roubles. This gap, she points out, is persistent from 1970 on and ranges from a 20 per cent gap in 1970 to a 36 per cent gap in 1987. Shelton concludes that the internal budget mess in the Soviet Union was quite severe even before Gorbachev.

38 See Richard Wagner, 'Economic manipulation for political profit: macroeconomic consequences and constitutional implications,' *Kyklos*, 30 (1977): 395–410; 'Boom and bust: the political economy of economic disorder,' *Journal of Libertarian Studies*, 4 (Winter 1980): 1–37; and 'Politics, central banking and economic order,' *Critical Review*, 3 (Sum-

mer/Fall 1989): 505–17. Also see Lawrence H. White, 'Problems inherent in political money supply regimes,' in *Competition and Currency* (New York: New York University Press, 1989), pp. 70–90.

39 See, for example, Tadeusz Kowalik, 'The costs of "shock therapy",' *Dissent* (Fall 1991): 497–504. Also see Valtr Komarek, 'Shock therapy and its victims,' *New York Times* (5 January 1992): section 4, 13.

40 See Michael Alexeev, 'Are Soviet consumers forced to save?,' *Comparative Economic Studies*, 30 (1988): 17–23.

41 For a discussion of why this dichotomy between monopoly price and competitive prices is analytically questionable see Rothbard, *Man, Economy and State*, pp. 560–660 (see Note 4). As Rothbard points out all we can really observe in a market economy is the difference between government established prices and market established prices. We do not have the *knowledge* to ascertain what the competitive price would be in comparison to some monopoly price.

42 This is the basic difference between the Pole and the Czech reforms. The Poles argued that price liberalization must be immediate to introduce market discipline and that privatization could come later. The Czechs, on the other hand, argued that this Polish strategy represented a 'reform trap' and that privatization must precede price liberalization.

43 See David Willis, *Klass* (New York: Avon Books, 1985) for a discussion of status, rank and privilege inside the Soviet Union prior to Gorbachev. Also see the classic studies by Milovan Djilas, *The New Class* (New York: Praeger Publishers, 1957) and Michael Voslensky, *Nomenklatura* (New York: Doubleday, 1984).

44 On the inability to recapture past losses from distorting government policies see Robert Tollison and Richard Wagner, 'Romance, realism, and economic reform,' *Kyklos*, 44 (1991): 57–70. On the political problems of redressing past wrongs consider the troublesome situation with the Czechs or Germans concerning the discoveries of ex-informers to the secret police of the Communist government. While historical understanding is a precondition for the awakening of civil society, endless debates about the compensation due to this or that group for past wrongs can tear the embryonic social fabric apart. One of the most important lessons of economics is that sunk costs are sunk, let bygones be bygones. One cannot influence the past, decisions must be focused on the future. Therefore, past imperfects inform the institutional rules that one may find desirable for future social interaction, but we cannot correct the past no matter how horrible it may have been.

45 This will also curb the monopolistic tendency of the domestic market by expanding the relevant market and, thus, expanding the availability of substitutes.

46 See Ronald McKinnon, *The Order of Economic Liberalization*, pp. 120–61 (see Note 36). On monetary reform also see Josef Brada, Vladimir Popov, Marie Lavigne, *et al.*, 'A phased plan for making the ruble convertible,' in Josef Brada and Michael Claudon (ed.) *Reforming the Ruble* (New York: New York University Press, 1990), pp. 93–131.

47 Steve Hanke and Kurt Schuler, 'Ruble reform,' *Cato Journal*, 10 (Winter 1991): 655–66. Also see Robert Hetzel, 'Free enterprise and central

NOTES

banking in formerly communist countries,' *Economic Review of the Federal Reserve Bank of Richmond* (May/June 1990): 13-19. As Hetzel points out

> A market economy . . . is not established by a one-time reform. It requires a lasting commitment to limiting the role of government in economic activity. The existence of a central bank provides a continuing incentive for politicians under pressure to confuse money creation with wealth creation. The resulting inflation then leads to myriad interventions in the economy in the form of wage, price, interest rate, exchange market, and capital controls. Eliminating the central bank is one way of committing to a limited role for the state (p. 19).

48 Abba Hetzel, 'Free enterprise and central banking in the formerly communist countries,' p. 19, fn. 4 (see Note 47).
49 See the discussion of free banking theory in White, *Competition and Currency*, and George Selgin, *The Theory of Free Banking* (Totowa, NJ: Rowman and Littlefield, 1988). For an historical discussion of the operation of a free banking system see Lawrence White, *Free Banking in Britain: Theory, Experience and Debate, 1800-1845* (New York: Cambridge University Press, 1984). A key episode in White's discussion is how the banking system handled the Ayr Bank failure of 1772. As White points out, the Ayr Bank, which was in operation from 1769 to 1772, engaged in reckless management and extended a great deal of bad credit through note issue. The bank's failure also led to the failure of eight other private bankers, but it did not threaten the financial system as a whole. The note exchange system that emerged in the Scottish system served as an important check against over-issuance by a single bank and provided market incentives to discipline those that attempted to engage in over-issue of its notes through the law of reflux. White, *Free Banking in Britain*, pp. 30-2, 126-8.
50 For a discussion of this problem with central banking see Selgin, *The Theory of Free Banking*, pp. 89-107 (see Note 49).
51 However, see the report in *The Economist* (29 February 1992): 78-9 on the surprising rise in the rouble since mid-January 1992. Since the January price liberalization, the rouble rose from 110 to the dollar to 70.
52 See, for example, Annelise Anderson, 'Monetary competition and monetary stability in the transition from plan to market,' in James Dorn and Larisa Piyasheva (eds) *From Plan to Market: The Post-Soviet Challenge* (Washington, DC: Cato Institute, forthcoming).
53 See Lerner, *The Economics of Control* (New York: Macmillan, 1944), pp. 302-22. Also see Lerner, 'Functional finance and the federal debt,' *Social Research* (February 1943): 38-51, and 'The economic steering wheel,' *The University Review* (June 1941): 2-8. For a criticism from the perspective of the political incentives functional finance engenders see James Buchanan and Richard Wagner, *Democracy in Deficit* (New York: Academic Press, 1977).
54 For a discussion of the analytical problems with the notion of public goods see Rothbard, *Man, Economy and State*, pp. 883-90 (see Note 4). Also see

Tyler Cowen, 'A public goods definition and their institutional context: a critique of public goods theory,' *Review of Social Economy*, 43 (April 1985): 53–63.

55 This argument is developed in Richard McKenzie and Dwight Lee, *Quicksilver Capital* (New York: Free Press, 1991).

56 This idea was directly challenged by Marxists. In the Marxist analysis of capitalism the logic of the system led to increasing monopolization. Since capitalism suffered from internal contradictions, monopoly capitalists would merge with the state to prop up their enterprises. These state monopoly capitalists would then seek to expand their market internationally and the competition between the various imperialistic state monopoly capitalists would breed war. This is how Lenin, for example, sized up the situation of the First World War. Socialism was the only logical leap to take. See Lenin, *Imperialism, The Highest State of Capitalism* (1916), in *Collected Works*, vol. 22 (Moscow: Progress Publishers, 1977), pp. 185–304.

57 Alexander Gray, *The Socialist Tradition* (New York: Harper & Row, 1968), p. 63. For a criticism of utopian reasoning from positions of moral purity see Isaiah Berlin, *The Crooked Timber of Humanity* (New York: Alfred Knopf, 1991). Berlin took the title from a quote of Immanuel Kant which reads: 'Out of timber so crooked as that from which man is made nothing entirely straight can be built.'

58 See Robert Nozick, *Anarchy, State and Utopia* (New York: Basic Books, 1974), pp. 297–334.

59 See the discussion on simultaneity in Janos Kornai, *The Road to a Free Economy* (New York: Norton, 1990), pp. 158–62.

60 This is also true for capitalist economies experiencing depressions. See Rothbard, *America's Great Depression*, 3rd edn (Kansas City: Sheed and Ward, 1975), pp. 25–9.

61 On this distinction see F. A. Hayek, *The Constitution of Liberty* (Chicago: University of Chicago Press, 1960), pp. 103–17.

8 CONCLUSION

1 F. A. Hayek, 'Individualism: true and false,' in *Individualism and Economic Order* (Chicago: University of Chicago Press, 1980(1948)), p. 32.

2 See Stephen Kinzer, 'East Germans face their accusers,' *New York Times Magazine* (12 April 1992): 24–7, 42, 50–2.

3 See 'Eastern Europe's past,' *The Economist* (21 March 1992): 24.

4 It was estimated in 1980 that 20 per cent of the Romanians over 18 years of age belong to the Communist Party, 18 per cent of East Germans, 14 per cent of Czechoslovakians, 13 per cent of Bulgarians, 12.5 per cent of Poles and 10 per cent of Hungarians.

5 Timothy Garton Ash has perhaps provided the best discussion of the intellectual and political movement behind the revolutions of 1989. See his *The Uses of Adversity* (New York: Vintage Books, 1990) and *The Magic Lantern* (New York: Random House, 1990).

6 In February 1992, however, a new blueprint for economic change was

unveiled in Poland. The new plan, announced by Prime Minister Jan Olszewski, intended to maintain some of the austerity measures of the original Balcerowicz program, but restore public confidence in the government's ability to manage the economy effectively. The emphasis in Poland's economic policy would shift from fighting inflation to stimulating the stagnant economy. The proposal met with sharp criticism from several different perspectives. See Stephen Engelberg, 'Polish economic about-face draws criticism,' *New York Times* (21 February 1992): A8. For a report on the attitude of some Polish economists see Barry Newman, 'Poles give lessons on capitalistic ways to ex-Soviet masters,' *Wall Street Journal* (2 April 1992): A1, A10. Mrs Bochniarz, the former minister of industry and now president of Nicom Consulting, argues that Western prescriptions for economic change are fundamentally flawed and led to many problems in Poland, including the loss of political will on the part of the government after the October 1991 elections. Mr Balcerowicz and Mrs Bochniarz lost their jobs after those elections. Mrs Bochniarz now counsels the Russians against following the Polish path exactly. Her most important advice is that reform is too important to be left to the market. Government must guide and manage the process from start to finish. Otherwise, the painful pill of transformation will simply be too hard to swallow.

7 See, for example, Vaclav Havel *et al.*, *The Power of the Powerless* (Armonk, NY: M. E. Sharpe, 1985). The papers in this book, written shortly after the formation of Charter 77 and just before the birth of Solidarity, argued that communist power did not derive from totalitarian control of the soul of subjects. The delirium of the Stalinist period was gone. Repression continued, but in a more anonymous way. And, while communist fictions concerning the past, present and future were constantly produced and reproduced by the state apparatus of information, no one believed in the promise any more. Communist power derived, instead, from the passivity, opportunism, cynicism and tacit acceptance of the way of life. Silent disagreement and conformity on the part of citizens assured that communist power was safe. Only with the development of civil society outside of the official state sector – an anti-political politics – can the communist system be defeated.

8 See the interview with Vaclav Havel conducted by Adam Michnik and published in *Gazeta Wyborcza* in 'A conversation with President Havel,' *World Press Review* (March 1992): 14–16. Also see Havel's reaction to the 'lustration' law passed by the National Assembly in 'Paradise lost,' *New York Review of Books* (9 April 1992): 6–8. Lustration derives from the Latin and means 'sacrificial purification.'

9 See, for example, Jeri Laber, 'Witch hunt in Prague,' *New York Review of Books* (23 April 1992): 5–8.

10 See, for example, Vasily Golovanov, 'A deep despair in Yeltsin's Russia,' *Literaturnaya Gazeta*, in *World Press Review* (April 1992): 18–21.

11 The exact figure was 18,856,113 members as reported in *The Europa World Year Books, 1990*.

12 See Michael Mandelbaum, 'Coup de grace: the end of the Soviet Union,'

Foreign Affairs, 71 (1) (1992): 168.

13 See Richard Pipes, 'Russia's chance,' *Commentary*, 93 (3) (March 1992): 28–33.

14 Richard Pipes, *The Russian Revolution* (New York: Alfred Knopf, 1990), p. 838.

15 The KGB has actually been abolished, but the AFB (the Agency of Federal Security) has been established to take its place. Also the *Moscow News*, no. 6 (9–16 February 1992): 2, reports that examination of the files has revealed that there were KGB agents among the hierarchy of the Russian Orthodox Church. There is an ongoing investigation of the files by a Parliamentary Commission of the Russian Supreme Soviet. The current commission is the third one to be established, the reports of the first two were suppressed.

16 See 'Behind democracy's façade,' *The Economist* (18 April 1992): 46. But see Oleg Vite and Dimitry Travin, 'Privatization as effected by the nomenklatura,' *Moscow News* (1–8 December 1991): 9. Vite and Travin argue that one must first distinguish between those who rose through the communist ranks as Party functionaries from those who rose as business executives. The business executives and factory managers had not only to master political horse trading required of all those who rose to prominence in the Party hierarchy, but also had to possess an ability to bargain in the bureaucratic market over resources, plan targets and personnel. Vite and Travin argue that those individuals possess the skills that will allow them to adapt to a free market environment quickly – much quicker, they argue, than the small-scale black market entrepreneurs would be able to adapt. The managerial elite is simply seeking to retain their control through privatization of what they have laid claim to as their own property. However unappealing it may be to the romantic, the managerial elite must become an ally of economic reform. The struggle against the managerial elite, they conclude, is not only dangerous to democracy, but economically pointless.

17 See Martin Malia, 'Yeltsin and us,' *Commentary*, 93 (4) (April 1992): 21–8. Also see John Morrison, *Boris Yeltsin: From Bolshevik to Democrat* (New York: Dutton, 1991).

18 An unfortunate consequence of our fascination in the West with the changes in Russia has been the personification in the public mind of reform with particular people. Personalities rather than fundamental ideas have dominated most discussion. This led to a bizarre inversion of the truth. Gorbachev was seen as a democrat even though he was never elected, and Yeltsin was seen as an authoritarian even though he was elected. The West tended to thank Gorbachev for the liberation of East and Central Europe, when in reality power was grasped from him by Solidarity, the Civic Forum, Sajudis and the Democratic Russia Movement. As Anders Aslund has pointed out, Yeltsin's record is much better than Gorbachev's on economics and politics. See Aslund, 'Russia's road from communism,' *Daedalus* (Spring 1992): 77–95.

19 See Boris Yeltsin's speech to the Congress of Russian SFSR People's Deputies, *Izvestia* (28 October 1991), translated in *Current Digest of the Soviet Press*, 43 (43) (27 November 1991): 1. Also see 'Yeltsin outlines

NOTES

radical economic reforms,' *Soviet/East European Report*, 9, no. 5 (20 November 1991): 1–2, 4.

20 See S. Razin, '10 decrees that shook the world,' *Komsomolskaya Pravda* (19 November 1991), translated in *Current Digest of the Soviet Press*, 43 (46) (18 December 1991): 1.

21 See Aleksandr Rutskoi, 'In defense of Russia,' *Pravda* (30 January 1992), translated in *Current Digest of the Post-Soviet Press*, 44 (4) (26 February 1992): 1.

22 See 'Building the new Russia,' *The Economist* (25 April 1992): 12–13. Also see the conversation with Yegor Gaidar, the architect of the Yeltsin program, *The Economist* (25 April 1992): 17–20.

23 See Olga Gerasimenko, 'The country doesn't have a Margaret Thatcher,' *Rossia* (29 January–4 February, 1992), translated in *Current Digest of the Post-Soviet Press*, 44 (5) (4 March 1992): 4.

24 Nikolai Petrakov, 'He who doesn't take risks doesn't get to drink champagne,' *Megapolis Express* (6 February 1992), translated in *Current Digest of the Post-Soviet Press*, 44 (7) (18 March 1992): 9.

25 See Mikhail Leontyev, 'The Pavlovization of liberal reform,' *Nezavisimaya Gazeta* (15 January 1992), translated in *Current Digest of the Post-Soviet Press*, 44 (3) (19 February 1992): 11–12.

26 See Yeltsin's speech to the Russian Federation Supreme Soviet on 16 January 1992, translated in *Current Digest of the Post-Soviet Press*, 44 (2) (12 February 1992): 1–3.

27 See 'Mere shock, or therapy too?,' *The Economist* (22 February 1992): 63. This editorial, however, argues against interpreting Yeltsin's raising of pensions and other concessions to ease the difficulties of the transition as a 'decisive retreat from the government's stabilization policy.' Such an interpretation, it is argued, is both too gloomy and too early. The real threat to the reforms will come, however, if privatization does not proceed quickly to curb the monopolistic situation. In November 1991, a parliamentary committee was empowered to approve any price increase by a monopolistic enterprise. Already 2,000 enterprises accounting for an estimated 70 per cent of industrial production have been named as monopolistic. Wholesale price control, though, could fundamentally destroy the liberalization efforts.

28 See *The Economist* (11 April 1992): 72.

29 See *The Economist* (11 April 1992): 71–2.

30 See the debate on privatization between the Gaidar team and the Piyasheva–Selyunin group in *Current Digest of the Post-Soviet Press*, 44 (9) (1 April 1992): 5–7.

31 To reach a Western ratio of public/private the former communist economies would still have to transfer about 50 per cent of GDP from government ownership to private ownership. In her twelve years in power, Margaret Thatcher privatized about 5 per cent.

32 See 'Russian government memorandum on economic policy,' *Izvestia* (28 February 1992), translated in *Current Digest of the Post-Soviet Press*, 44 (9) (1 April 1992): 1–4.

33 See *New York Times* (27 April 1992): A1, A6.

34 Jeffrey Sachs, 'Managing the LDC debt crisis,' *Brookings Papers on*

NOTES

Economic Activity, 2 (1986): 402. Sachs develops an argument for debt relief in this paper similar to the argument used in the law and economics literature to justify court imposed contract renegotiations. Due to the low probability of certain contingencies, contracts are often incomplete. The cost of accounting for every conceivable contingency would be too great. It is sometimes the duty of the judge or the adjudicating party to reduce the costs of renegotiating a contract between parties by offering terms that the parties would have agreed to had they negotiated the restructuring of the contract. Debt relief is in essence a renegotiation of a contract due to unfortunate and unforeseen events occurring to the debtor nation. Debt contracts, Sachs argues, should be renegotiated either when the debtor nation is in such dire economic straits that continued servicing of the debt would threaten the political and social stability of the country, or the ability of the debtor nation to repay the debt would be improved by partial forgiveness.

35 On the development of the 'Grand Bargain' idea see Grigory Yavlinsky, Mikhail Zadornov and Aleksei Mikhailov, 'Plus the " Group of Seven": program for an organized return to the world economy,' *Izvestia* (20 May 1991), translated in *Current Digest of the Soviet Press*, 43 (20) (19 June 1991): 1–5. Also see Graham Allison and Grigory Yavlinsky, *Window of Opportunity* (New York: Pantheon, 1991). In addition, see Jeffrey Sachs, 'Helping Russia,' *The Economist* (21 December 1991–3 January 1992): 101–4.

36 See Israel Kirzner, 'The entrepreneurial process,' in *Discovery and the Capitalist Process* (Chicago: University of Chicago Press, 1985), pp. 68–92. Also see Alfredo Irigoin, 'Economic development: a market process perspective,' PhD thesis, Department of Economics, New York University (1990).

37 See Jude Wanniski, 'The future of Russian capitalism,' *Foreign Affairs*, 71 (2) (Spring 1992): 17–25.

38 Stephen Howe, 'Hiccup in the long march of history,' *New Statesmen and Society* (6 March 1992): 12–14, argues to the contrary that socialism never amounted to much in Eastern Europe anyway. After the 1930s, communism ceased to be a coherent ideology. The traumas of post-communism have little to do with communism, he argues, because communism was mostly a gigantic ideological façade. However true these sentiments, expressed by Howe and others, are, they fundamentally confuse the issue of the intellectual vision behind the experience of socialism and what that means for us today. The ideological façade and the economic disaster were the unintended consequences of trying to pursue an incoherent and impossible utopian vision of how to organize social relations of production. The failure of this vision had nothing to do with the particular problems of political leadership in East and Central Europe or the former Soviet Union, but was the result of the inherent structural weaknesses of the idea.

39 For a discussion of modernism and the ambiguities surrounding postmodernism see Peter Scott, 'The postmodern challenge I–IV,' *Times Higher Education Supplement* (10, 17, 24 and 31 August 1991). Scott, however, argues that post-modernism is too ambiguous to mount much of

193

a challenge to modernism. Moreover, he argues against interpreting modernism strictly as a rationalistic philosophy. In the end, though, Scott's essays fail to capture the strength and weaknesses of modernism because he does not distinguish between the French and Scottish Enlightenment. While the French Enlightenment embodied the Age of Reason and Science, the point of the Scottish Enlightenment was, in large part, to employ rational analysis to whittle down the claims of reason. See F. A. Hayek, *The Constitution of Liberty* (Chicago: University of Chicago Press, 1960), pp. 54–70.

40 Vaclav Havel, 'The end of the modern era,' *New York Times* (1 March 1992): E15.

41 Martin Malia, 'Yeltsin and us,' 24. Also see Z (Malia), 'To the Stalin mausoleum,' *Daedalus* (Winter 1990): 295–344, and 'Leninist endgame,' *Daedalus* (Spring 1992): 57–75.

42 See Fukuyama, 'The end of history?,' *The National Interest* (Summer 1989): 3–18.

43 Timothy Garton Ash points out that there are many questions to ask about the new Europe. The most common question raised by commentators is how can the West help the transition of formerly communist countries to liberal democracies. But, Garton Ash thinks that the more interesting question is how might these former communist countries help the West. What, after all those years of hard experience under communism, can they teach us about life and social order? Garton Ash, however, goes too far when he suggests that the new Europeans can offer us no new ideas. 'They can,' he states, 'offer no fundamentally new ideas on the big questions of politics, economics, law or international relations. The ideas whose time has come are old, familiar, well-tested ones. (It is the new ideas whose time has passed.)' See Garton Ash, *The Magic Lantern*, pp. 150, 154(see Note 5). While true on one level, this assessment misses the great opportunity that the new Europe holds for starting anew, of redefining the basic relationship between the citizen and the state, and what that may mean for the development of social theory.

44 See Richard Ericson, 'The classical Soviet-type economy: nature of the system and implications for reform,' *Journal of Economic Perspectives*, 5 (4) (Fall 1991): 26.

INDEX

195

INDEX

63–4; and interest groups 6–8,
74–5; and reform 76–7, 84, 130–1
DeSoto, Hernando 43
distribution 32–3
Djilas, Milovan 69

economics: aggregate 4, 21;
development of, in the West 15–
21; model for transition 42–3; *vs.*
politics 76–7, 84–6, 108; and
socialism 50
Erhard, Ludwig 42
Ericson, Richard 145
error: and information 114–15; and
market system 62–3, 91–2, 137;
politics 136–7
exchange rate 98, 123, 125, 139

Fabian socialism 68
Fernandez, Racquel 76
Finer, Herman 20
fiscal policy 116–17, 119–20, 125–9
Fischer, Stanley 78
food 4, 35, 41
France, revolution 73
Friedman, Milton 76, 92
Friedman, Rose 76
Fukuyama, Francis 144

Gaidar, Yegor 138, 141
Galbraith, John Kenneth 74
Germany, Democratic Republic 4,
35, 119, 132–3
Germany, Federal Republic 42
glasnost 38, 44, 85, 88
Gorbachev, Mikhail: and
bureaucracy 36–7, 45, 83–4; and
collapse of Soviet Union 3, 84, 99,
104; and coup 13–14, 103–4;
credibility 12–14, 86, 99–104, 107,
137; inconsistency 2, 41–2, 103;
problems facing 32–8; reform
package 1–2, 38–42, 137, 138; and
Soviet history 13–14, 136
Gorlin, Alice 39
Gosplan 60–1
government *see* state
grain, price fixing 29, 97–8

gross national product (GNP),
Soviet Union, estimates of 21–4
growth 35, 143–4; assessment of
77–8; Soviet illusion 13, 15–25

Hanke, Steve 123
Havel, Vaclav 133–4, 144
Hayek, F. A. 19, 20, 51–2, 55–6, 109,
111–12, 115, 132
health care 36
Hetzel, Robert 123
Hill, Howard 18–19
history 14–15, 111; Soviet Union 13,
25–32, 136
Hobbes, Thomas 109, 110–11
Homan, Paul 17–18
Hough, Jerry 81
housing 36
Hume, David 109, 111–12
Hungary 35
Huxley, Julian 19

ideas 1, 6, 8
illusion of Soviet economic strength
3–4, 12–45; Gorbachev's challenge
32–8; Gorbachev's reform
package 38–42; history 25–32;
industry 117–19; measurement
malpractice 21–5; model for
transition 42–3; and Soviet people
61–5; and Western understanding
15–21, 71
incentives 9, 90–3; capitalism 55,
62–3, 91–2; and public ownership
52, 91–2
independence, states 39, 127–9
individual economic activity, law on
100–1
individualism 132
industry 10, 32, 41, 117–19
inflation 121, 123, 125
information 9, 90–3; and democracy
6–7, 63–4, 76–7; and error 114–
15; and planning 52–4, 61–2
institutions 43
interest groups, and democracy 6–8,
74–7, 84–5, 145
International Monetary Fund (IMF)
78–9, 142–3

196

Soviet Union 3, 84, 99, 103–4; credibility 1–2, 41, 99–104; failings of 83–4, 86–7, 137–8, 139; inconsistency 2, 41–2, 103; laws 39–40, 99–103; price reforms 40; problems confronting 35–8
Peru 43
Petrakov, Nikolai 41, 140
Pipes, Richard 135
Piyasheva, Larissa 140
planning, economic 58–9; Bolshevism 26–9; illusion of 61–5; impossibility of 31, 51–4, 58, 108; and politics 19–20; Soviet infrastructure 59–61; Stalinism 29–32, 58–9; theory 17–19
Plato 52
Poland 35, 133
policy: commitment to *see* credibility; fiscal 116–17, 119–20, 125–9; monetary 119–20, 123–5
Politburo 60, 81, 83
politics: agency problem 63–4; *vs.* economics 76–7, 84–6, 108; error 136–7; logic of 6–8, 74–7, 84–6
Popov, Gavriil 12
power: Communist Party 27–8, 69–70, 81–4, 135; *nomenklatura* 69–70, 84–5; and reform 38, 80, 87
Presidential Plan 2, 41
price reforms 120–2; Gorbachev 40; NEP 97–8; Yeltsin 139–41
prices, and resource allocation 50–1, 55, 62–3, 91–2
private enterprise within Soviet system 27–8, 95, 96–7, 100–3 *see also* black market; underground economy
private ownership of property 31, 112; and resource allocation 50–1, 55, 91
privatization 121, 122–3, 140
production 10, 32, 117–19; commodity 26, 31, 59, 69
Public Choice school of economics 2, 51
public goods 126–7

queuing 11, 67

Rabuskha, Alvin 43
rational abstention/rational ignorance 6–7, 63, 75
rationing 30, 66–7
Rawls, John 110
Reagan, Ronald 3
reform 10, 106–31; aims of 32–3, 35, 36–7; of bureaucracy 36–7, 45, 83–4; credibility 8–9, 93–104; and democracy 76–7, 84, 130–1; fiscal policy 125–9; logic of 77–80; monetary 123–5; NEP (*q.v.*) 27, 68; and politics 6–8, 74–7, 84–6; pre– perestroika 33, 88; price liberalization 120–2; privatization 122–3; problems of 117–20; shock therapy 120, 129–30; state role 112–17; Yeltsin 138–44
rent-seeking 5–6, 74–7; democratic politics 55
resource allocation: and market system 50–1, 55, 62, 71, 91; state monopoly 64–5; without competition 30–1 *see also* planning
rights 109–10
Rodrik, Dani 76
Roosevelt, Franklin D. 18
rouble, the 107, 121, 123–5
rules 111–12; economic 33; market 10, 71, 92, 104
Rutskoi, Aleksandr 139–40
Ryan, Alan 48–9
Ryzhkov, Nikolai 41

Sachs, Jeffrey 78, 142
Schroeder, Gertrude 35
Schuler, Kurt 123
Schumpeter, Joseph 18
Selyunin, Vasily 13, 22–3, 31, 37, 80
Shakespeare, William 88
Shatalin, Stanislav, 500-Day Plan 2, 41, 103
Shmelev, Nikolai 13, 37
shock: exogenous 8, 77, 85–6, 103–4; therapy 120, 129–30
Simis, Konstantin 36
social contract 110–11
socialism 4–5, 46–56, 108–9; failure